JEREMY DUMMETT is an expert on the history of Sicily and author of *Syracuse, City of Legends: A Glory of Sicily*. He read history at Trinity College, Cambridge, where he became interested in the history and culture of Italy. His professional career took him to Athens and Milan, where he lived and worked for many years. Now retired, he is a frequent visitor to Sicily. His website is at www.jeremydummett.com

JEREMY DUMMETT

PALERMO
CITY OF KINGS
THE HEART OF SICILY

I.B.TAURIS
LONDON · NEW YORK

FSC
www.fsc.org
MIX
Paper from
responsible sources
FSC® C007584

Published in 2015 by
I.B.Tauris & Co. Ltd
London • New York
www.ibtauris.com

ISBN: 978-1-78453-083-9
eISBN: 978-0-85773-716-8

A full CIP record for this book is available from the British Library
A full CIP record is available from the Library of Congress

Library of Congress Catalog Card Number: available

Typeset in Perpetua by Tetragon, London
Printed and bound in Sweden by ScandBook AB

We are grateful to the following for permission to quote from their works: Boydell
Press, Cambridge University Press, CEMERS Publications, Collector's Library, Editori
Laterza, Granta Books, Harvard University Press, Hodder & Stoughton, Professor
Graham Loud of the University of Leeds, Osprey Publishing, Penguin Books, Pietro
Vittorietti Edizioni, the Random House Group, Rizzoli, Salvatore Sciascia Editore,
Sellerio Editore, Thames & Hudson and the University of Chicago Press.

We are also grateful to the British Library for permission to
reproduce the map on the endpapers of this book.

Every effort has been made to contact copyright holders. Any errors or omissions
brought to the attention of the publishers will be made good in future editions.

Contents

List of Illustrations

Black-and-white illustrations

All images are from the author's collection.

Colour-plate section

Unless stated otherwise, all images are from the author's collection.

1. Santa Rosalia, Palermo's patron saint.
2. The cathedral.
3. Church of San Domenico (St Dominic).
4. Fontana Pretoria (Pretoria Fountain).
5. Mosaic, church of the Martorana (Wikimedia Commons. Photograph by Marie-Lan Nguyen, 2008).
6. Mosaic, Cappella Palatina (Palatine Chapel) (Wikimedia Commons. Photograph by Urban, 2005).

Maps

Endpapers: Palermo in 1580. A. Majorchus, Rome, by permission of the British Library. © The British Library Board, 24240.1.

Preface

Whicle there are many books on Sicily, there are very few in English dedicated to the principal Sicilian cities. Yet these cities have the most dramatic, varied and fascinating histories. I set out to fill this gap firstly with my book on Syracuse (*Syracuse, City of Legends: A Glory of Sicily*, published by I.B.Tauris in 2010), to which I now add this book on Palermo. My books are complementary, for Syracuse was the leading city in Sicily until conquered by the Arabs in 878, after which Palermo took on the leading role and became the island's capital, the position it still holds today.

This book presents the history of Palermo together with a commentary on the principal monuments. It is intended for the general reader interested in the Mediterranean as well as for the visitor looking for specific guidance on the city. The combination of history and guide (the first on Palermo) links past and present with the aim of bringing the city alive.

Part I tells the story from the city's foundation as a Phoenician settlement in the eighth century BC, through the height of its civilisation in the Middle Ages, up to the events of modern times. It is written in narrative form based on contemporary sources, making full use of eyewitness accounts. Part II contains a commentary on the monuments and works of art to be seen today. They come from different eras and for the sake of clarity are presented in their historical context together with maps indicating their locations.

Given the complexity of Palermo's history and the range of its monuments, this book represents a selection of the events and sites which appeared to me to be the most important and relevant. In terms of the monuments, visitors should note that it is a good idea to check in advance as changes and closures are frequently made due to restoration work.

In a shrinking world where originality is increasingly hard to find, Palermo has a lot to offer. The city has not yet been overwhelmed by tourism and remains a regional centre full of local character with much to be explored. It is also well placed for visiting the ancient Punic and Greek sites, the beaches and nature reserves of western Sicily. I am in agreement with Patrick Brydone, who on his visit to Palermo in 1770 reported to his friend William Beckford: 'I shall have a great deal to write you about this city; we are every day more delighted with it, and shall leave it with much regret.'¹

Acknowledgements

My thanks go to my editor at I.B.Tauris, Joanna Godfrey, for publishing this book. The team at I.B.Tauris is to be congratulated on the quality of production. For the research, the British Library provided its usual first-class service.

In Palermo, I was greatly helped by Massimo Palloni and Patty Marchetti, whose B & B, the BB22 behind the church of San Domenico, became my home from home. Their advice on the city was invaluable. I am indebted to Aldo Saccaro, the author of a book on the Jews of Palermo, who shared his deep knowledge of the city with me. For tours of the monuments, I have to thank my friend and guide, Sergio Morabito. Many of the prints that appear in my book were supplied by Salvatore Pilocane from his stall, which appears in Piazza Marina on Sundays. My thanks also to Adriana Viaggi for their friendly and efficient transport service in and around Palermo.

Friends and family provided valuable assistance and I would like to thank the following for their contributions: Daniel and Virginia Worsley, and Mark and Henry Dummett, for their comments on draft chapters; Georgina Kirk and Iain Moran for developing my website; and Hermione for her support throughout the project.

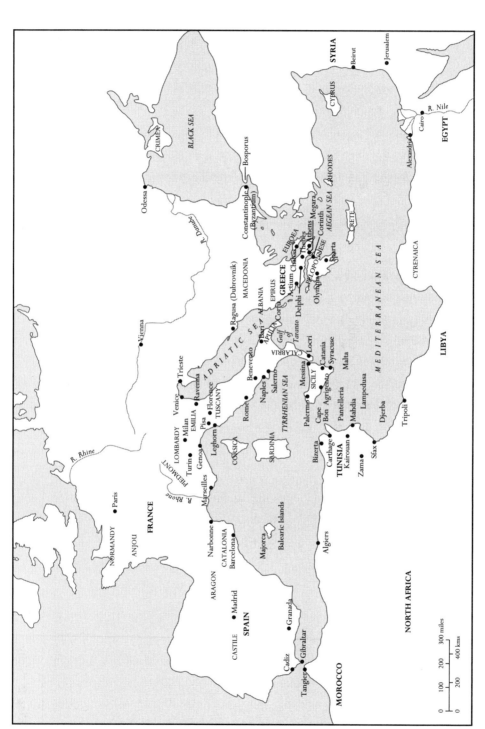

Map 1 The Mediterranean Sea

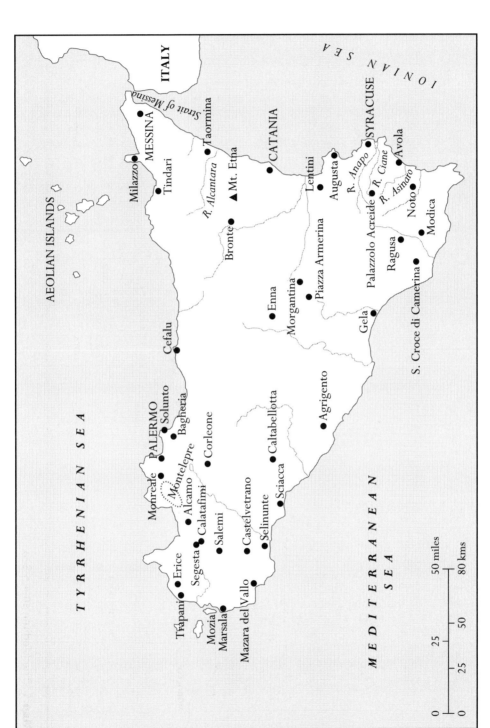

Map 2 Sicily

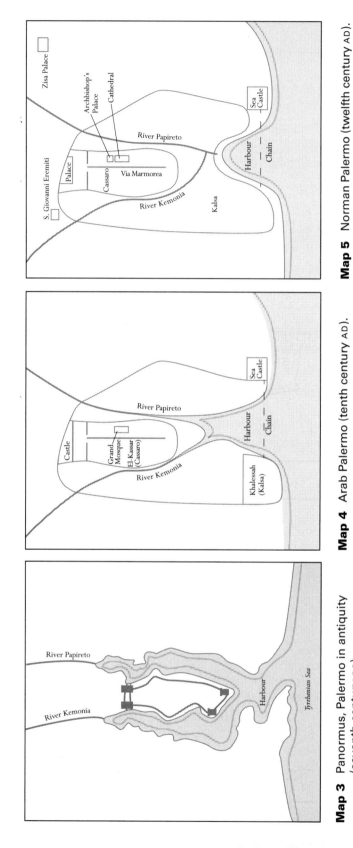

Map 3 Panormus, Palermo in antiquity (seventh century BC).

Map 4 Arab Palermo (tenth century AD).

Map 5 Norman Palermo (twelfth century AD).

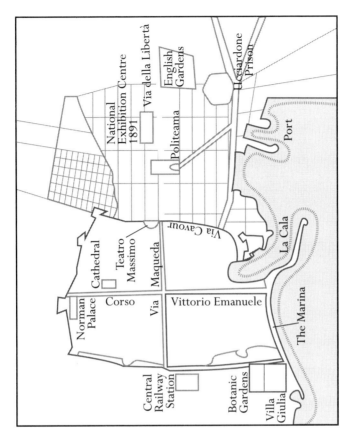

Map 7 Palermo in the belle époque (c.1880 to 1914).

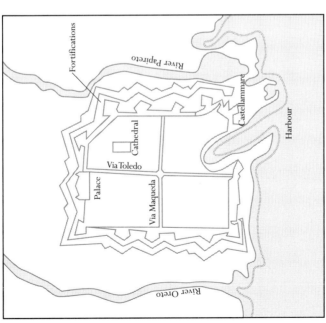

Map 6 Spanish Palermo (second half of the seventeenth century).

To Max, Milo, Freddie and Emma

Prologue

S ince ancient times extraordinary events have taken place in Palermo, making it one of Italy's most fascinating cities. Repeatedly a target for foreign powers, the city was drawn into major conflicts in European history including the Punic Wars, the Crusades, Western Europe's struggle with the Ottoman Empire, the Napoleonic Wars and World War II. So many armies invaded and so many different people ruled Palermo that layer upon layer of history built up, each one leaving its own cultural imprint. Palermo's history is written in its buildings, its art and literature, its language and food.

For the visitor, Palermo is a destination with a difference, offering an adventure in an ancient Mediterranean city with a rich cultural heritage. Palermo is a treasure trove of original monuments and works of art which are largely unknown outside Sicily. The most striking are the Norman churches with their brilliant mosaics, the Norman cathedrals in Palermo and Monreale, the fine medieval sculptures and paintings on display in galleries, plus the array of highly decorated baroque churches, oratories and palaces. The Museo Archeologico Regionale (Regional Archaeological Museum) contains exceptional exhibits from the ancient Punic and Greek cities of western Sicily while the opera house, the Teatro Massimo, puts on lively performances by young Italian singers. Exotic public gardens provide walks amid giant ficus trees, orange groves and statues commemorating fallen heroes. Most of the monuments are located in the historic centre which runs from the seafront to the foot of the mountains, and is divided into four quarters by the intersection of two main roads, Corso Vittorio Emanuele and Via Maqueda. There is a strong North African feel to the busy street markets, the Islamic-style churches with their red domes, and the squares filled with palm trees.

***

In antiquity Sicily was a mysterious wooded island with a mountainous interior from which streams flowed down into the sea. In the hot sunny climate, lush vegetation filled the coastal plains while at several points around the coast inlets of the sea formed natural harbours. To the east rose the massive outline of a volcano whose lava enriched the surrounding land. Coastal waters teemed with all kinds of fish, including swordfish and tuna. The island acted as a magnet to settlers, to whom it seemed an earthly paradise.

The history of Sicily, however, has been traumatic. Too large to integrate easily with the Italian mainland and yet too small to go it alone, its destiny was one of frequent and violent invasion. Its strategic position at the centre of the Mediterranean and rich natural resources made it the target for ambitious states expanding in the region. The result was periods of domination by foreign powers, some long, some short, the best contributing to the island's prosperity, the worst just exploiting it for the invaders' own ends.[1]

The story of Sicily is the story of its relations with the people who colonised it, the Phoenicians, Greeks, Carthaginians, Romans, Byzantines, Arabs, Normans, French, Spanish and finally the Italians. During the periods of foreign domination, and the wars they generated, Sicily experienced extremes of fortune from the heights of power and prosperity to the depths of oppression and poverty.

The domination by foreign powers has gone, leaving deep scars. For while there is energy and creativity here, there is sadness and resignation too. Although since 1947 the island has been run by Sicilians as an autonomous region of Italy, the violence and the injustices remain. In the years following World War II conditions were so bad that half a million Sicilians, out of a total population of 5 million, left home to find work in northern Italy and other regions of the industrialised world. Since then much on the surface has improved. The island is less cut off, living standards have risen, young Sicilians are travelling and learning foreign languages and society is becoming more open. However, the underlying structure of society remains unaltered, the divide between rich and poor is as great as ever, and there is still a long way to go before Sicilians benefit from an effective rule of law. Sicily's problems are not easy to solve, as past rulers discovered to their cost. According to Leonardo Sciascia:

> Sicily proved fatal to all those who governed her, most of whom left their reputations buried there, in such a way that even posterity was unable to revive. A land that is difficult to govern, then, because it is difficult to understand.[2]

***

Palermo, the capital of Sicily, is situated on a bay on the north-western coast of the island, facing the Tyrrhenian Sea. A fertile coastal plain known as the Conca d'Oro (the Golden Shell), famous for its orange and lemon groves, has provided the city with rich agricultural produce since ancient times. A ring of mountains encircles the city, the most prominent being Monte Pellegrino to the north, shielding it from the territory inland.

Founded by Phoenicians in the eighth century B C, Palermo was developed as a trading and military base by the Carthaginians. While in ancient times eastern Sicily was the territory of the Greeks, the west was largely controlled by the Carthaginians. At this time the city was called Panormus, the Greek for 'all harbour', reflecting the size of its port. It was never a Greek city, though it was ruled for a short while by the Greek general Pyrrhus. During the long Roman era that followed, Panormus became the main port for supplying Sicilian grain to Rome.

Palermo rose to prominence in the ninth century A D when the Arabs made it their capital of Sicily. Until then Syracuse, a city on the east coast founded by the Greeks, had been the leading city on the island. Under the Arabs Palermo grew to become a flourishing centre of trade containing 300 mosques. Palermo's most brilliant period followed in the twelfth century under the Normans when it became one of the most powerful cities in the Mediterranean. From their palace in Palermo the Norman kings ruled the rich kingdom of Sicily through a unique blend of cultures: Norman, Arab and Byzantine Greek. In describing the cities of Sicily, al-Edrisi, the Arab geographer to King Roger II, wrote:

> First in importance comes Palermo, that beautiful great city, the largest and most sublime metropolis in the world, whose praises never end; the city decorated with such elegance; seat of kings ancient and modern. Located on the sea, on the western side of the island, surrounded by mountains, her beaches are clear and sparkling […] The countryside around Palermo is well irrigated and filled with freshwater springs. The city has an abundance of fruit and her buildings and elegant villas defy description. In summary, to look at this city is enough to make one's head spin.[3]

The long Spanish era, when the aristocracy and the Church dominated the island, brought a decline in Palermo's fortunes. This was followed by a short period under the protection of the British during the Napoleonic Wars. Palermo was then freed from the Spanish Bourbons of Naples by Garibaldi in 1860.

After an uneasy entry into the new Italian nation, the city went on to become a fashionable destination for Europe's aristocracy during the belle époque of the late nineteenth and early twentieth centuries. Since 1947 Palermo has been the seat of the Sicilian Regional Government.

Today Palermo, with a population of 655,000, is the largest city in Sicily and the fifth largest in Italy. The province of Palermo contains 1.2 million of Sicily's total population of 5 million.[4] The city spreads far beyond the historic centre, extending up the valleys towards the mountains and along the coastline in both directions. The plain running from the city's centre to the seaside resort of Mondello, and the coastline out towards the airport, have been developed with residential areas and holiday homes. Many of these outlying districts, created in an uncontrolled housing boom, are now shabby and run-down and receive a minimal level of services. There are few large employers to absorb the working population so that much of the work on offer is part time and precarious. For a city of this size and location there is a notable lack of investment. Palermo has to contend with some deep-seated problems.

***

Palermo is represented by symbols from the past that portray different aspects of the city's character. One is the eagle, the symbol of power given to the city by the Romans, adopted by the Holy Roman Emperor Frederick II in the thirteenth century, and widely used by the Spanish. In the sixteenth century the coat of arms included the motto *Senatus Populusque Panormitanus Urbs Felix et Regni Caput* (The Senate and People of Palermo, the Happy City and Capital of the Realm). The eagle forms part of the coat of arms, which appears in many places around the city.

Also with roots in antiquity is the Genio di Palermo (Genius of Palermo), a mythical figure representing the genius or spirit of the city, who is portrayed in many statues and pictures. While the details vary, these commonly consist of a seated man with a beard, wearing a crown and holding a serpent to his breast. This strange image probably dates back to pre-Roman times. One statue known as *Palermu lu Grandi* (Big Palermo) can be found in Piazza Garraffo in the Vucciria district, another *Palermu u Nicu* (Little Palermo) in the Palazzo delle Aquile (Palace of the Eagles) in Piazza Pretoria. The latter statue, which dates from the 1470s, carries a curious statement: *Panormus conca aurea suos devorat alienos nutrit* ('Palermo, golden shell, devours its own and nourishes foreigners'). A third statue of the Genius, in Piazza Rivoluzione, became a rallying point in 1848 against the occupying Bourbon forces, who had it removed. The return of the statue, after Garibaldi freed the city in 1860, was met with general rejoicing.

From the time of the plague in the seventeenth century comes the most important symbol of them all, Santa Rosalia, Palermo's patron saint. Rosalia came from a noble family and lived under the Norman kings in the twelfth century. She withdrew at an early age to live the life of a religious hermit. On 15 July 1624, when the plague was ravaging Palermo, her bones were found in a cave on Monte Pellegrino and were used by the archbishop to raise the morale of the people and to combat the plague. In the following year she was made Palermo's patron saint and the first festival in her honour, known as the *festino*, took place. This became the most important event in the city's calendar and takes place every year in mid-July. Visitors have described the *festino* over the years, noting the huge public outpouring of emotion in support of Santa Rosalia and the intensely personal regard in which she is held by Palermitans. During the *festino* the saint's statue, riding on a huge, colourful carriage, is borne from the cathedral to the sea through packed streets. At the Quattro Canti (Four Corners), the baroque square at the city's centre, the mayor welcomes the procession with the words '*Viva Palermo e Santa Rosalia!*' to a tumultuous welcome from the crowd.

***

When in Palermo the subject of food is never far away. Eyes light up and gestures become more animated as people discuss their favourite dishes. The variety, freshness and intensity of flavour make eating in Palermo an experience to remember. Local specialities include *pasta con le sarde* (pasta cooked with fresh sardines, pine nuts, currants and wild fennel) and *caponata* (a sweet and sour vegetable dish based on aubergines). Palermo is famous for its sweet pastries, thanks to the Arabs who introduced sugar cane to Sicily. The classics are *cannoli* (crisp pastry tubes filled with sweetened ricotta) and *cassata* (a cake made from marzipan, sponge cake and sweetened ricotta).

The variety of food can be seen in the street markets, whose character was captured by Renato Guttuso in his painting of the Vucciria, the most famous of the markets. Painted in 1974 and on view at the Palazzo Chiaramonte in Piazza Marina, it shows the rich profusion of produce on sale, the fruit and vegetables, the meat and cheeses, in a visual feast. Today the Vucciria is much reduced in scale, though it does retain some of its old atmosphere.

The full colour and vitality of the street markets are to be found in the Capo and Ballarò districts where rows of stalls fill a maze of small streets and alleyways in an endless open market. Shoppers push their way down a narrow gap between stalls piled high with tomatoes, artichokes, aubergines, peppers, oranges, peaches, watermelons and aromatic herbs. Gleaming piles of fish are displayed on slabs, with huge tuna and swordfish waiting to be sliced up. Behind the stalls men prepare street food as they have always done, using deep pans to fry *panelle*, *crocchette* and *arancini* (chickpea fritters, croquette potatoes and rice balls filled with cheese or ham) while dishes of pasta are prepared such as *anelletti al forno*, small rounds of pasta baked in a tomato sauce with aubergines, boiled eggs, peas and cheese.

Palermo's food is now matched by a thriving wine industry, which in recent years has greatly increased the quantity and the quality of production. Sicilian wines from a variety of producers are increasingly appreciated by visitors and are becoming well established in international markets. The wine from the white grape Grillo is a favourite of Montalbano, the police inspector featured in the novels of Andrea Camilleri.

***

Unlike the famous cities of northern and central Italy, such as Venice and Florence, Palermo's history is still being made. The battle with Cosa Nostra, the Sicilian mafia, continues on a daily basis, the outcome of which is vital not only to Sicily but to the whole nation. Organised crime has reached epidemic proportions in Italy, with the annual turnover of the major mafia groups estimated at 7 per cent of national GDP, which makes them Italy's largest enterprise. In times of expansion the costs of their criminal activity can be absorbed into the wider economy without major disruption. In times of recession the extra costs become a burden which the country can ill afford. The effects are particularly felt in the south, where a close relationship exists between the density of organised crime and low economic growth.[5] With its vast wealth, the mafia has an impact far beyond southern Italy. Investments have been made in the legitimate economy in northern Italy and around the world. Writing in the 1960s, Leonardo Sciascia anticipated the export of Cosa Nostra's activities to mainland Italy, a process he described as 'the palm tree line that is moving from south to north', and he wondered if the whole of Italy was not becoming like Sicily.[6]

While the mafia gets the publicity, the forces of antimafia are less well known, especially outside Italy. A formidable antimafia drive has been developed by the police, magistrates and politicians in Palermo fighting to enforce the rule of law. It includes the introduction of new legislation to deal with organised crime, some of which is being adopted in Brussels for use across the European Union. The authorities are supported by several popular antimafia movements, the most prominent being Addiopizzo, whose aim is to unite businesses against the payment of protection money.

Two of the outstanding antimafia figures were the judges Giovanni Falcone and Paolo Borsellino, both from Palermo, assassinated by the mafia in 1992. In 1987 their investigations led to the convictions of 360 mafiosi in what was known in Italy as a 'maxi-trial'. They were part of a pool of investigating magistrates who made serious inroads into mafia power. These magistrates and those who followed them were remarkable, working with little support in conditions that would be inconceivable in most Western democracies. They were described by the Sicilian writer, Vincenzo Consolo:

> They were men of a new breed, of sound moral background and total commitment, who were forced to fight a battle on two fronts, internal and external. Internally they had to deal with corrupt officials within the institutions, even inside the judiciary, who secretly supported the mafia. Externally they were in the front line against the military wing of the mafia, the sworn enemy of the state.[7]

Investigations are currently focussing on the political connections of the mafia at national level. These include the negotiations between state and mafia which are alleged to have taken place in the 1990s in the aftermath of the assassination of the judges. The interweaving of elements of the state with organised crime, which goes back to the 1860s, is a dangerous grey area which has yet to be fully exposed. Undoubtedly many of its secrets lie in Palermo.

***

Palermo is both light and dark, *chiaroscuro*, like a painting by Caravaggio. It is a city of many faces: a city of art, of original and memorable monuments; a historic city and tourist destination; a port and commercial centre; a university city; the seat of Regional Government; and a city of mafia and antimafia.

All this exists amid the loud chaos of a traffic-infested historic centre which nevertheless retains its character and charm. Seagulls' cries and ships' sirens from the port compete with the roar of motorbikes as they accelerate through the narrow streets. It is a gritty place, not yet sanitised by global influences and remains, above all, authentic. There is richness and intensity to life here made up of the climate, the clear skies and hot sun, the colours, the directness and humour of the people, the rich food and the history, combined with the works of art. It is an exhilarating mixture for the visitor with time to spend in the city.

PART I

The Story of Palermo
From Phoenician Settlement to Modern Times

CHAPTER 1

Panormus, Palermo in Antiquity

The Phoenicians in their sleek, fast galleys explored the Sicilian coast in the first half of the eighth century BC. On trading missions the galleys were followed by their merchant ships, wide and spacious, propelled by a characteristic square sail. On the north-western coast of Sicily, on a stretch of land facing an inlet of the Tyrrhenian Sea, the Phoenicians established a settlement which became known as Panormus, from the Greek meaning 'all harbour'. The name referred to the site's large, natural harbour, described by Diodorus Siculus as 'the finest harbour in all Sicily'.[1] In the Phoenicians' own language the name was Ziz, which appeared on some of their coins. The foundation date is unknown but was probably in the mid-eighth century BC, while archaeological evidence of a settlement here starts in the seventh century.[2] Edward Freeman, the nineteenth-century historian of ancient Sicily, described the site as follows:

> An inlet of the sea, making its way inland by a narrow mouth, presently parted off into two branches, and left a tongue of land between them. Of these two branches, each had a stream running into it. Such a site as this, a little inland sea, with the land sheltering the water and the water sheltering the land, was indeed a haven of rest for the wearied merchantman of Phoenicia, seeking a safe harbour for his ships and their burdens. The spot was seized on; the well-placed piece of land, with water on both sides of it, became the site of the Phoenician settlement.[3]

The nearby plain offered fertile land for cultivation, suitable for crops and fruit, while the site was ringed with mountains providing a plentiful supply of water and protection from the interior. Evidence of human habitation in the area dating back to the Stone Age comes from cave drawings of human figures in the Grotta dell'Addaura on Monte Pellegrino.

Only an outline story exists for Palermo in antiquity. The reason is that the city played a secondary role in this period and rarely attracted the attention of the ancient historians who were, in any case, Greek and Roman. The Phoenicians, and the Carthaginians after them, left no written record of their lives in Sicily and are usually portrayed as barbarians in comparison to the heroic Greeks. In antiquity Syracuse was the leading city in Sicily and, together with the other Greek cities in eastern Sicily, received the lion's share of historical coverage. The Phoenicians were, in fact, a remarkable people who had much in common with the Greeks.

The Phoenicians in western Sicily

Sicily was unknown in the civilised world until merchant adventurers from the eastern Mediterranean began to explore the island in the eighth century BC. At the time it was a place of densely wooded hills with rivers flowing to the sea and fertile coastal plains where flocks of wild goats roamed freely. Mount Etna's huge outline, with plumes of smoke at its peak, dominated the east coast, adding to the island's mysterious image. Three different tribes were already established in small numbers. In the centre were the Sicans, the first to arrive, from Spain according to Thucydides. Then there came the Elymians, who settled in the north-west. The Sicels, who came from Italy, were the most populous and settled in the east of the island. Originally called Trinacria for its triangular shape, Sicily took its name from the Sicels.

The merchant adventurers, who came to explore the island initially seeking metals and other precious material, were Phoenicians and Greeks. After the early explorers came the settlers, who established permanent communities along the coastline, the Phoenicians in the west and the Greeks predominantly in the east. The Phoenicians preceded the Greeks in Sicily, according to Thucydides:

> There were also Phoenicians living all round Sicily. The Phoenicians occupied the headlands and small islands off the coast and used them as posts for trading with the Sicels. But when the Hellenes began to come in by sea in great numbers, the

Phoenicians abandoned most of their settlements and concentrated on the towns of Motya, Soloeis and Panormus where they lived together in the neighbourhood of the Elymi, partly because they relied on their alliance with the Elymi, partly because from here the voyage from Sicily to Carthage is shortest.[4]

The Phoenicians were a Semitic people whose origins can be traced back to biblical times when they were known as the Canaanites. They lived under constant threat from their more powerful neighbours, the Egyptians and the Assyrians. The geography of their homeland, Canaan in modern Lebanon, squeezed between mountains and the sea, led them to become a seafaring people. They developed new techniques in navigation based on the study of astronomy and in shipbuilding which enabled them to sail by night and to undertake longer voyages than had previously been possible. They developed shipping routes along the North African coast as well as via Greece and Sicily that took them as far west as Spain. The Phoenician fleet, with its characteristic horse's head on the ship's prow, became the first naval power in history. Their famous port cities of Tyre and Sidon were designed as maritime centres and incorporated double harbours, one commercial and the other military, as well as inland waterways, all to facilitate shipping. This model was copied by the Greeks when they developed their city of Syracuse on the east coast of Sicily.

The origin of the name 'Phoenician' lies in the Greek for a dark-red colour, *phoinix*, referring to a purple dye made from a mollusc found near Tyre. The king adopted it as the royal colour and it became widely used in textile manufacture, famous in Homer's time. It was one of a number of high-value export products, including silverware and gold jewellery, which formed the basis of the Phoenicians' commercial empire, begun in the tenth century BC under King Hiram I. Their most important legacy was an alphabet designed for use in commercial transactions consisting of 22 symbols, all consonants. Concise and practical, it was adapted by the Greeks to their own language, adding vowels, and was later used by the Romans. It is the ancestor of all Western alphabets.

To support their overseas commerce, the Phoenicians established trading outposts across the Mediterranean from Italy to Spain and North Africa, including on the islands of Malta, Ibiza, Sardinia and Sicily. Their most important settlement was Carthage, in modern Tunisia, which would eventually take over from their homeland as their most powerful base.

The western expansion of the Greeks was spurred by unrest and over-population at home, together with the difficulty of producing enough food. Greek communities became established in southern Italy, from the bay of Naples to the toe of Italy, in southern France and in Sicily. Naxos was the first Greek settlement in Sicily, founded on the east coast in around 734 BC, fol-lowed in the next year by Syracuse. Further settlements were established on the east coast, as well as inland and on the south coast, in particular Akragas (Agrigento). Himera was founded on the north coast while the furthest Greek city to the west, on the south coast, was Selinus. These cities grew rapidly thanks to the fertile, lava-enriched soil and well-stocked coastal waters. A thriving export trade in agricultural produce built up, which formed the basis of their prosperity, and the Greeks became the most powerful force in Sicily for the next 500 years.[5]

While the Greek cities grew and prospered in the east, the Phoenicians consolidated their presence in the west of the island in three settlements, Panormus and Solus on the north coast, and Motya on the west coast. According to Thucydides, the Phoenicians withdrew to these centres when the Greeks began to arrive in Sicily in large numbers.

Panormus was important from the beginning as a port. Due to a higher sea level, in ancient times the harbour extended into what is now the modern city, reaching as far as Via Roma. The early settlement became a walled city with deep water up to the city walls which provided a safe mooring in all conditions. On either side was a river, the Papireto to the north and the Kemonia to the south, flowing into an inlet of the sea so that the ancient city was surrounded by water on three sides. Over the centuries the sea slowly retreated, with the inlets drying up and the rivers being diverted below ground.

Little is known about Solus, Thucydides' Soloeis, which was a smaller city on the coast, probably located near the modern Santa Flavia. In 350 BC Solus was refounded by the Carthaginians up the hillside on a promontory overlook-ing the sea. This is the modern site of Solunto.

Motya (modern Mozia) was the most important of the Phoenician settlements and also the closest to Carthage. A small island located in a large, protected bay at the midpoint of the west coast, it provided ideal conditions. The bay offered a safe anchorage for a fleet of ships. The island's natural defences were strengthened by a high wall, with a mole added, linking the North Gate to the mainland. Farms were established inland and maritime trade flourished.[6]

The Phoenicians' position in western Sicily was strengthened by their alliance with the local tribe of Elymians, who had two settlements in the area, Eryx and Segesta. Eryx (modern Erice) was the site of an important sanctuary in the ancient world, with multi-ethnic appeal.

Eryx was a legendary Elymian hero who received Heracles on his visit to Sicily. In one version of the story, Eryx was killed by Heracles in single combat. Eryx was the son of Aphrodite, to whom the sanctuary was dedicated. The cult of Aphrodite, whose origins were linked to the Phoenician goddess Astarte, was widespread in the Mediterranean. A temple and sanctuary crowned the peak of Eryx, a rocky hill 800 metres high, clearly visible to sailors at sea. Sacred prostitution, a Phoenician custom, was practised here. A settlement was built lower down the hill and a port established to the south, Drepana (modern Trapani).

Segesta, an inland settlement to the west of Panormus, was the main Elymian base and commercial centre. Agricultural produce was exported from their port, Emporio, on the Castellammare bay. Despite its political allegiance with Carthage, Segesta later became thoroughly Hellenised in terms of culture, as its temple demonstrates.

The Carthaginian–Greek wars

In the early years Phoenicians and Greeks lived peacefully with one another in Sicily. The prosperity of the Greek cities such as Akragas and Selinus on the south coast, for example, was initially based upon trade with Carthage. Sicily is a large island and must have seemed like a continent to the early settlers. The Greeks, however, were continually expanding their cities and competing for territory. In 510 BC, Dorieus, son of the Spartan king, led a Greek expedition to establish a new settlement in western Sicily. He was defeated and killed by a combined army of Elymians and Phoenicians. Sicily became divided into two zones of influence, the west Punic, first Phoenician and then Carthaginian, and the east Greek.

By the sixth century BC Carthage had grown into a major city and maritime power with influence across the Mediterranean. The Phoenician settlements, including those in Sicily, became Carthaginian dependencies. The absorption of the Phoenicians by Carthage was a long and subtle process, for there was much in common between the two cultures. They had the same ancestry, spoke the same language and were both skilled in trading and shipping. The position of Carthage as a land power, however, was a new factor. Unlike the old Phoenician cities, Carthage controlled substantial territory inland and could call upon a large supply of manpower. This led to a build-up in military strength and aggression.

Meanwhile the situation in Sicily was becoming increasingly unstable as the Greeks continued to quarrel amongst themselves. The situation was made more volatile by the fact that the major Greek cities came under the control of tyrants backed by mercenary forces. When Theron, tyrant of Akragas, deposed Terillus so as to add Himera to his territory, Terillus appealed to Carthage for help. Determined to contain the ambitions of the Greeks and to defend their own position in Sicily, the Carthaginians invaded Sicily with a large force under Hamilcar, which landed at Panormus. The Battle of Himera which followed in 480 BC was a triumph for the Greeks and coincided with the victory of the Athenians over the Persians at the Battle of Salamis.

So began the Carthaginian–Greek wars in Sicily, which lasted from the Battle of Himera until 264 BC when the Romans entered the conflict. In the long run the result of these wars was a stalemate, the advantage swinging first one way and then the other, with neither side gaining decisive victory. The destruction to Sicily was enormous. Cities like Selinus, Himera, Akragas and Motya were sacked and destroyed, their populations massacred, sold into slavery or forcibly transferred elsewhere. Temples and other public buildings, among the finest of the Greek era, were demolished and much of the countryside was laid to waste. At times the Greeks lost control over parts of eastern Sicily. Syracuse was frequently under siege though the city succeeded in holding out and was never taken. Carthaginian losses in terms of troops, equipment and ships were enormous but the vital port cities were retained. After each phase in the war the dividing line between east and west, the Greek and the Carthaginian zones of influence, tended to revert to the same position along the line of the Halycus river (the modern Platani river).

The Greeks were rarely capable of presenting a united front to invaders. Individual cities preferred to seek advantage for themselves against a troublesome neighbour by calling for help from an overseas power. One such case led to the Battle of Himera and another was a contributory cause of the Athenian attack on Syracuse in 415–413 BC. Segesta was constantly fighting Selinus over territory and appealed to Athens for help. This became an additional reason for the Athenian expedition, which put Syracuse under siege. The expedition ended disastrously for the Athenians in a battle in the Great Harbour of Syracuse. Thucydides mentions that the treasures at the temple of Eryx, which was under Segestan control, were offered as an inducement to the Athenians. The Greek temple at Segesta, which may have been built to impress the Athenians, was never finished.

After the Athenian expedition Syracuse became the focus of the war with Carthage, with the tyrants who ruled the city relentlessly pursuing their campaigns. Dionysius I led an army into western Sicily which captured and destroyed the Carthaginian base at Motya in 397 BC.

Motya was never rebuilt, for in the aftermath of the siege the Carthaginians decided to create a new base at Lilybaeum (modern Marsala) a little further down the coast, as it offered a stronger defensive position. Timoleon won a famous victory in 340 BC against a much larger Carthaginian force at the river Crimisus, near Segesta. Agathocles took the war to North Africa but was unable to break the defences at Carthage. Then one of Alexander the Great's generals, Pyrrhus, who was seeking to carve out a kingdom for himself, was encouraged by Syracuse to come to Sicily. Here he defeated the Carthaginians, taking their strongholds at Eryx and Panormus, during a two-year campaign in 278–276. Lilybaeum, the Carthaginian base, however, proved too strongly defended to be captured. After falling out with the Sicilians, Pyrrhus returned to Italy in 275.[7]

Except for the interlude under Pyrrhus, Panormus and Eryx remained in Carthaginian hands. The role of these cities was to act as outposts of Carthage, supporting trade and military operations, and they provided a base for the armies brought over to Sicily to fight the Greeks. They were never highly populated in comparison to the Greek cities. Motya at its peak had perhaps 16,000 inhabitants and Panormus, at the time of the Roman siege, 27,000. By contrast, Syracuse in the early fifth century BC, under the Deinomenids, was a city of 200,000.

Greek cities in the west were also casualties of the wars. Selinus, a city of 60,000 inhabitants, was largely destroyed in 409 BC. While the Carthaginians used it later as a base, it was finally abandoned in 250, with its remaining population forcibly moved to Lilybaeum. Segesta, which had managed to maintain independence through a shrewd use of alliances, playing one side off against the other, was brutally treated by Agathocles, tyrant of Syracuse, in 307 for siding with Carthage. The city was partially destroyed by Agathocles and never recovered its former status.

Roman Panormus

The fighting in Sicily reached a new phase with the arrival of the Romans. Having conquered Italy the Romans saw Sicily, with its abundant natural produce, as the logical next step. The island's strategic position between Italy and North Africa made its conquest essential. Landing first at Messana to gain control of the straits between Sicily and the mainland, the Romans began a hugely destructive campaign to subdue the whole island. The Carthaginians responded by building up their forces in the cities they controlled. By this stage Syracuse and the nearby cities in eastern Sicily, ruled by Hiero II, were allies of Rome. The war for Sicily between Rome and Carthage, known as the First Punic War, lasted from 264 to 241 BC.

Once they had secured eastern Sicily with the help of their Syracusan allies, the Romans set out to take Carthaginian territory in the west of the island. Panormus fell to the Romans in 254, as described by Diodorus:

> There [at Panormus] they [the Romans] moored their ships in the harbour close to the walls, and after disembarking their men, invested the city with a palisade and a trench; for since the countryside is heavily wooded right up to the city gates, the earthworks and trenches were made to extend from sea to sea. Thereupon the Romans by making constant assaults and by employing engines of war broke down the city wall, and having gained possession of the outer city slew many; the rest fled for refuge to the old city, and sending envoys to the consuls asked for assurances that their lives would be spared. An agreement was made that those who paid two minas apiece should go free, and the Romans then took over the city; at this price 14,000 persons were brought under the agreement upon payment of the money, and were released. All the others, to the number of 13,000, as well as the household goods, were sold by the Romans as booty.[8]

The city must have been relatively prosperous to make such substantial payments possible.

The Carthaginians counter-attacked under Hamilcar Barca, the father of the famous Hannibal, who put Panormus under siege from his base on Monte Pellegrino. Eventually the fighting went Rome's way and western Sicily fell under Roman rule. After a long siege Lilybaeum finally capitulated in 241 and the Carthaginians made a peace treaty with Rome. In it they agreed to leave Sicily, release all Roman prisoners and pay a substantial indemnity. Syracuse was finally taken after a two-year siege in 212, as the city had joined the Carthaginians after the death of Hiero II. When Agrigentum followed, the whole of Sicily was in Roman hands.

Little is known about Panormus in the later Punic Wars, during Rome's titanic struggle with Carthage and the armies of Hannibal. Sicily came into the story again when Scipio, the brilliant young Roman general, collected and trained his army in Syracuse before crossing over to Africa from Lilybaeum to defeat Hannibal at the Battle of Zama in 202 BC.

Under the Roman Republic, Sicilians settled down to work the land and to support trade with Rome, in a period of relative peace and prosperity. Woodlands were cleared and the island became Rome's major source of grain, dominated by large estates known as *latifundia*, worked by slaves. Sicily was the first province of Rome, where the Romans learned the benefits of overseas possessions. Sicilians were largely left alone as long as they paid their taxes and delivered sufficient quantities of grain.

After the Civil Wars of the late Republic, which resulted in the foundation of the Roman Empire and which brought more destruction to Sicily, the emperor Augustus introduced a programme of regeneration to the island. Six cities were granted the status of *coloniae*, which brought with it full Roman citizenship. They were Syracuse, seat of the Roman governors, Panormus, Tauromenium, Catania, Tyndaris and Thermae. An ambitious public building programme was undertaken across the island, veterans from the legions were settled on the land and administrators arrived to collect taxes. One of these was Cicero, who in 76–75 BC was based in Lilybaeum. After a later visit to Sicily to collect evidence, Cicero went on to win his famous court case against Verres, the corrupt Roman governor of Sicily.

Panormus increased in size and importance under the Romans, developing into the main Sicilian port for supplying goods to Rome – especially grain, but also wine, oil and fruit. Jewish immigrants arrived from the Near East and Panormus became a multi-ethnic port city where the languages spoken included Punic, Hebrew, Greek and Latin.

The Romans became followers of the cult of Aphrodite at Eryx, renaming it Venus Erycina, and assigning 200 soldiers to protect the temple and sanctuary. According to Livy there was a temple to Venus Erycina on the Capitoline Hill in Rome in 215 BC.[9] The cult became more popular after Virgil described the site and its legend in *The Aeneid*, when Aeneas stops at Eryx before going on to found Rome: 'Next, where the crest of Eryx is neighbour to the stars, a sanctuary is founded to Venus the Idalian.'[10]

The emperors Tiberius and Claudius both contributed to the maintenance of the temple at Eryx.

Byzantine rule and the coming of the Arabs

During the break-up of the Roman Empire, tribes from northern Europe descended upon the Mediterranean, at first carrying out raids and then seeking to carve out kingdoms for themselves. Sicily was a target and Panormus was besieged in AD 440 by the Vandals, who went on to establish themselves in Carthage. The Goths then took the main cities of Sicily in 476, including Panormus. The centre of the Roman Empire had now moved to the new capital, Constantinople, in the eastern Mediterranean and from there the emperor Justinian I sent an army under his general Belisarius to retake the lands lost to the Vandals and Goths. Belisarius landed in Sicily in AD 535 and took the island for Byzantium, which ruled it for the next 300 years. Procopius, who accompanied Belisarius, described the capture of Panormus as follows:

> the Goths who were keeping guard in Panormus, having confidence in the fortifications of the place, which was a strong one, were quite unwilling to yield to Belisarius and ordered him to lead his army away from there with all speed. But Belisarius, considering that it was impossible to capture the place from the landward side, ordered the fleet to sail into the harbour, which extended right up to the wall. For it was outside the circuit-wall and entirely without defenders. Now when the ships had anchored there, it was seen that the masts were higher than the parapet. Straightway, therefore, he filled all the small boats of the ships with bowmen and hoisted them to the tops of the masts. And when from these boats the enemy was shot at from above, they fell into such an irresistible fear that they immediately delivered Panormus to Belisarius by surrender.[11]

Under the Byzantines civil administration was run from Constantinople, which imposed a heavy tax regime upon the population. The Christian Church became well established in Sicily, owning large areas of land. Pagan temples were consecrated as Christian churches and the bishops became powerful local figures. Sicily once again came under the influence of Rome, this time from the Church, with the Pope playing an important part in Sicilian affairs.

After the death of the Prophet Muhammad in 632 the Arabs, united in their new religion of Islam, began a major campaign of conquest. The emperor Constans II, who was unpopular in Constantinople, moved his court in 663 to Syracuse partly to protect Sicily from the threat of Arab raiders. After Constans was assassinated in 668, his successor took the court back to Constantinople. Sicily continued to be ruled by the Byzantines until the Arabs launched an invasion of the island in 827.

CHAPTER 2

Arab Palermo

A new power appeared in the Mediterranean in the seventh century which presented a challenge to the states of Christian Europe. This was the Arabs, who after the death of their Prophet Muhammad in 632 advanced out of their Arabian homeland on a wave of military conquest. Islam appealed to the Christian Arabs with its doctrine of one God, and its recognition of Jesus as a prophet. United by their new religion, the Arabs exploited the power vacuum left by the old empires of Byzantium and Persia which had fought each other to the point of exhaustion. First to fall to their advance were the great Christian cities of Damascus, Antioch and Jerusalem. Within 30 years all of Syria, Egypt and Persia had been taken, the advance going as far as Afghanistan and India. Nothing like it had been seen since the days of Alexander the Great. The Arabs went on to overrun Tunisia, then to invade Spain, taking Toledo and Cordoba, eventually to be stopped at Tours, in France, in 732. They also raided southern Italy and Sicily, which they invaded in 827.

Desert tribesmen, who were natural warriors, formed the core of their armies, which were made up of tribal groups whose fierce family pride added to their fighting spirit. Behind their success lay a mixture of discipline, a sense of brotherhood and boundless self-confidence.

As they advanced from their homeland the Arabs, or Saracens as the Italians called them, became a diverse people. The tribes of North Africa were absorbed into their culture: Berbers and the descendants of Carthaginians, Romans and Vandals, all followers of Islam and the teachings of the Qur'an.

Sicily was transformed by the Arabs. Like the Greeks before them, the Arabs came as settlers seeking a new life. Around half a million immigrants arrived in the Arab era, settling for the most part in the west and the south-east of the island. They brought with them a sophisticated culture, advanced in the arts and sciences, introducing what amounted to a revolution in agriculture, to the benefit of Sicilians. They also brought a new source of conflict, their Muslim religion. For while the Arabs were tolerant of the Christian and Jewish religions, allowing freedom of worship, the establishment of a Muslim state so close to the Italian mainland was seen as a threat by the popes in Rome.

The Arabs left a strong imprint upon western Sicily and especially upon Palermo. This can be experienced in the winding alleyways and street markets of the city, in the food and in the Sicilian language. No monuments from the Arab era, however, have survived. Islamic art and architecture are represented in the Norman buildings due to the collaboration of the Arabs with the Norman rulers. Unlike the Greeks, the Arabs did not leave a history of their time in Sicily so their story is incomplete and their leaders remain shadowy figures. They were, however, inquisitive travellers who wrote journals describing the island.

The Arab conquest of Sicily

The Arab invasion force, transported by a fleet of 70 ships, landed at Mazara del Vallo on the south-western tip of Sicily in June 827. The elite army of 10,000 infantry and 700 cavalry, a mix of Arabs, Berbers and Spanish troops, was led by the 70-year-old Asad ibn al-Furat. The cities of Sicily, guarded by garrisons led by Byzantine Greeks, were on their own in facing this new threat. Constantinople was exhausted from fighting the Persians and was unable to support its Sicilian province. Hungry for land and close to their home base, the Arabs presented a strong challenge for the control of Sicily and the war they started lasted for 50 years. The invasion was prompted by a call for help from Euphemius, a renegade admiral in charge of Byzantine forces in Sicily. When Euphemius abducted a beautiful nun from her convent, her brothers appealed to the emperor in Constantinople. Rather than be arrested, Euphemius declared himself emperor in Syracuse and actively joined the Arab side, encouraging an invasion by the Aghlabid dynasty in Tunisia. He met the Arabs at Mazara, adding his partisans to the invasion force.

After defeating a Byzantine force at Mazara, the Arabs proceeded down the south coast and then cut inland towards Syracuse via the ancient city of Akrai (modern Palazzolo Acreide). Syracuse was the capital of Byzantine Sicily and the most powerful city on the island. It was well defended and offered strong resistance. When disease spread among the invaders from the marshes around the harbour, killing many of the troops including their commander, the Arabs withdrew. Their attack was then directed towards towns of the interior, in particular Enna, which they failed to capture. Euphemius was killed in one of these actions.

Then, strengthened by reinforcements from North Africa, the Arabs made their way to Palermo which they put under siege in July 830. Palermo was a well-fortified city of 70,000 inhabitants and put up a spirited defence. But the fighting, combined with disease and an increasing shortage of food, took its toll and the loss of life became enormous. When in August 831 the Byzantine governor finally negotiated surrender there were only 3,000 people left in the city still alive. After the governor and his family left for Constantinople on a safe passage the population was sold into slavery.[1]

The capture of Palermo was a breakthrough for the Arabs. It was the first major city they had taken and it gave them a secure base. Up to this point they had been living rough in the countryside and small villages. The empty city, which was rapidly occupied by the Arab, Berber and Spanish troops, became their capital. It was an ominous development for the remaining Byzantine garrisons on the island, for in Palermo the Arabs were able to consolidate their forces and prepare sorties to attack the other cities.

Almost immediately infighting broke out between the tribal groups over the allocation of land and property. While a strength in battle, the fiercely competitive nature of tribal loyalties proved to be a handicap when it came to governing new territories. A more deep-seated division arose between the rulers of Palermo and their counterparts in Tunisia. The Palermo Arabs wanted independence from North Africa, while the Tunisians saw Sicily as their colony. Later this led to civil war, with Palermo under siege in 900. In the long run the Arabs in North Africa were too preoccupied with their own affairs to impose their will and in due course Sicily became an independent Arab state.

Western Sicily was secured by 840, with colonies being settled by immigrants from North Africa, and slaves brought in to work on the fields. The fighting continued with Modica falling in 845 and Cefalù in 857. The toughest battle was for Syracuse, the largest and most powerful city and the key to Sicily. After several attempts to take the city had failed, the Arabs attacked once more in 877 with a larger army led by Ibrahim ibn Ahmad. The defence was in the hands of 15 to 20,000 citizens and soldiers, those who were left after many had fled inland. The city's strong natural defensive position on Ortygia, a promontory jutting out into the harbour, kept the Arabs at bay for nine months. No relief came from Constantinople for the vastly outnumbered defenders. Theodosius, a monk who was present at the siege, wrote of huge boulders being hurled at the walls from catapults and surprise attacks being made at night, while all escape routes were blocked. When at last the city fell in May 878, a massacre took place. None of the Syracusan soldiers survived and the remains of the population were sold into slavery. The treasure taken was reputedly greater than that from any other Christian city in the Arabs' advance. Syracuse, the glory of ancient Greek Sicily for 1,600 years, and for a while the most powerful city in the Mediterranean, was left in ruins. This gave the Arabs control of Sicily with the last centres of resistance, the hilltop cities of Taormina and Rometta, being taken in 902 and 965.[2]

The monk Theodosius, together with the archbishop of Syracuse, who at the point of a sword had led the Arabs to the city's treasure, were among the few prisoners to be taken to Palermo. Theodosius described their arrival in 878 as follows:

> We arrived at the famous and well-populated city of Palermo where we were met by a lively crowd of people, singing songs and loudly welcoming the victors of Syracuse, who were laden with booty. Entering the city and seeing the mass of citizens and foreigners gathered together, we realised that Palermo was just as vast as its reputation had foretold. For it seemed as if the whole Arab race was here. And there were so many houses that it looked like several cities rolled into one. After five days we were taken before the emir who was seated upon a raised throne behind a veil.[3]

Clearly Palermo had grown rapidly since its capture by the Arabs nearly 50 years before.

Palermo in the 970s

Palermo – Bal'harm or al-Madinah (the city) to the Arabs – blossomed in this period. A great Muslim city compared to Baghdad, Cairo and Cordoba, Palermo was the seat of the emir (governor) who ruled Sicily, and was filled with palaces, parks, mosques and minarets. In the centre lay the ancient city surrounded by high walls and towers. Around it extensive new suburbs grew up containing villas with walled gardens and housing for the working population. The busy port was filled with ships which carried goods around the Mediterranean in a flourishing trade with the Arab cities of North Africa. Well-irrigated orchards and vegetable gardens were tended on the plain outside the city gates. Palermo became one of the great cities of the world, with a population of around 100,000 by the end of the tenth century, a powerful trading centre well before the rise of the maritime cities of northern Italy.[4]

Ibn Hawqal, an Arab geographer and chronicler who visited the city in 972–3, provided a description. Born in Baghdad, Ibn Hawqal travelled across Europe, India and Africa for 30 years before publishing his *Cosmology* in Baghdad in 977. In it he describes the countries he visited, especially the Muslim territories, which included Sicily. This is how he found Palermo:

> Siqilliyah [Sicily] is an island of seven days' journey long and four wide; she is covered in mountains, castles and fortresses, populated and cultivated all over. Palermo, the largest and best-known city, is the capital. Situated on the sea, on the north coast, Palermo is divided into five distinct *harat* [districts].
>
> El-Kassar: the ancient city centre surrounded by a formidable, high stone wall. This district, which is inhabited by nobles and wealthy merchants, has nine gates. A grand mosque stands here, once a Christian church.

This was the Cassaro, or castle district, occupying the high ground, stretching down to where the Quattro Canti stands today. The grand mosque stood on the site of the present cathedral.

> Khalessah: the seat of the emir and his court, with lower stone walls. It contains the arsenal and prison, baths, a mosque and government offices. There are four gates, the most famous being the Bab al-bahr [Marine Gate] next to the sea. There are no shops or markets in this district.

This was the Kalsa district, stretching down to the sea. Originally the Arabs had their base in the Cassaro until about 937 when they decided to move it to the Kalsa district. Here they built a fortified palace close to the Marine Gate and the port.

Sacalibah: the port and the largest and most heavily populated district, the home of sailors and foreign merchants. It has no surrounding walls. The harbour is filled with ships, in the evening their prows pointing towards the sunset.

Mosque: so called for a large mosque known as Ibn Saclab. This is also a substantial residential district.

El-Jadid: new suburbs with residential housing.

The army is based west of the El-Kassar district in its own quarters. Irregular troops and volunteers, hired for specific campaigns, congregate down by the waterfront, causing trouble for passers-by. The public markets are situated between the Mosque and El-Jadid districts, where 150 butchers' shops can be found. The butchers have their own mosque, a sign of their prosperity, which is estimated to hold 7,000 people. Outside the city walls tradesmen offer their goods and services. They include sellers of oil, money-changers, chemists, tailors and armourers. Papyrus grows nearby which is used to make rope for the navy and paper for the emir. In total there are over 300 mosques in the city. Clean water is abundant, brought in by canals and aqueducts, and is available in the houses of wealthy residents. The shape of the city is oblong and it is paved with stone.[5]

Muslim rule in Sicily

The fighting to control Sicily was very destructive, comparable to the Punic Wars in the third century BC, and many cities were left in ruins. Once it was established, Arab rule relaxed and life for the local population became more stable. Unlike Byzantium, which had sought to exploit the island, the Arabs brought progress and developments in commerce and agriculture. Taxes were set at a reasonable level and the local economy boomed to the benefit of much of the population. The ancient cities received new life, especially Palermo, but also Mazara and Trapani in the west, and Agrigento in the south. To the east, Syracuse was rebuilt and refortified after the destruction caused by the siege, while Messina and Catania were also developed. In the tenth century, the Aghlabids of Tunisia were defeated by the Fatimid dynasty, which transferred its capital to Cairo, from where they ruled Tunisia and Sicily. The emirate in Sicily became largely independent, the hereditary territory of the Kalbid dynasty based in Palermo.

Arab Sicily was multi-ethnic, a loose confederation of peoples rather than an integrated state. The Christian and Jewish religions, both recognised in the

Qur'an, were tolerated and freedom of worship was allowed within certain regulations. Christians, for example, were not allowed to carry arms or to build tall
houses which could be defended. Following a famine in 940 due to bad harvests,
the Arabs threw many of the Christians out of western Sicily, using the army
to search through villages and farms. The west became predominantly Muslim,
with Christian and Jewish communities concentrated in the big cities. In the
centre most people converted to Islam, while the majority of Christians lived
in the east under the rule of noble landowners. The dispersion of Muslims and
Christians across the island thus broadly followed the old Punic/Greek division.

For administrative purposes, Sicily was divided into three provinces, the Val
di Mazara (with Palermo its capital) covering the west, the Val di Noto (Noto)
covering the south-east, and the Val Demone (Messina) covering the north-
east. The name Demone came from the Arabic for 'woods', referring to the
wooded territory around Mount Etna. The division into these three provinces
lasted until the nineteenth century. Four levels of citizenship emerged for non-
Arabs: independent, for a few community leaders; tribute, for freemen paying
defined duties; vassal, for those who were secure but with property under Arab
ownership; and slaves who provided the workforce.

The Arabs applied their talents to agriculture and, encouraged to find new
methods by the difficult conditions in North Africa, drew upon experience
in Persia and Egypt. From this they developed a scientific approach that revo-
lutionised farming and food production. It combined the study of plants, and
their suitability for different climates, with new techniques of planting and
growing crops. A central feature was the provision of irrigation. The Arab
approach was summarised in the *Book of Agriculture*, which included examples
from Sicily, written around 1158 by Ibn al-'Awwam, an Arab living in Spain.
It contained a wealth of practical information, in 34 chapters accompanied by
diagrams, on subjects such as pruning fruit trees, growing herbs for medicinal
use, raising pigeons, rearing and training horses, preserving dried fruit, bread-
making and methods of treating the soil and laying out crops. This handbook,
which represented the most advanced knowledge of its time on horticulture
and husbandry, was widely read across Europe.[6]

In Sicily the Arabs found a familiar climate combined with fertile soil and
a plentiful supply of fresh water from numerous rivers. The early settlers had
positioned cities by the rivers, so that improving the water supply through canals
and aqueducts did not present a problem. In the countryside, water towers and

tanks were used, as well as water wheels driven by mules. New crops such as cotton, rice, silk and sugar cane were introduced. A thriving business in luxury silk garments developed. Sugar was used to make the intensely sweet desserts and pastries still to be found in Sicily. Grain continued to be the principal crop, especially hard durum wheat suitable for making dried pasta for storage and export. Semolina, made by crushing the berry produced by the wheat, was used to make couscous, an Arab dish still to be found in western Sicily. New varieties of fruit and vegetables appeared, including oranges and lemons, aubergines and cucumbers, melons, pistachios and almonds. Two crops that were reduced in quantity under the Arabs were olive oil, due to the destruction of olive trees in the fighting, and wine, which was not widely consumed by Muslims.

Fishing was another area of Arab expertise. Muslim immigrants, many of whom came from just across the sea in Tunisia, were practised fishermen. In Sicily they found similar conditions and introduced their method of fishing for tuna using interconnecting nets to lead the fish into a trap. This became a hallmark of the Sicilian tuna-fishing industry which exists up to the present day.

Arab influence extended to the Sicilian language and Arab words entered the mainstream, including place names used by Muslims settlers. The port in western Sicily known in antiquity as Lilybaeum became Marsala from the Arabic 'Marsa-Allah' meaning 'Harbour of God'. Derivatives of *qal'ah*, meaning 'fortress', can be found in the names of towns such as Caltagirone, Caltanissetta and Calatafimi. Similarly *jibel*, Arabic for mountain, appears in Gibilmanna and Gibellina. Cassata, the sweet ricotta cake and Sicilian speciality, takes its name from the Arabic *qashatah*, the bowl used to make it. The water tanks the Arabs placed in their gardens, *gabiyah* in Arabic, continued to be used in Sicilian as *gebbia*. The best-known inheritance from Arabic in Sicily is the word admiral, which is derived from *Emir-al-Bahr*, meaning 'commander of the sea'. Sicilians shortened the Arab title to *amiral*, which in Italian became *ammiraglio*. The word admiral was introduced to Northern Europe by the Crusaders.

Arab civilisation with its roots in the simple desert life reached its peak in the opulent cities like Palermo, captured during the Arab advance. Here prosperity grew on the back of successful trading with other cities around the Mediterranean. Arts and sciences flourished and Arab learning impressed the world. But the gap between the new urban culture and tribal origins was too great. The cultured and progressive side was counterbalanced by a backward looking mentality which bred suspicion and violence. Stability was undermined by rebellion and infighting between emirs of the different cities so that in the end the Arabs proved unable to create a lasting empire.

Byzantine attack on Sicily

On the orders of the emperor Michael, the Byzantines made a last attempt in 1038 to re-establish themselves in Sicily. George Maniaces, a Byzantine Greek general and governor of the Byzantine territories in southern Italy, collected a large army of Greeks strengthened by mercenaries. Maniaces was a forceful character with an impressive physique. A chronicler noted: 'Nothing in him was worthy of praise except his handsome appearance. He was proud of mind and overflowing with fearsome cruelty.'[7] Landing first at Messina, Maniaces made his way down the east coast and succeeded in retaking Syracuse. Other cities along the coast were also recaptured and eastern Sicily briefly returned to Byzantine control. Maniaces refortified Syracuse, building a fort on the southern-most point of Ortygia. Another castle, built on this same site in the thirteenth century, is known today as the Castello Maniace.

When Maniaces was recalled to Constantinople in 1039 he took with him one of the most revered Christian relics in Sicily as a gift to the empress. This was the body of Santa Lucia, patron saint of Syracuse, who was martyred in 304 in the persecutions of the emperor Diocletian. After the departure of Maniaces the Greek army dispersed and the Arabs quickly reasserted their control of eastern Sicily.

Among the force led by Maniaces was a group of Norman mercenaries who had been fighting in Apulia. One of the mercenaries was William de Hauteville, a member of the Norman family whose exploits in the south became famous. The Normans noticed the rich potential of Sicily and, once they turned their full attention to the island in the 1060s, the days of Arab dominance were numbered.

CHAPTER 3

Roger I, Norman Conqueror of Sicily

The Normans were a powerful force in medieval Europe. While their conquest of England in 1066 is well known, not so well known are their conquests in southern Europe where they controlled southern Italy, Sicily and Malta by 1091. They went on to establish themselves in Tunisia, join the first Crusade and set up a principality in Antioch. In so doing they played a decisive role in Western Europe's efforts to reclaim the Mediterranean from the Arabs. The effect of the Norman campaigns in the south was very great, for their conquests laid the basis of the Kingdom of the Two Sicilies, which in various forms lasted until the nineteenth century.

Wherever they went the Normans left monuments to their power and Christian faith: great castles, churches and cathedrals. Nowhere are these monuments more striking than in Palermo. The men who led these exploits were exceptional, tough, shrewd and hugely ambitious. One of the most successful was Roger de Hauteville, a leading figure in the story of Palermo. Roger's career began as a soldier of fortune, fighting in southern Italy with his fellow Normans under the leadership of his elder brother Robert, known as the Guiscard ('the Cunning').

The Norman campaign in the south was not a planned invasion like the conquest of England. The young Norman knights seeking their fortunes left in small groups and called for reinforcements as opportunities arose. But the Normans went south in such numbers that when William was preparing to invade England, he called for help and a contingent of knights from Italy fought at the Battle of Hastings.

The conquest of Sicily was recorded by chroniclers, one of whom, Geoffrey Malaterra, opened his account as follows:

> That most renowned prince Roger, familiar with many such authors, having had
> the histories of the ancients recited to him, decided, on the advice of his men, to
> commit to writing for the sake of posterity his laborious and perilous victories,
> specifically how he subjugated by force first Calabria and then Sicily with his army
> and ordered me to devote myself to the task of dictating this work.[1]

One family, the Hautevilles, of which Robert Guiscard and Roger were members, dominated the leadership in the south. A certain Tancred owned lands around the village of Hauteville in Normandy. He produced as many as 12 sons from his two marriages. Muriella, his first wife, bore him five: William, Drogo, Humphrey, Geoffrey and Serlo. Fressenda, his second wife, bore him seven: Robert, Mauger, William, Aubrey, Humbert, Tancred and Roger. Tancred must have been a wealthy man to have brought up so many sons as knights, as the training and equipment were expensive. However, his estate could not support such a large family, so that eight of the Hauteville sons and a number of their descendants made careers for themselves in the south. Several of them spent most of their lives in Italy where life was precarious but the rewards great. The brothers were very competitive and fought each other on occasion, coming back together in moments of crisis. They were a tough bunch, professionals who led from the front, and took on enemy champions with their lances in single combat.

The Normans in southern Italy

Southern Italy at the time was a melting pot of competing religious and political interests. In Campania, the region around Naples, three small principalities fought each other for control, Benevento, Capua and Salerno. They were in the hands of the Lombards, who, like the Normans, had come south in search of their fortune. Originally a Germanic people from northern Europe, the Lombards had settled in the region that bears their name around Milan. They were supporters of the Christian Church in Rome and were in conflict with the Byzantine Greeks, who retained control of Apulia and Calabria, with Bari as their capital. The papacy, which opposed the Church in the east, used its influence to undermine the Byzantine states while the German emperors followed the situation ready to intervene in their own interests. Saracen raids down the coast added another dimension to the anarchy.

Some Norman knights visiting a shrine to the Archangel Michael on Monte Gargano in 1016 met a Lombard leader named Melus. He came from a noble family in Bari from where he had been thrown out by the Byzantine Greeks. When Melus asked for help against the Greeks, the Normans agreed. The following year they returned with a group composed of the younger sons of nobility, mercenaries and adventurers, and together with the Lombards were initially successful. The Byzantines, however, sent reinforcements and subsequently inflicted a heavy defeat upon Melus and his combined force of Lombards and Normans.

The Normans by this time had established a reputation as fighting men and were aware of the spoils to be won. As mercenaries have so often done, they switched sides and went over to support Byzantium. They continued to use this tactic as it suited them and, while playing one side off against the other, gradually built up their strength. The first breakthrough came in 1030 when the king of Naples awarded the territory of Aversa, just north of Naples, to Rainulf who called for support from Normandy. Among the contingent to arrive were three Hautevilles, William, Drogo and Humphrey.

When Byzantium made its last attempt to regain Sicily, their general George Maniaces landed at Messina with a large force including a group of Norman mercenaries. William, the eldest of the Hautevilles, was among them and gained his nickname of Iron Arm for killing the Arab emir of Syracuse with his lance. Eastern Sicily was briefly restored to Byzantine control but the campaign collapsed in 1039 once Maniaces was recalled to Constantinople.

Returning to the campaign in Apulia, William won control of Melfi in 1042, and was elected Duke of Apulia by his fellow knights. Drogo succeeded to the title when William Iron Arm died, while Richard took over from his uncle Rainulf in Aversa. Rainulf had been the pioneer for the Normans in the south and the first to see its potential. The initiative now passed to the Hautevilles, among them Robert, who now came south. Leaving Normandy with five knights and 30 foot soldiers he stopped in Lombardy for a while, living off the land and stealing horses and weapons for his men.

Robert was powerfully built, fair-haired and hugely self confident, his dominant personality matched by a commanding voice. While fighting was his main claim to fame he also used cunning, as his nickname 'the Guiscard' implied. He was wilier than Cicero or Ulysses, according to William of Apulia:

Robert was a young man inured to hard work, prudent and ingenious, ready to turn his hand to anything that needed doing, always seeking advancement and rejoicing in honour and praise. He was just as ready to seek success by stratagems as by force, if this was necessary, because a sharp mind can often achieve what violence cannot accomplish.[2]

As there was no role for him in Apulia, he set off with a group of knights to Calabria, a wild and untamed region. Here he fought as a mercenary for the local barons over the next few years. It was in this period that his cunning was first recognised. On one occasion a monastery, which banned entry to armed men, was captured by smuggling in swords hidden in a coffin. A Greek leader, who had agreed to talks in private, was personally abducted and ransomed by Robert. Unscrupulous tricks such as these worthy of Machiavelli, together with his fighting ability, built Robert a fearsome reputation.

The conquest of Sicily

The conquest of Sicily took the Normans 30 years, a whole generation, due to inadequate resources and the decentralised nature of Arab Sicily. By contrast the conquest of England was completed in a matter of months thanks to an invasion force of around 7,000 and the fact that Harold, the English king, and many of his followers died at the Battle of Hastings. With the king and his entourage removed from the scene, the Normans were able to take advantage of the centralised English state and rapidly assume power. While resistance in the countryside continued and was not totally eliminated for several years, William was crowned king of England on Christmas Day 1066, three months after the invasion took place.

In Sicily the situation was different. Robert's first priority was to protect his Apulian territory where he often faced rebellion. So while he was present at the big battles in Sicily, playing a decisive part, the subduing of the island was left to Roger. This suited Roger well for it gave him the opportunity to come out from under his brother's dominant influence and acquire territory of his own. It was the drive of these two leaders that realised the conquest of Sicily, with Robert Guiscard the architect and Roger the executor.

The nature of Arab rule in Sicily, which had lasted for 200 years, had altered over the years to become decentralised. The Aghlabid dynasty, which initially ran Sicily from Tunisia, gave way to the Fatimids, who were based in Egypt. A hereditary emirate, the Kalbid dynasty, took control of an independent Sicily ruled from Palermo. Different emirs, or governors, ran Syracuse, Mazara, Agrigento and the interior of the island, in competition with each other. Outside the cities were the smaller towns, heavily fortified and often located on hilltops. Despite their lack of organisation, the Arabs had demonstrated during the invasion by Maniaces that they would fight hard to defend their island. These conditions made for slow progress for an invasion force.

As the time the Normans spent campaigning in the south lengthened, so the make-up and capability of their forces changed. Their success attracted followers, knights and other combatants, from different parts of France and Italy. Always few in number compared to the local population, the Normans welcomed these additions and absorbed them into their army. The campaigns continued to be led by the mounted, heavily armoured Norman knights. Typically fighting in squadrons of 25 to 50, the knights would advance in a solid line, knee to knee, starting at a trot and reaching a gallop as they approached the enemy, lances outstretched. A medieval form of blitzkrieg with huge shock value, one charge was often enough to break the enemy's line. If the defence proved stubborn, a second group of knights would be launched to attack the enemy's flank. The impact of the cavalry charge goes some way to explain how the Normans repeatedly defeated much larger armies. Their military techniques adapted to local conditions to include siegecraft, for the capturing of cities became as important as fighting set-piece battles. Crucially, after the capture of Reggio, the Normans began to make use of ships captured in the port and elsewhere along the coast.[3]

During the 1060s the Normans built up a navy that played a vital part in the conquest of Sicily. Their opponents in the region, the Byzantine Greeks and the Arabs, both had long seafaring traditions and it says much for the Normans' adaptability and operational skills that they were able to compete so soon in naval terms. Learning from the Greeks in Calabria, their navy included three types of vessel: the warship, the supply ship and the horse transport. The warships, known as *dromons* (from the Greek for 'runner') were a type of galley – narrow, fast ships, propelled by oar and sail. Developed from the ancient trireme, they came in different designs and carried crews of between 100 and 200. Horse transports, vital to the Normans, had also been developed by the Greeks. Carrying around 20 horses and their knights, the transport incorporated a ramp using a door in the side or in the stern which could be lowered upon reaching land. The knights thus rode straight off onto the beach from an early form of landing craft.[4]

Messina was the Normans' first target, a port that could act as a bridgehead for their forces. The Normans were helped by the emir of Syracuse, Ibn al-Tumna, who enlisted their support against his brother-in-law, Ibn al-Hawas, who ruled the interior of Sicily. Preparations for the invasion began in 1061 with Roger carrying out exploratory raids to test his ships and the city's defences. This experience of combined operations was used five years later in the conquest of England.[5] The invasion force consisted of 2,000 men, perhaps half of them knights. The advance party led by Roger was so successful that when Robert arrived with the main force, Messina was already in Norman hands.

Once Messina was secured, the brothers returned to the mainland, Roger to his base at Mileto in Calabria. Here he was married to Judith d'Évreux, daughter of a cousin of William the Conqueror, described as 'beautiful and of excellent parentage'.[6] It was a love match that went back several years. It did not prevent him returning shortly afterwards to Sicily. Here he was welcomed by the Christian citizens of Troina, in the interior of the island, a city Roger made his temporary base.

Campaigning continued in Sicily around the towns of the interior near Troina. Matters came to a head in 1063 when the Arabs, with reinforcements from North Africa, collected a large army near the fortress of Cerami. Here the Normans won a major victory, followed by another at Misilmeri to the south of Palermo. In the Arab camp at Misilmeri Roger found carrier pigeons, which he used to send a macabre message to the citizens of Palermo. He had them released carrying notes written in blood describing the Norman victory.

The capture of Palermo

The siege of Palermo lasted for five months and was fiercely contested. Palermo was one of the great Muslim cities, with a population of around 100,000, and was renowned as a centre of culture and trade. The Arabs were well prepared, with the city strongly fortified and the harbour protected by chains and towers. They were determined to defend their capital city to the best of their abilities. But among the population morale was low due to the earlier Norman victories.

Roger's army was joined outside Palermo by Robert's fleet of 60 ships. Their combined force consisted of knights, possibly over 1,000, together with infantry, siege engines and the equipment necessary for storming a city. The Norman ships, which were moored away from the harbour, were shortly put to the test by an Arab fleet sailing in towards Palermo. The Normans gained the initiative in the ensuing battle, with the Arab ships fleeing into the harbour. After they had entered, the defensive chain was put across the harbour's mouth but several Norman ships in close pursuit crashed through the barrier, causing damage to the Arab fleet. Palermo was now completely surrounded with supplies to the city cut off.

At first the land battle was concentrated upon the citadel, the heavily fortified El-Kassar (Cassaro) district on the high ground. Roger led the attack, putting a third of the city's walls under siege. Amid fierce fighting, javelins and arrows flew down from the ramparts on the attackers while Roger armed his infantry with bows and slings with which to return the fire. The Arabs made sorties outside the walls, which were defeated by the Normans who otherwise made little progress. Meanwhile conditions inside the city deteriorated rapidly through sickness and a lack of food. Leaving Roger to continue the main assault, Robert led an attack on the less well-defended Khalessah (Kalsa) district, down by the harbour.

> Skilfully assembling machines and ladders for scaling the walls, the duke secretly entered the orchards with 300 knights to attack the city from the other side, namely the side where the ships lay, and instructed his brother by all means to do the same from his side. When the signal was given, they rushed in without hesitation and with great clamour to carry out what they had planned. All the citizens, rushing to arms, were terrified by the noise of the tumult and hastened to their own defence. In the process they carelessly left empty that part of the wall that normally had the fewest guards. There the wall was breached by Guiscard's forces, which had placed ladders against it. Thus they took the outer city and opened the gates with iron bars so their allies could enter. The duke and the count and the entire army camped inside the city walls.[7]

Once the Normans were established within the walls, the Arabs realised that the city was lost. But despite heavy casualties they were still in a strong position, in command of the citadel, and they decided to negotiate. They called a truce and offered to accept Norman rule, paying tribute, as long as their personal safety and freedom to follow their religion were guaranteed. These terms were accepted by Robert, who saw the advantages of avoiding a long and debilitating siege. It was the beginning of a new phase in Norman–Arab relations. While there were many more battles to come in other parts of Sicily, in the capital Palermo the interests of Muslim citizens were protected by the government. A surprising alliance had been born between Christians and Muslims.

In January 1072 the Normans formally took control of Palermo. They entered the city led by Robert Guiscard, his wife Sichelgaita and Roger, followed by the other leading knights. They celebrated Mass at the basilica of Santa Maria, which had been rapidly reconverted from a mosque, taken by the reinstated Greek archbishop Nicodemus. Remains of the ancient basilica can be found in the modern cathedral.

Robert, having divided the Sicilian territories they had won between himself and Roger, remained in Palermo throughout the summer, establishing a garrison and strengthening fortifications. Repairs were made to the fort known as Castellammare (meaning 'sea castle') located at the harbour's mouth. The Normans chose the highest part of the citadel for their base. Robert started work on the castle complex, which had been an Arab fort, building a walled perimeter on the high ground. A Norman governor was appointed to run the city's administration, which was superimposed upon the existing Arab system. He retained the Arab title of emir, or *ammiratus* in Latin. This was Robert's last contribution to the conquest of Sicily, for after he returned to Apulia in the autumn, he never returned to the island.

Roger, Count of Sicily

The task of completing the conquest of Sicily was now in the hands of Roger de Hauteville, who took the title of Count of Sicily. So far it had taken the Normans ten years, in which they had gained Palermo, Messina and the Val Demone, and won every major battle they had fought with Arab forces. The Arabs, however, remained an obstinate enemy, prepared to fight long and hard to defend their territories. When Robert returned to the mainland, Roger was left with scant resources, perhaps as few as 100 knights, with which to continue the campaign. Due to the lack of Norman manpower, the campaign developed into a drawn-out war of attrition which lasted for another 20 years. During this time Roger kept close control of Sicilian territory, creating no new fiefdoms, but ruling captured cities through close relatives and associates, and so avoiding the rebellions that plagued Robert in Apulia.

Norman perseverance paid off and Trapani was taken in 1077, followed by Taormina two years later. After the siege of Syracuse in 1085 the news arrived of the death of Robert Guiscard. Having left Sicily, Robert had campaigned tirelessly, at one stage entering Rome to protect Pope Gregory. He died, probably of typhoid, on the island of Cephalonia in Greece campaigning against Byzantium. His body was brought back to Apulia where it was buried at Venosa alongside his brothers William, Drogo and Humphrey. Unlike Roger, Robert never settled down to consolidate and rule his territories, preferring the life of a soldier of fortune to the end. He was succeeded as Duke of Apulia by his son by Sichelgaita, Roger Borsa.

The capture of Syracuse was followed by that of Enna, Agrigento and Noto. Then to protect Sicily from attack by Arab shipping, Roger led an expedition to take Malta, an important Arab stronghold and naval base. When Malta fell in 1091 many Christian prisoners, pilgrims and traders captured by pirates were released and brought back to Sicily. The Norman conquest of the south was now complete, giving Sicily 100 years of peace and prosperity under Hauteville rule, widely regarded as the greatest period in the island's history.

During the last decade of his life Roger turned his attention to governing Sicily. Until then he had campaigned almost continuously at the head of his knights. He proved to be a shrewd and able governor, successfully balancing the interests of the different communities. A new ruling class emerged of Normans, French and Lombards, all of whom supported the Roman Church. The Arabs continued to run much of the administration while Arab soldiers were recruited into Roger's army. A number of Greeks with experience of Byzantine government were promoted to prominent positions. Freedom of worship and the right to be judged by their own laws were granted to Latin peoples from the north, Greeks, Jews and Arabs. In this way Norman adaptability and openness to other cultures created strength out of diversity. In recognition of Roger's status, Pope Urban II bestowed on the count and his successors the apostolic leadership in Sicily. This put Roger in control and established the principle of a national Church led by a ruling family for the first time in Europe.

Acting as champions of the Roman Church while being tolerant of Islam provided a difficult balancing act for the Normans in Sicily. Partnership with the Arabs was crucial for ruling the island. However, the objective of the Roman Church was to reclaim Sicily for Christianity. These conflicting attitudes to the Muslim population built tension at the heart of Norman Sicily.

In his family life Roger made a contribution to the Hauteville line by fathering 17 children in his three marriages.[8] His first two wives, Judith and Eremburga, who were both Norman, gave him more than ten children but no surviving male heir. In his fifties Roger married Adelaide del Vasto, who came from a prominent family in northern Italy. When Jordan, Roger's illegitimate son and presumed heir, died a few years later, prospects for the succession looked bleak. But in 1093 Adelaide bore the count a son, Simon, and two years later a second son, whom they called Roger. By this stage the count's reputation was such that his daughters were sought after by the royal families of Europe and two of them were married to kings.

Count Roger died in June 1101 at the age of 70. He was buried in the Benedictine abbey of Santissima Trinità (Holy Trinity), which he had founded at Mileto in Calabria. His tomb was an ancient Roman sarcophagus covered by a canopy of porphyry, the red stone usually reserved for royalty, identified with the Byzantine emperors. It was sign of his status, for the man who had begun his adult life as a mercenary soldier ended it as one of the most respected princes in Europe. He left Sicily enjoying a new level of prosperity, with Palermo established as a centre of Mediterranean trade. His government ruled peacefully over a population of mixed races and religions. To his heirs he passed a stable state of Sicily.

The Countess Adelaide was determined and resourceful. She ruled as regent for her sons, relying upon the officials appointed by Roger to govern Sicily. Rebellions were put down and the succession was ensured. After Simon died young, Roger II inherited the title and went on to become one of the outstanding rulers of the Middle Ages.

CHAPTER 4

Roger II, King of Sicily and Southern Italy

The Norman achievement in the south reached its peak under Roger II. He united Sicily and southern Italy into a kingdom recognised by the Pope and the crowned heads of Europe with himself as king. A consummate statesman, he steered his kingdom successfully through treacherous waters to become one of the most powerful in Europe. Roger had a formidable presence. He was clever, quick and domineering, both an intellectual and a man of action. As king he was apparently 'more feared than loved by his people'.[1]

His reign represented something new in medieval Europe. Feudal principles of landownership and service to the Crown were superimposed upon well-developed administrative practices taken from Islam and Byzantium. The result was a state with a remarkably efficient organisation that anticipated future bureaucratic forms of government. Its unique character came from a brilliant fusion of Latin, Greek and Arab cultures, recorded for posterity by the Norman monuments in Sicily. For Palermo the rule of Roger II was the most glorious period in the city's entire history.

The early years

While acting as regent, Countess Adelaide made an important decision for her family and for the future of Sicily when she moved the court to Palermo. During the long campaign to subdue Sicily and thereafter for the rest of his life, Roger I's preferred base had been Mileto in Calabria. Adelaide and the court moved first to Messina and then to Palermo. The move made good sense for many reasons. Palermo had been the Arab capital of Sicily for 200 years and offered palaces, castles, administrative offices, arsenals, a mint and a safe harbour. The economy was booming based on trade with the eastern Mediterranean and North Africa. The city's environment was cosmopolitan, with a Muslim majority, and the Normans were able to build on the infrastructure created by the Arabs.

It was here that Roger II came of age in 1112, was made a knight and took up the reins of government as Count of Sicily and Calabria. His mother provided him with a Greek tutor, Christodoulos, who instructed him in the traditions of Byzantium. In Palermo he became strongly influenced by Arab culture and he grew up speaking French, Greek and Arabic.

When Simon died aged 12, Roger became heir to the title. He married Elvira, daughter of Alfonso VI, king of Castile and León, in 1117. Dynastically it was a good marriage, for Alfonso had built a strong position for himself throughout the Iberian Peninsula. Elvira, whose mother was Moorish, was brought up in an atmosphere of coexistence with the Muslim population and it seems likely that she viewed the Arabs in Sicily sympathetically. Although arranged for reasons of state, it appears to have been a happy marriage. The succession was secured when within a few years Elvira bore Roger four sons, Roger, Tancred, Alfonso and William.

The first campaigns

As Count of Sicily, Roger's first move was to impress his authority upon the island. According to his biographer, the Abbot Alexander of Telese:

> When as a young man he had been made a knight and was in a position to exercise his rights as the count, he was so firm and decisive in his actions, ruling the whole of Sicily so well and strongly, and exercising such terrible authority, that no robber, thief, plunderer or other criminal dared to stir out of his lair.[2]

Having secured Sicily, Roger turned his attention to southern Italy where the Hauteville territories were once again under threat. Until 1111 these territories had been controlled by two powerful figures, Roger II's cousin Roger Borsa and Bohemond I, but in that year both died leaving underage successors. The inherent instability of the region resurfaced with rebellions breaking out and the Pope exerting his influence against Norman interests. Roger crossed to the mainland to help William, Roger Borsa's young son, who became Duke of Apulia, providing him with troops and equipment. But William was not a natural leader and soon became dependent on Roger for military support. In return, Roger made a hard bargain, acquiring Robert Guiscard's half-share in Palermo, Messina and Calabria. In this way control of the whole of Sicily and Calabria passed to Roger II.

In 1127 came the news of the death of William of Apulia. Roger took his army to Salerno. Fighting took place over the next three years to secure the main towns. In the long run the strength of Roger's army and navy prevailed and the coalition was forced to concede defeat. Roger's right to the dukedoms of Apulia and Calabria was confirmed by the Pope. Roger collected the barons and the leading churchmen together at Melfi and had them swear an oath of loyalty to himself and his two eldest sons.

In 1130, the year that Roger added the duchy of Apulia to his possessions, Pope Honorius II died and a schism took place in the papacy. The College of Cardinals was unable to decide between two candidates, both of whom claimed the throne of St Peter, and who took the names Anacletus II and Innocent II. Innocent went to France. Anacletus, who appeared the stronger candidate, remained in Rome. When both candidates started lobbying for support among the European powers, Roger began talks with Anacletus. In return for his support Roger demanded a crown. To accommodate him a new kingdom was created, with Palermo the capital, based on dubious historical evidence that the city was the site of an ancient kingdom. In September 1130, Pope Anacletus invested Roger with the Kingdom of Sicily and Southern Italy, the latter including Capua and Naples.

The coronation

On Christmas Day 1130 Roger II was crowned king at the cathedral in Palermo. It was a sumptuous occasion, on which Roger put his wealth and celebrity status on show. Huge crowds thronged the streets while barons and churchmen from all over the kingdom attended the ceremony to witness Roger, dressed like a

Byzantine emperor, receive his crown. Roger's vision of kingship was distinctly oriental, as demonstrated by a famous mosaic in Palermo, in the church known as the Martorana. The mosaic shows him receiving his crown directly from Christ. It is not clear from the chroniclers who actually placed the crown on his head. One version claims that for political reasons it was one of the powerful barons, Robert of Capua, while others name Archbishop Peter of Palermo. According to Telese:

> The duke was led to the cathedral as befits royalty. There he received unction with the holy oil and assumed the royal dignity. It is impossible to describe just how glorious he looked, how regal in his dignity, how splendid in his richly decorated robes. For it seemed to the crowd that all the riches and honours of this world were present.
>
> The glory and wealth of the royal palace was such that it caused wonder and amazement to the extent that it made those who had come from so far away not a little afraid. For the reality was even more extraordinary than that which they had been led to believe.[3]

Following the coronation, Roger attended to affairs of the Church, strengthening his patronage of the great abbeys and monasteries in his kingdom, which had become major landowners. The monasteries, of which there were more than 30 in Sicily, held strong influence in the countryside so there was probably a political motive in Roger's support. Messina had become an important port serving the eastern Mediterranean and now became an archbishopric. To support Pope Anacletus a new cathedral was built at Cefalù, with mosaic craftsmen brought in from Constantinople. Christian orders were brought onto the island, including Cistercians, Augustinians, Templars and Hospitalers. In his patronage of the Church Roger was continuing his father's policy of re-establishing the Roman Church after the Muslim domination. The process was aided by the arrival in Sicily of increasing numbers of men from the north, followers of the Roman Church including knights and churchmen, attracted to the flourishing Norman state.

Rebellion in southern Italy

The triumph of the coronation was followed shortly by news of rebellion in southern Italy. This time it came from Amalfi, a recent addition to Roger's territories. It marked the beginning of a ten-year war to consolidate the new kingdom, something that presented Roger with the most difficult challenge of his career. Brought up in peaceful court surroundings, Roger II was not a soldier by training and, while he was brave in action, military leadership was not one of his strengths. Romuald, the archbishop of Salerno, who knew him well, wrote of him: 'King Roger was large of stature, corpulent, leonine of face, somewhat hoarse of voice; wise, far-seeing, careful, subtle of mind, great in counsel, preferring to use his intelligence rather than force.'[4]

Living in Palermo, he regularly underestimated the turbulent nature of the barons in the southern cities of the mainland and their desire for independence. The major powers that had seen their territories taken over by the new Norman kingdom made the most of the rebellion to reassert their interests in the region. The Pope and the German and Byzantine emperors lined up to cut the Norman king down to size.

Roger handled the crisis shrewdly. His spies told him of weaknesses within the coalition's army. It was not united and many of their soldiers, who were not professional, were suffering from the length of the campaign. Roger waited as cracks appeared in the unwieldy invasion force, and when the septuagenarian German emperor Lothar and his army returned to Germany, he launched his response. Capua and Avellino were rapidly retaken while Naples capitulated.

The death of Pope Anacletus in 1138 ended the papal schism. Innocent II became pope and Roger offered his support in return for his confirmation as king. The investiture took place in July 1139 when the Pope confirmed Roger as king of Sicily and his sons Roger as Duke of Apulia and Alfonso as Prince of Capua. When Tancred, Roger's second son, was made Prince of Bari, all three major cities in the region came under direct control of the Hauteville family. Roger's sons went on to subdue the Abruzzi region so that by 1140 all of Italy south of the Papal States was firmly in the hands of the king. After Roger had re-embarked for Sicily he could refer to himself as *Rex Siciliae et Italiae*.

Palermo as the seat of government

With peace restored, Roger turned his attention to government and introduced a number of reforms. He was a hard worker and keen administrator who insisted upon careful accounts being kept of royal expenditure. His officials had a hard time keeping up with him, for a close companion said of Roger that 'he got more done asleep than most men did awake'.[5] Reforms were made to the currency, which was based on the Arab tarì, or quarter dinar. For the first time a standard monetary unit appeared, the ducalis or ducat, named after the Duchy of Apulia. The ducat was a silver coin, typically showing an image of Christ Pantocrator (Christ All-powerful) on the obverse, and on the reverse portraits of the king and his eldest son, Roger. While not used for long in Sicily, when later introduced in Venice as a gold coin the ducat became a standard trading currency across much of Europe.

The prosperity of the kingdom attracted talented individuals from many countries to serve in Roger's government in Palermo, as recorded by Romuald: 'And although the king himself was possessed of great wisdom, intelligence and judgement, he also gathered men of good sense of different classes from the various parts of the earth and made them partners in his decisions.'[6] The purpose of this policy was to offset the influence of the Norman barons, who were independent, unruly and too irresponsible to hold high office.

For most of Roger's reign the top position in government was held by George of Antioch. His title in Latin was *ammiratus ammiratorum*, or 'emir of emirs', and for the Greeks archon of archons. The position combined government responsibilities with those of commander-in-chief and was the equivalent of prime minister with an active service role as great admiral. Originally responsible only for Palermo, the role had expanded to cover Sicily and then the entire kingdom. In charge of both military and government affairs, as in the Arab states, George 'ruled by the sword and the pen'.[7]

Christodoulos, a Greek Christian, had been the first to hold this position, appointed by Roger I and then ruling Sicily during Roger II's boyhood. Adelaide had chosen him as Roger II's tutor. After Christodoulos died in 1126, his deputy George was promoted first to emir and then in 1132 to emir of emirs. A Greek Christian and an accountant by trade, George was born in Syria and served the king in Constantinople, from where he left for the Arab court at Mahdia in North Africa. Here he rose to prominence in charge of financial administration. When he fell out of favour, George made contact with the government in Palermo and was employed by Christodoulos for his financial expertise, fluent Arabic and knowledge of the Mediterranean.

As emir of emirs George of Antioch became Roger's right-hand man and the most powerful man in the kingdom after the king, a position he held until his death around 1150. He was largely responsible for the later expansion of the kingdom into North Africa. George had a fiery personality and was a daring and lucky commander. As his biographer al-Maqrisi tells us, he played a central role in the kingdom.

> [George] amassed the revenues and organised the foundations of the kingdom. He veiled Roger from [his] subjects and arranged for him to dress in clothes like the Muslims' and not to ride out, nor to show himself in public, except on holidays when he would process, preceded by horses adorned with saddles of gold and silver and with caparisons studded with gemstones and by domed letters and gilded banners with the parasol above him and the crown upon his head.[8]

Two monuments to the great admiral have survived in Palermo. One is a seven-arched bridge over the river Oreto which stands outside the historic centre to the south-east of the city. The other is the church known as the Martorana, the full name of which is Santa Maria dell'Ammiraglio (St Mary's of the Admiral). The church, which was founded by the admiral and dedicated to the Virgin Mary, contains mosaics showing the admiral prostrating himself before the Virgin Mary, and King Roger II receiving his crown from the hand of Christ.

The top government institution was the *curia regis*, an assembly of chief subjects, nobles, barons, bishops and other churchmen. Its role was to take note of the king's wishes, to advise him on policy and to help in the drawing up of legislation. The *curia* acted as the supreme court of the kingdom to which magistrates could refer cases. High officers of state included the chancellor, responsible for issuing government acts, a position held from 1137 to 1152 by Robert of Selby, an Englishman from Yorkshire. Robert was a robust character who took part in suppressing the rebellions and was highly influential at court. Vice chancellor in this period was Maio of Bari, a shrewd and talented administrator from Apulia, who succeeded Robert as chancellor, and who played a leading role under William I. Thomas Brown, another Englishman, held the post of master of the king's chapels.

One of the strengths of the kingdom was its financial administration, overseen by Greeks such as George of Antioch, and administered by Arab civil servants. Properties were registered and valued and taxes were efficiently collected. Peaceful conditions around Sicily, enforced by a powerful navy, led to boom conditions in trade. Sicilian agricultural produce was, as ever, in great demand. Wheat, oranges, lemons, almonds and salt tuna were among the items supplied to cities around the Mediterranean. Sicilian timber for use in shipbuilding was another export. Arab and Jewish traders flourished, attracting others from Venice, Pisa and Genoa, who established their communities in the city. Through these activities, his military campaigns and his own large estates, Roger had at his disposal revenues that far outstripped those of most contemporary states. The revenue from Palermo alone was reputed to exceed that of England.

Roger's court in Palermo was one of the most brilliant in Europe, with the king acting as a great patron of the arts and sciences. Scholars, scientists, writers and artists flocked to the city with its unique mix of cultures. French and Latin, the languages of the barons, were spoken at court. Greek was the language of top officials and parts of the government. Arabic was the language of science and the arts as well as of the financial administration. Palermo developed into an intellectual centre of high achievement. Classical Greek works by Plato, Euclid and Ptolemy became better known in the West through Latin translations prepared in the city. Doctors from the famous medical school in Salerno practised there. Arab poets such as Ibn Hamdis presented their poems at court. The Greek historian Nilus Doxopatrius wrote his treatise on Church dogma in which he claimed that Rome had lost its primacy to Constantinople when the city was overrun by barbarians. Astronomy was studied and scientific experiments were encouraged. The atmosphere of the court was distinctly Muslim, with Roger most at his ease when discussing scientific subjects in the company of Arab experts.

The most significant work to emerge from Roger's court in Palermo was the study of world geography by the Arab scholar Muhammed al-Edrisi. Born in Ceuta of a noble Moroccan family, al-Edrisi studied in Cordoba and travelled extensively in Africa and Asia Minor. After his arrival in Palermo in 1139 he became a close friend of the king. Interested in the topography of his realm, Roger commissioned al-Edrisi to carry out a monumental study of world geography that took him 15 years to complete. Under Roger's patronage and with his close involvement, information was collected from far and wide, from the Normans in northern Europe, from ships' captains and by men sent out on voyages. The works of ancient and contemporary geographers were consulted. The result was published in January 1154 and was known as *The Book of Roger*. Its title, which may have been suggested by the king himself, was *Amusements for Him Who Longs to Travel the World*. It was the outstanding work of geography of its time and became famous across the Muslim world. Due to the king's death shortly after publication it was not immediately translated into Latin and remained unknown in the West until the sixteenth century. It contained the most accurate maps and descriptions of the world then available, starting with the statement that the world is round like a sphere, and was copied by geographers for the next 300 years. The book was accompanied by a gigantic world map engraved on a solid silver dish, with a diameter of about two metres, which has not survived. *The Book of Roger* contained descriptions of the countries of the world, from the Mediterranean to northern Europe, from Africa to the Middle East, India and China. England gets the following mention:

> England is set in the Ocean of Darkness. It is a considerable island, whose shape is that of the head of an ostrich, and where there are flourishing towns, high mountains, great rivers and plains. This country is most fertile; its inhabitants are brave, active and enterprising, but all is in the grip of winter.[9]

The Normans adapted Palermo to their needs, leaving the outline of the Arab city essentially unaltered. The main change was the location of their headquarters, which they moved from the Kalsa district to higher ground inland. The Arab emirs had latterly preferred to be based near the port from where they were close to the fleet. The choice of the higher ground was made by Robert Guiscard after the capture of Palermo in 1072 and his successful storming of the lower city. As in the Arab days, the upper city known as the Cassaro was a city within a city, protected by high walls interspersed with towers. It reached down in a semicircle to take in the territory around the modern cathedral, extending to where the Quattro Canti stands today. The Cassaro was the home of the barons while Kalsa, the lower city, was where the Arabs lived with their markets and mosques. At the entrance to the harbour Roger extended the castle known as Castellammare to include residential apartments.

At the highest point of the Cassaro, defended by impressively high walls, stood the palace of Roger II, known today as the Palazzo dei Normanni (Norman Palace). It incorporated the king's apartments, courtyards, chapels and gardens. The treasury was located within its walls on the north side in the Torre Pisana (Pisan Tower) under the watchful eyes of Arab guards. There were servants' quarters, guardrooms and a harem. The king's personal servants were eunuchs, a practice inherited from the Arab emirs, who also looked after the children and the harem. An Arab cook supervised the kitchens. The palace grounds also contained workshops to supply the court with their finery. Goldsmiths, jewellers and silk workers were employed here and a fine silk mantle has survived which is on display in Vienna. It carries an inscription in Arabic stating that it was made in the royal workshop in Palermo in 1133–4.

Roger's greatest monument, the Cappella Palatina (Palatine Chapel), built on the first floor of the palace, was consecrated on Palm Sunday 1140. Dedicated to St Peter, the basilica contains a rich array of mosaics depicting biblical as well as oriental scenes with a huge image of Christ Pantocrator at its centre.

Within a short distance below the palace, Roger founded the Benedictine monastery, San Giovanni degli Eremiti (St John of the Hermits), which in its day was the richest of all the Sicilian monasteries. Its five red cupolas and intimate cloisters, recalling the Arab influence, are one of the great sights of Palermo.

As well as his palace in Palermo, Roger built for himself a country estate not far from the city at a place called Favara. Here he created an artificial lake, which he stocked with fish, and an extensive park, which he filled with deer. On the side of the lake he converted an old Arab building into a palace, the remains of which can be seen today. Roger left one other outstanding monument, his cathedral at Cefalù, which is among the greatest Norman monuments in Sicily.

In *The Book of Roger*, al-Edrisi left the following description of Palermo:

First in importance comes Palermo, that beautiful great city, the largest and most sublime metropolis in the world, whose praises never end; the city decorated with such elegance; seat of kings ancient and modern. Located on the sea, on the western side of the island, surrounded by mountains, her beaches are clear and sparkling.

The city is divided into two, Cassaro, the upper city, and Kalsa (also referred to as the borgo or suburb) the lower. Cassaro is the ancient fortress, famous throughout the world. It covers three districts; the central one filled with towered palaces and nobles' houses, mosques, warehouses, baths and the grand merchants' shops. The other districts also contain palaces, richly decorated buildings, baths and warehouses. Cassaro is the location of the cathedral, first a Christian church and then a mosque, and now returned to its original religion. It is hard to imagine the beauty of this monument with its decorations, rare works of art and sculpture. When the Arabs ruled Palermo, the Kalsa was the seat of the emir, whose palace was close to the Bab al-Bahr (the Marine Gate) and the port where the ships were built.

The countryside around Palermo is well irrigated and filled with freshwater springs. The city has an abundance of fruit and her buildings and elegant villas defy description. In summary, to look at this city is enough to make one's head spin.

Cassaro is surrounded by such high walls as to make it impregnable. At its highest point Roger has built a new palace from large blocks of stone defended by high towers which contains mosaics, minarets, well-constructed rooms, architectural decorations, rare ornaments and elegant images of all kinds. Visitors praise the splendours of Palermo to the skies, saying that they know nowhere else with such impressive buildings.

The Kalsa, which surrounds the ancient Cassaro, covers a wide area. It is full of warehouses, shops, markets, baths and residential houses and is protected by a wall and a moat. The gardens and villas of the Kalsa are supplied with fresh water brought in by canals from the mountains surrounding the city. Water mills, to supply the needs of the city, are established along the river to the south.[10]

Roger's last years

The turning point in Roger's fortunes came when he lost several of the people closest to him during the years 1148–52. His eldest son Roger, Duke of Apulia, was killed fighting in southern Italy at the age of 30. This was a serious blow for the duke had shown many of the best Hauteville qualities, had taken control of southern Italy and had been first in line to succeed his father. Tancred and Alfonso, Roger's other two sons who had been tested in government, had already died, leaving William, reputedly the least able of them all, heir to the throne. Worried about the succession, Roger had William crowned co-ruler of the kingdom in 1151. He also married again, to Sibylla of Burgundy, who died in childbirth shortly afterwards. His third marriage followed, to Beatrice of Rethel in Germany. This union brought no sons but a daughter, Constance, whom Roger never saw. Roger also lost two key officials, Robert of Selby and George of Antioch in 1151–2. Both men had been Roger's close and trusted associates, and George had been the power behind the throne for the past 25 years. Their deaths left a great gap at a critical time.

The pro-Catholic and anti-Muslim forces in Sicily had been growing steadily for years. Knights from France, Lombardy and southern Italy had arrived in large numbers to join the flourishing kingdom, swelling the elite ruling class. Monks and other clergymen arrived to help build the Christian Church, serving in Palermo or joining the newly established abbeys and monasteries. A combination of powerful barons and leading churchmen, many of them with an interest in landowning, upset the balance between Christian and Muslim communities. The guarantee of tolerance for the Arabs, first made by Robert Guiscard after the capture of Palermo, came under increasing threat. Muslims were pressured to convert to Christianity and those who did not were increasingly marginalised in society.

To replace George of Antioch, Roger chose Philip of Mahdia, who was a eunuch and a converted Christian, probably of Greek origin. Enslaved by the Arabs in North Africa, he may have escaped to Palermo with George of Antioch. Philip was brought up in the royal household and became close to the king through many years of service. According to Romuald: 'Since he [Roger] had faith in Philip's dealings and found him to be capable of carrying out his affairs, [he] put him at the head of the whole palace and appointed him master of his household.'[11]

Upon George's death Philip was appointed admiral of the fleet and was sent to North Africa to capture the town of Buna. This was rapidly achieved and he returned in triumph to Palermo. Here, however, Philip found himself arrested and thrown into prison on charge of renouncing the Catholic faith, of secretly following Islam, and of attending services in the mosques. The implication was that his earlier conversion had not been genuine. Fellow eunuchs close to Philip were arrested on the same charge.

When Roger heard the nature of the charges he ordered the case to be heard by the *curia*, an event which took place late in 1153. Philip, confident of the king's support, firmly denied the charges. Witnesses then came forward and testified for the prosecution. Philip, faced with the hostility of the *curia*, appealed to the king for a pardon, making an oath to follow the Christian faith in future. In a tearful speech Roger said that he would have pardoned Philip of any crime except one against his religion.

> I would not pardon an affront to our faith, nor an offence to the Christian religion, by my own son, nor would I ever set free even my nearest relative. Let the whole world know that I love the Christian faith with complete affection and will not hesitate to avenge an affront even among my ministers.

The case was passed to the *curia* for sentencing: 'Then the counts, justiciars, barons and judges who were present, considering the statement of the king, took themselves off to one side and having discussed the case for some time, pronounced their sentence: death by fire.'

The sentence was carried out shortly afterwards.

> Philip was tied by the feet to wild horses and violently dragged up to a lime furnace in front of the palace. From there, released from the horses' feet, he was thrown into the middle of the flames where he was consumed in an instant.[12]

The others accused of the same crime also suffered capital punishment. To the Arabs, Philip's brutal execution was an act of treachery made worse by the fact that it took place in the holy month of Ramadan.

The facts of the trial and execution are not in doubt. The account by Romuald, archbishop of Salerno, is confirmed by Arab sources.[13] According to the Arabs, the pretext for Philip's arrest was the leniency he had shown towards some wealthy Muslim families whom he had allowed to escape during the capture of Buna. The reason for the execution remains unclear but it does not seem likely that Philip was guilty of secretly following Islam. He had served for years in the royal household in close proximity to senior officials and to the king himself. Reliability and loyalty were essential qualities for serving the king and Philip's character and habits would have been well known.

The probable truth of Philip's case is that he was sacrificed by Roger in a show trial to protect the succession of his son William. Roger was well aware of William's shortcomings and with the barons gaining in strength he could see dangers ahead. The barons and the Church were united in their anti-Muslim stance and probably demanded some high-profile, pro-Christian sign from Roger. Religious persecution was in the air at the time. Another factor was also at play. By 1153 Roger was showing signs of the illness that would soon kill him. The precise nature of the illness is unknown, with reports mentioning angina, a constriction of the throat and a fever. In any case his health had been deteriorating for some time. Given Roger's normally robust nature, his sympathy with the Arabs and his customary loyalty towards his officials, it can only be supposed that when severely reduced by illness he succumbed to overwhelming pressure.[14]

Philip's execution marked the end of peaceful coexistence between Christians and Muslims in Sicily. The Christian elite had sent a clear message to the Muslim community: no one was now safe. In the words of the German historian Eric Caspar:

> In the flames of the fire also perished the tolerance which had made the Norman
> state great. The solidarity and internal unity, vital in countering threats from abroad,
> began to break up. A new era opened for the kingdom, one of internal divisions,
> which proved even more dangerous than that of the rebellions.[15]

As the Arabs predicted, Roger did not survive long after Philip's death. He died three months later, in February 1154, aged 58. He had ruled in total for 42 years, for 24 as king. The chronicler Hugo Falcandus commented: 'Not long afterwards he himself surrendered to fate, overcome by early old age, both worn down by his immense efforts and more devoted to sexual activity than the body's good health requires.'[16]

Despite his wish to be buried at Cefalù, where a sarcophagus had been prepared for him, he was buried in the cathedral in Palermo. His tomb made of porphyry, the red stone associated with the Byzantine emperors, can be seen there today.

CHAPTER 5

The Last Norman Kings

A t the death of Roger II storm clouds were gathering over the Norman kingdom of Sicily. The Pope, Adrian IV, was challenging the legitimacy of the Sicilian Crown. Germany, under the leadership of Emperor Frederick Barbarossa, was planning an expedition to southern Italy, while Byzantium wanted revenge for the attacks on her territory. The Arabs in North Africa were looking for an opportunity to free themselves from rule by Palermo. In Sicily the barons were demanding a more active role in government and posed a greater threat to stability than ever before. The small Sicilian state could not handle all these pressures at once. In addition, the character of the Norman king was a crucial factor. Roger II, while ruling his kingdom with an iron fist, had used shrewd diplomacy in dealing with foreign powers. His successors were just not of the same calibre and were incapable of preventing the descent into chaos.

William I, the Bad

The succession passed without incident and William I was crowned king at Easter 1154 in Palermo. The king was striking in appearance, tall and power-fully built, with a handsome face partially obscured by a large, intimidating black beard. William had been married young to his Spanish wife, Margaret, who bore him four sons. Despite the mounting problems at home and abroad, he inherited a powerful kingdom. Sicily and southern Italy were united under an efficient government based on sound finances, backed by strong armed forces. As Falcandus noted, the achievements of his father Roger II had been extraordinary.

His son William, whom he had made king while he still lived, succeeded him, and took control of the palace and the treasure and the responsibilities for the realm. It was a time when the kingdom of Sicily was rich in hard-working and famous men, had the greatest power by land and sea, was feared by all the peoples around it, and enjoyed complete peace and all possible tranquillity.[1]

William was, however, temperamentally unsuited to govern. Lazy and pleasure-loving, he preferred the luxury of his royal palace and harem, where he ruled like a sultan, to the responsibilities of government. As fourth in line to the throne for much of his life, he had received little early training and was ill equipped for the role of king. He showed none of his father's appetite for the hard work necessary to control the affairs of state and chose to delegate administration to his ministers. On becoming king William appointed Maio of Bari emir of emirs. Maio, who was capable and intelligent, had started his professional life as a notary and had worked his way up to become chancellor to Roger II in his final years. He was a controversial figure hated by the barons, who resented the promotion of an Italian of humble origins to the top post in the kingdom, while they remained outside government. Falcandus is scathing about Maio, of whom he writes: 'This man was a beast than whom no more repellent pest could be found.'[2]

William's first moves in government were diplomatic, with the aim of defusing the threats from abroad. His peace offers were turned down by Byzantium and the Pope, the Englishman Adrian IV, who hoped with German help to reduce the power of Sicily. When an attack on southern Italy became imminent, William crossed to Salerno in 1155 to organise the defence. Having done so, he returned to Sicily, leaving his chancellor, Asclettin, in command in Apulia. The barons of southern Italy were encouraged to rebel, led by the king's cousin Count Robert of Loritello and Prince Robert of Capua, who returned from exile in Germany. The expected attack from Germany did not come, but when the rebels were reinforced by troops from Byzantium, it was not long before most of southern Italy was under their control. The position became perilous when William fell ill, with rumours circulating of his death. The rebellion gathered strength, even spreading to Sicily, something that had never happened under Roger II.

William showed his ability as a military commander in the spring of 1156 when, having recovered from his illness, he collected his army and navy at

Messina and launched an attack on the mainland. First taking Brindisi where his troops still held the citadel, he went on to inflict a series of crushing defeats upon the Byzantine forces and the rebels.

While William and his army were occupied in Apulia, the Almohad dynasty in North Africa seized the opportunity to break free from Sicilian rule. Christian communities were attacked and first Sfax fell, then Tripoli and finally Mahdia, with its large Sicilian garrison, was placed under siege. A fleet was sent from Palermo under the command of Caid (an Arab term for 'leader') Peter, William's chief eunuch and a converted Muslim, to relieve the garrison. Romuald reports: 'Caid Peter, the king's eunuch, who was in command of the fleet, came to Africa and fought with the fleet of the Almohads, but was driven back in flight and lost many of his galleys.'[3]

It was decided in Palermo to abandon the African territories as the kingdom was already at full stretch on other fronts. The garrison in Mahdia finally surrendered and was given a safe passage back to Sicily.

Finding himself abandoned by Germany and Byzantium, the Pope came to terms with William in a comprehensive settlement known as the Treaty of Benevento. William swore allegiance to the Pope and was invested with the Crown by Adrian. The full territory of the kingdom in Sicily and southern Italy was confirmed, together with the right to arrange the succession of the Crown. It was a significant achievement by William for he gained more concessions from the Pope than those granted to his father. The kingdom was strengthened by the treaty, which created a firm alliance with the papacy. Negotiations had been handled by Maio, who, now at the peak of his power, demonstrated diplomatic skills of a high order. In formulating the treaty, Maio had been aided by his protégé Matthew of Ajello, a notary originally from Salerno. William was content to leave the government of the kingdom in Maio's hands.

Opposition to Maio from the barons in Sicily soon reached boiling point. Palermo was filled with rumours of plots and counterplots, some even suggesting that Maio was plotting against the king. The plan gaining support was to assassinate Maio and to remove William from power, replacing him with his young son, with his mother, Margaret, as regent. Under such a regime the barons thought they could increase their influence on government. The problem was how to get close to Maio, who was well protected and who had his spies all over the city. He was astute and had already survived several attempts on his life. The barons chose a young nobleman, Matthew Bonellus, as their champion. Bonellus, whose family owned estates in Sicily and on the mainland, had an impeccable background. Crucially, as Bonellus was betrothed to Maio's daughter, he was above suspicion.

One evening in November 1160 when Maio was visiting Hugh, the archbishop of Palermo, in his residence, Bonellus placed knights at intervals down Via Coperta, the street with a covered portico that connected the residence to the royal palace. He positioned himself near the entrance to the residence, close to the gate of Sant'Agata. When Maio emerged he was approached by Matthew of Ajello, who having caught wind of the plot, warned him that he was in danger. Maio called for Bonellus to be sent to him. Hearing his name, Bonellus realised the moment had come to strike and ran forward, sword in hand. According to Falcandus, Maio

> shifted to one side and avoided the blow of the raised sword, turning the striker's force to nothing. But he was not able to avoid the impact as he came at him again with greater power; he sustained a mortal blow, and fell to the ground dying.[4]

Matthew of Ajello, who was wounded in the fight, managed to escape. Bonellus and the other conspirators then fled to the fortress at Caccamo outside Palermo. Maio's assassination was celebrated in the city.

> But once the traitor's death became known, the entire city — which until then had been in a state of suspense with contradictory rumours — exploded with such joy, that it was only then that Maio's unpopularity with the people became apparent.[5]

Unnerved by the absence of Maio, his trusted right-hand man, and uncertain as to the strength of the rebels, William opened negotiations with the conspirators, offering pardons. As a temporary measure, two trusted associates, Henry Aristippus, archdeacon of Catania, and Count Silvester, were appointed to head the government. Before long, Matthew Bonellus was back in Palermo, basking in popular support, where he became a powerful figure. The conspirators decided to implement the next stage of their plan. They encouraged a hostile crowd to advance on the royal palace, where in a coordinated attack aided by bribing the guards, the prisoners in the palace jail were released. The combined mob then went on the rampage through the palace, looting the portable items of value.

Jewellery, gold and silver vases and royal garments, the collection of years by the Hautevilles, including al-Edrisi's silver map of the world, were smashed or carried off. Gold coins were thrown out of the windows to the crowd below. Anti-Muslim feeling ran high. The palace eunuchs were killed and the girls in the harem were raped or abducted. The Muslim quarter in the Kalsa, the lower city, was also attacked.

For a while the king was held prisoner in the palace, until he was rescued by a small group of loyal associates led by Romuald, the archbishop of Salerno, and Richard Palmer, the bishop of Syracuse. In an attempt to restore calm, William was persuaded to go to the window of the Torre Pisana and address the masses below. Assuring everyone that he was still in charge, the king appealed to the crowd to lay down their arms. His appeal was successful and the crowd, assuming that the coup had failed, began to disperse. When more of his followers reached William they found him in a state of collapse, for his young son Roger, the heir to the throne, had been mortally wounded in the eye by an arrow. The rebel barons withdrew to their fortress outside Palermo and there followed a period of stalemate with no decisive action on either side.

More revolts took place in Sicily and on the mainland with Christians and Muslims at each other's throats. Many of the Muslim intellectuals, al-Edrisi probably among them, left Sicily at this time for the Muslim territories. Slowly the king regained confidence and began to reassert his authority. The rebels failed to make any further progress and eventually their inland stronghold at Butera, in the centre of the island, was taken and destroyed. Captured ringleaders suffered the full fury of William's revenge and were executed or mutilated and thrown into prison. The king, learning from his earlier mistake, no longer held prisoners within the palace grounds but in an adjoining prison or at the Castellammare by the port. Matthew Bonellus, arrogant as ever, still saw himself as untouchable and a favourite with the crowd. He misread the mood of the people who were growing tired of the troubles. Bonellus was told to report to the palace where as a precaution the gates were heavily guarded. When he arrived he was arrested and thrown into a dungeon where, blinded and hamstrung, he was left to die.

With the rebellions put down, William retired to a life of leisure, leaving government in the hands of his ministers, Matthew of Ajello, Caid Peter and Richard Palmer. The king was tired of affairs of state and just wanted to be left in peace.

Afraid of any event that would interrupt the enjoyment of his leisure, he had given his officials orders not to bring him any news that might cause him sadness or stress and he went on to devote himself totally to pleasure.[6]

Earlier in his reign William had contributed to the splendour of his royal palace in Palermo with embellishments to the Cappella Palatina. He decorated another room in the royal palace with spectacular mosaics, the so-called Sala di Ruggero (Room of King Roger), which has been well preserved. Towards the end of his reign he also built for himself a new palace, known as the Zisa, as a retreat in hot weather. It was well ventilated and designed so that the apartments on the upper floors provided complete privacy and included a great hall for entertainments.

The Zisa was not yet complete when William began to suffer from ill health. He was attended by several doctors, including Romuald, who had studied at the famous medical school in his hometown of Salerno. At first William's condition improved and then worsened again. He died in May 1166 at the age of 45.

Historians labelled William I 'the Bad' in the fourteenth century largely based on the evidence of Falcandus. It now seems a harsh judgement. When roused to action he could be effective and he proved to be a better military commander than his father. The Treaty of Benevento was a diplomatic triumph. On the other hand his lack of commitment to government meant that he was never in control of events and by opting out of his responsibilities, and leaving others in charge, he fatally undermined the authority of the Crown. It was his misfortune to have been in charge when the worst rebellions took place in Palermo.

William II, the Good

On his deathbed William I had stated that he wished his eldest surviving son, also called William, to succeed him. His other son, Henry, was to be prince of Capua. Accordingly William II was crowned king at the age of 12 by Romuald of Salerno in the cathedral at Palermo. The young king was an immediate success with the crowd: 'Since he was very handsome and seemed even more handsome on that day – how, I do not know – and bore a monarchical beauty on his brow, he won the goodwill and support of everyone.'[7]

For the next five years until William came of age his mother acted as regent. Margaret, described as a wise and sensible woman, began her rule by bestowing benefits upon the population. Prisoners were released, slaves were freed, tax concessions were granted and more nobles were created. The atmosphere in Palermo and across the kingdom had changed since the rebellions and Sicilians were ready for peace. The new reign got off to a good start.

Margaret, however, had seen enough of the intrigues at court to be suspicious of those around her and called upon her French cousin, Stephen of Perche, to act as her senior minister. The title of emir of emirs, last held by Maio, was not renewed and on his arrival in 1068 Stephen took up the reins of government as chancellor and archbishop of Palermo. The arrival of Stephen, together with a group of some 30 Frenchmen, caused renewed friction in Palermo. Anti-Muslim feeling led to the defection of Caid Peter, who left Palermo for North Africa, where he continued his career as admiral for the Arabs. Eventually opposition from the established ministers, Romuald, Richard Palmer and Matthew Ajello, backed by the barons, forced Stephen, to whom Margaret had become very attached, to return to France.

William II assumed control of government in 1171 at a time when the external threats to the kingdom were receding. Frederick Barbarossa had led an army into central Italy which reached Rome but which was destroyed by an epidemic. On a desperate return journey to Germany, cities closed their gates to him and only remnants of the original force arrived home. In 1177 at the Peace of Venice, the emperor, the Pope and the Norman kingdom finally reached a peace agreement.

William had been brought up in a Muslim environment and his Arabic, spoken and written, was fluent. Apart from the palaces and gardens in and around Palermo, he also had a palace in Messina, built in pure white stone and overlooking the seashore. William added one more pleasure palace in Palermo, similar to the Zisa, known as the Cuba. Like his father he was distracted from work by easy living and was described by a Muslim visitor as pleasure loving and enjoying the luxuries that came with his position.[8] By nature mild and tolerant, William once calmed a crowd shaken by the effects of an earthquake by encouraging both Christians and Muslims to pray to their own gods. But of the original Hauteville abilities in military affairs and diplomacy there was little sign.

For some time William had been seeking to make a suitable marriage. When the suggestion came that he should take as his bride Joanna, the daughter of the

English king Henry II, William agreed. Joanna was young and beautiful and the marriage would strengthen ties with England. The ceremony took place in February 1177 in the Cappella Palatina in the royal palace, where Joanna was crowned queen of Sicily by the English archbishop of Palermo, Walter of the Mill. She was just 11 years old. It proved to be a happy marriage.

Regular contacts had existed between the Norman kingdoms of Sicily and England since the time of Roger I. Under Roger II there were Englishmen such as Robert of Selby and Thomas Brown in official posts in Palermo, invited to Sicily to help the re-establishment of the Catholic Church. Richard Palmer, bishop of Syracuse and an ambitious politician, rose to prominence as a minister under William I and continued to play a leading role in Palermo under William II. The most influential of the Englishmen to make their careers in Sicily was Walter of the Mill, known in Sicily as Gualtiero Offamilio. Walter arrived in Sicily with Stephen of Perche and was employed by Margaret as tutor to her children. He came from a humble background and is thought to have been born in England to a French mother. He was a man of towering ambition who rose through the ranks to become canon of the Cappella Palatina and archdeacon of Cefalù. On Stephen's return to France, Walter became archbishop of Palermo after using a mob to employ strong-arm tactics to ensure his election. In this position, which he combined with being first minister to William II, he made himself into one of the most powerful men in the kingdom. The court in Palermo had been in touch with the most important English churchman of the time, Thomas Becket, archbishop of Canterbury. Henry II's quarrel with Becket over the right of Rome to intervene in English affairs was well known in Europe. Becket had been in correspondence with Margaret and Richard Palmer, both of whom were sympathetic to his cause.

William's other senior minister was Matthew of Ajello, who held the post of vice chancellor, and between them Walter and Matthew were the twin pillars of the king's government. Walter built himself a following of the leading barons and churchmen and began to represent a dangerous concentration of power. The king, with Matthew's help, looked for means of curbing Walter's power and hit on the idea of creating a second archbishopric. The opportunity was offered by the presence of an old Greek church in Monreale, a village to the west of the city, which could be used as the site. Work on the immense Benedictine abbey began in the spring 1174 and was completed in 1183. It was William's greatest act of patronage and created a unique complex, a mix of Eastern and Western styles, containing the largest expanse of mosaics depicting

1. Palermo's cathedral – section by the Palazzo Arcivescovile (Archbishop's Palace) (Rouargue Frères, *c.*1800).

scenes from the Old and New Testaments to survive from the twelfth century. Possibly at Joanna's request, Thomas Becket, who had been canonised in 1173, featured in one of these scenes. Walter, not to be outdone, rebuilt the main cathedral in Palermo (figure 1).

In 1184, with peace concluded with Germany, William agreed to a dynastic marriage of his aunt Constance to Henry, son of Frederick Barbarossa. Constance, who was the daughter of Roger II, had been living in a convent, and the marriage took place two years later. In giving his agreement William was encouraged by Walter but strongly opposed by Matthew, who as a southern Italian was well aware of German ambitions in the region. On the face of it the succession of the Norman monarchy was safe enough. William was 31 and Joanna 19 and there should have been plenty of time for an heir to the throne to be born. But it was not to be and only three years later in 1189 William II died. According to a drawing by the contemporary Peter of Eboli, William died in his bed surrounded by Muslim attendants. He was 36 and his marriage to Joanna was childless.

The myth of William II as 'the Good' was probably created by historians because of his mild character and for the largely peaceful nature of the kingdom under his rule. It was a superficial judgement, for by engaging in pointless wars abroad, he weakened the kingdom so that when the real test came there was no strength left. William had been spending the kingdom's capital at a critical time. His biggest mistake, however, was the agreement on Constance's marriage to Henry Hohenstaufen, which sealed the kingdom's fate.

Descriptions of Palermo

Palermo under the later Norman kings displayed all the splendours of Norman–Arab culture. Palaces, chapels, gardens and a great cathedral with mosaics were added to the city, which seemed a fabulous place to visitors. Two descriptions of Palermo in this period have survived.

The first is attributed to Hugo Falcandus and refers to the reign of William I. He described the seafront protected by the Castellammare with high walls interspersed by towers encircling the city. The royal palace, at the far end of the city from the sea, was built 'with amazing effort and astonishing skill out of squared stones, the outer side with walls which wind far and wide'. The interior of the palace, which contained apartments and workshops, was 'remarkable for its great splendour of gems and gold'. The Cappella Palatina came in for particular praise. Falcandus described it as being

> paved with a floor of costly craftsmanship and with walls whose lower level is decorated with plates of precious marble, and the higher one with mosaic stones, some gold and others of different colours, with representations of the story of the Old and New Testaments. The uppermost level is adorned by an outstanding elegance of carvings and an amazing variety of sculpture, with the splendour of gold shining all around.[9]

The second description is by Ibn Jubayr, a Muslim who worked as secretary to the governor of Grenada in Spain, and who left on a journey to perform the hajj, the pilgrimage to Mecca, in 1183. He reached Palermo in late December 1184 where he stayed for a week in a hostel frequented by other Muslims. His account refers to the reign of William II, whom he met, and was written for a Muslim audience. Ibn Jubayr compared conditions on the island to those in his native Spain. Noting the high standard of living, he wished to see Sicily return to Muslim rule. He was well aware of the contradictions of life for Muslims under the Normans. Muslim influence was strong at the royal court and in public around Palermo, where Christian women could be seen wearing Muslim dress. At the same time, while not actively persecuted, Muslims suffered from religious discrimination and did not feel safe.

Ibn Jubayr found Palermo magnificent, filled with gardens divided by wide roads and a river running through the centre. As with Cordoba in Spain, there was an ancient centre, the Cassaro, which contained the mansions of the nobility. The king's palaces, at the high point of the city, were compared to a string of pearls around a lady's neck. The spacious royal estates included gardens, courtyards and summer houses for the king's pleasure.[10]

End of the dynasty

When William II died childless, legally the Crown passed to his aunt, Constance, the daughter of Roger II. As Constance was married to Henry Hohenstaufen, son of the German emperor, the kingdoms of Sicily and Germany were now in theory united. William had nominated Constance as his successor in the event of his having no children at an assembly of barons and churchmen. Despite this, the ruling elite in Palermo decided to contest the succession rather than be subjected to German rule. Led by Matthew of Ajello they elected Tancred of Lecce as king. Tancred had proved himself as a military commander under William II, but as the illegitimate son of Duke Roger, Roger II's eldest son, he had no legal claim to the throne. As a local man Tancred was widely supported in Sicily but was less well accepted on the mainland. Matthew of Ajello became Tancred's chancellor.

Initially Henry Hohenstaufen was preoccupied with affairs at home. But in 1190 his father, Frederick Barbarossa, died while travelling to Palestine on the Third Crusade, which prompted Henry to claim the Sicilian kingdom. Henry established the Hohenstaufen dynasty, which would play a major part in the affairs of Europe. The dynasty is also referred to as Swabian (*svevo* in Italian) from the family's original territory near Bavaria. In April 1191 Henry and Constance travelled to Rome where they were crowned emperor and empress by Pope Celestine III.

In Sicily Tancred faced mounting problems. In the aftermath of William II's death Christian gangs attacked Muslims in Palermo, many of whom fled the city for the mountainous regions inland. Others began to leave Sicily altogether for North Africa. In the centre and east of Sicily Muslims rebelled and for a while civil war raged. In southern Italy the barons, as so often in the past, took the opportunity of unrest in Sicily to go their own way. Tancred, though a good military commander, was not up to the task of uniting the kingdom in its current predicament.

In the spring of 1194 Henry led the German imperial army to southern Italy. They were transported by a powerful fleet, largely supplied by the Pisans and Genoese. Naples quickly surrendered. Salerno was taken and destroyed in a revenge attack for the city's earlier defiance to Henry. As a result, most of the other cities in the region opened their gates to the invading army. By the time Henry reached Sicily many of the kingdom's leaders had died, including Tancred, Roger his eldest son and co-ruler, Matthew of Ajello and Walter of the Mill. The main survivors of the Hauteville dynasty were Tancred's younger son, William III, his three sisters and Tancred's widow, Sibylla, who was acting as regent.

Landing at Messina, Henry and his army met with little opposition. The kingdom was leaderless and demoralised, with public order breaking down. The gates were thrown open and Henry was welcomed into the city with the streets decorated in his honour. At the royal palace no resistance was met and the keys to the treasury were handed over. Huge quantities of gold coins, jewels and precious garments worn by the Norman kings were shared out among the German generals. The famous mantle of Roger II found its way to Vienna, where it can be seen today.

The Germans were astonished at the beauty and prosperity of Sicily. To Henry all that mattered was the island's treasure, which he intended to use to extend his ambitions in southern Europe. German expeditions to the south had failed repeatedly and he was determined to deal decisively with the Norman kingdom. Palermo was systematically stripped of its riches, which were packed up and transported by mule over the Alps to Germany. Land was granted to German generals, establishing a permanent presence on the island with which to enforce Henry's control. A special target was made of the Norman barons, many of whom were arrested and sent off to prison in Germany.

At first Tancred's family was well treated. Sibylla was offered the territories of Lecce and Taranto in southern Italy and the family was present in the cathedral of Palermo on Christmas Day 1194 when Henry VI was crowned king of Sicily. Shortly afterwards came the news of a plot against the German emperor. Whether genuine or not, it gave Henry the excuse to remove a potential threat posed by the remains of the Norman leadership. His response was immediate and bloody. Calling an assembly, Henry had Tancred's son, William, the queen regent and numerous barons and bishops condemned for treason. Tancred's family was sent to Germany where William was thrown into prison, castrated and blinded. He died a few years later. Sibylla and her daughters were placed in a convent from where they were able to escape and flee to France. Among those condemned in Palermo some were blinded, some burned alive and some hanged. The survivors ended up in prison in Germany. A revolt against German rule followed later, and was savagely put down. Jordan, a descendant of the Hauteville family, was singled out and had his head impaled upon an iron crown ringed with spikes. Revenge was even taken on Norman prisoners in Germany, some of whom were mutilated in their cells. A three-year reign of terror descended upon Sicily.

The invasion by Henry VI was one of the worst disasters to befall Sicily in her entire history. For Palermo the effect was catastrophic. From being the capital of a prosperous, independent kingdom the city became an outpost on the periphery of the German Empire with her freedom and her riches gone. Once more Sicily showed her extraordinary ability to experience extremes of fortune, as noted by Falcandus: 'Nowhere else does Fortune give her wheel a more sudden twist, or sport more hazardously with mortal men.'[11]

Epilogue

So ended the Norman kingdom of Sicily: ripped apart by internal dissension, and finally swept away by a foreign power. The paradox of a Christian state hand in glove with a large Muslim population at the time of the Crusades was always likely to end in trouble. Just as destabilising was the continued inability of the Norman barons to remain loyal to the Crown. Most crucial of all was the character of the ruler himself. After the dynamic leadership of the two Rogers, the two Williams, undermined by the luxury of their lifestyles, could only offer a pale reflection of earlier achievements. Fate also played a part, for the decline of the kingdom can be measured in the longevity of its rulers. Roger I lived to the ripe old age, for his time, of 70, Roger II to 58, William I to 45 and William II to 36. The untimely deaths of heirs to the throne, especially Duke Roger, Roger II's eldest son, were also critical.[12] The *coup de grâce* was given by William II when he agreed to Constance's marriage to Henry Hohenstaufen, thereby at a stroke giving away the kingdom to Germany, the old enemy.

The end came only 64 years after the kingdom had been established by Roger II. It was an extraordinary time. In these years Sicily reached a peak of civilisation not seen since the days of the ancient Greeks, while Palermo enjoyed prosperity and a cultural brilliance never attained before or since. Underlying this achievement was the Norman tolerance of different cultures and the ability to make them work together.

It is our good fortune that some of the greatest Norman treasures survived. In the Cappella Palatina, the Martorana, the Palazzo Zisa and the cathedrals at Monreale and Cefalù are world-class monuments to be enjoyed today, which give us an insight into the unique civilisation created by the Normans in Sicily.

Constance was not present in Palermo when her husband Henry VI, the German emperor, was crowned king of Sicily. She was on her way south, travelling slowly for she was heavily pregnant. At 40 years old her pregnancy was unexpected and she was determined to protect her child's royal inheritance. When she reached Jesi in southern Italy, knowing the birth to be imminent, she had a tent pitched in the main square. Here, on 26 December 1194, the day after Henry's coronation in Palermo, she gave birth to her son. By arranging the birth in a public place Constance avoided any possible claim that the child was not hers. She and the baby went on to Palermo to join Henry. Their son was named Frederick Roger, recalling both his German and Hauteville forebears. When Henry returned to deal with affairs in Germany, Constance was left as regent in Sicily. In 1197, having returned to Sicily, Henry died of a fever in Messina, probably malaria, a month short of his 32nd birthday.

For a brief period Constance ruled the kingdom of Sicily from Palermo, relying on local advisers, sending Germans home and seeking to prolong the Hauteville inheritance. In this aim she was supported by the Pope, Innocent III, who viewed with apprehension the union of Sicily and Germany. Constance developed good relations with the Pope, who became guardian to her son. Frederick was anointed co-ruler of Sicily at the age of three and a half at the cathedral in Palermo in May 1198. Constance did not survive much longer and died in November of the same year. She was buried alongside her husband Henry in the cathedral. But Constance's diplomacy and decisive action had done enough to ensure her son's future. Innocent III acted as regent and the continuity of the Sicilian kingdom was assured.

Frederick was brought up in Palermo under Muslim influence, like the Hauteville kings before him. As the grandson of Roger II on one side and Frederick Barbarossa on the other, his was an extraordinary inheritance. He grew up to become the most powerful ruler of his age.

CHAPTER 6

Frederick II, Wonder of the World

F rederick II was the most extraordinary ruler of medieval Europe. For more than 30 years he was a dominant figure, astonishing people with his wit and learning, at the same time shocking them with his controversial ideas. The impact of his personality was such that years after his death rumours were spread that he had returned and was back in charge.

He took up his responsibilities as king of Sicily and Southern Italy in 1208 at the age of 14. Four years later he was crowned king of Germany and in 1220 he was crowned Holy Roman Emperor by the Pope in Rome. As emperor he ruled lands from the North Sea to the Mediterranean, including Germany, northern Italy, Burgundy and the Sicilian kingdom. King of Jerusalem was later added to his titles. He became the most powerful ruler in Europe.

Frederick's combination of political power and personal charisma drew extravagant praise from commentators. Matthew Paris, an English monk and chronicler, famously described him as 'the greatest of the princes of the earth, wonder of the world.'[1] Paris' phrase *stupor mundi* ('wonder of the world'), has been associated with him ever since. A legend grew up of Frederick as a political genius, an intellectual giant and dynamic man of action. He was compared to the Roman emperors and it was claimed that that he had no equal between Charlemagne and Napoleon. For centralising the Sicilian state he was called 'the first ruler of the modern type who sat upon a throne' by the historian Jacob Burckhardt.[2] He has been cast in a variety of roles including that of a Renaissance prince before his time, the father of Italian poetry and the forerunner of modern German statesmen.

Early days in Palermo

When his mother Constance died in November 1198, Frederick was left an orphan with no brothers or sisters just before his fourth birthday. The situation in Palermo was perilous, for in the aftermath of the German invasion different factions fought for control of the kingdom. Fortunately for the succession Constance had established the Pope, Innocent III, as her son's guardian, which proved vital in the turbulent years to come. Frederick grew up in a highly volatile and insecure environment and was aware from an early age that the men looking after him could not be relied upon.

While he was largely self-taught, a series of tutors provided Frederick with the rudiments of a formal education. He showed a thirst for knowledge, becoming an avid reader with a particular fascination for scientific subjects. He loved hearing the stories of his Norman forebears. His time was spent in the royal palace, which was still Muslim in culture, and on the country estates where he discovered a passion for wildlife and hunting. Running wild as a boy, he roamed the streets of Palermo, conversing with people from diverse ethnic backgrounds and acquiring a facility in their languages. He was fluent in the Sicilian dialect of the streets, the Norman French spoken by the court and the Arabic of his servants. Later he learned Latin and was able to speak German and Greek.

The young king took up the reins of government for the kingdom of Sicily, known as the *regno*, in 1208 at the age of 14. Frederick's first move was to reassert the rights of the Crown in the face of the barons who had taken over Crown property. In the following year he married Constance of Aragon, at the Pope's suggestion, in a political marriage aimed at strengthening the *regno*. Constance, who was about ten years older than Frederick, was the widow of the Hungarian king. Despite the age difference it was a happy marriage, with Constance bringing a sophistication and knowledge of courtly behaviour lacking in the young king. While Frederick could be charming, as a young man he had his rough side, and the marriage taught him the manners needed to succeed in the wider world.

Frederick was crowned king of the Romans, effectively a preliminary to coronation as Holy Roman Emperor, at Aachen in 1215. After the ceremony he spontaneously took up the cross in the spirit of Charlemagne and declared he would lead a Crusade to the Holy Land. But it was not for another five years, and after more negotiations with the Pope, that Frederick was finally crowned Holy Roman Emperor. Frederick's coronation at St Peter's in Rome in November 1220 was a sumptuous affair. The new Pope, Honorius III, crowned Frederick and Constance emperor and empress, Frederick wearing the mantle of his grandfather, Roger II of Sicily. At the age of 26, after a meteoric rise to power, Frederick had achieved the pinnacle of his ambition and yet had managed to keep his Sicilian kingdom.

Campaigns in Sicily

The conditions Frederick faced in the *regno* were chaotic as the barons and churchmen had continued to expand their estates at the expense of the royal demesne. The Muslims in Sicily remained in open revolt against the Christian establishment. Frederick rapidly imposed his authority and set about reinstating the Norman legal system. All castles built since the time of William II were declared illegal, with the property reverting to the Crown, and a state army was established with citizens obliged to serve the Crown. Royal castles were strengthened to form part of the *regno*'s defences.

Fierce fighting took place in western Sicily in difficult terrain, with the Arabs defending their mountain strongholds. Frederick mounted an attack on Iato, the stronghold of the Arab emir and leader of the revolt, Ibn Abbad. After a siege lasting two months Frederick's forces captured the fort together with the emir. When brought before the emperor, Ibn Abbad threw himself on the ground and begged for mercy. Furious at the prolonged Arab revolt against him, Frederick ripped open the emir's body with his spur and had him sent to Palermo to be hanged along with the other ringleaders.

Frederick decided upon a drastic solution to the Muslim question to protect the kingdom from further revolts. He had a colony built for them on the mainland near Foggia, named Lucera, and over the next few years transferred 15 to 20,000 Arabs to the new city. Here the Arabs were governed by their own laws and were free to engage in agriculture and trading. Arab intellectuals and . skilled professionals had already begun to leave Sicily for North Africa in the time of William I. Those remaining on the island were the poorer people who either converted to Christianity or lived like hermits in the mountains. Sicily lost many small traders and farmers who had made a positive contribution to the economy, leaving tracts of land untended and abandoned. The story of Muslim Sicily ends around 1225 with the transfer of the Arab population to Lucera. The Arabs left few visible traces behind them of their long residence in Sicily, apart from the Islamic-style monuments built under the Normans. But many aspects of their culture lived on as part of Sicilian life in the language and place names, in the food and agriculture, in crafts and design, and in the souk-like street markets of Palermo.

Jewish settlers from North Africa were encouraged by Frederick to come to Sicily to fill the gap left by the Arabs. Jews from this region had developed similar skills on the land to their Arab neighbours and their religion posed no threat. The Sicilian Jewish community grew substantially in this period.

Frederick's court

Frederick's personal interests, which went from government and lawmaking to science, literature, the natural world and philosophy, attracted talented people to his court. Among his inner circle of advisers were Piero della Vigna, the lawyer and administrator, Hermann von Salza, grand master of the Teutonic Knights, Berardo, archbishop of Palermo, and the Scotsman Michael Scot, philosopher and astrologer. Frederick loved good company and flourished at the centre of his court. The Italian monk Salimbene noted:

> Frederick was a worthy man, and when he wished to show his good, courtly side, he could be witty, charming, urbane, and industrious. He was adept at writing and singing, and was well-versed in the art of writing lyrics and songs. He was a handsome, well-formed man of medium height. I saw him and he pleased me much.[3]

In 1235 Frederick's third marriage took place to Isabella, sister of Henry III, king of England. She bore him one child, a son named Henry. It was another political marriage, which lasted for six years before the queen's premature death. Frederick's happiest relationship was with Bianca Lancia, who came from a wealthy Italian family, the counts of Loreto in Piedmont. Her uncle, Manfred Lancia, was a close supporter of Frederick's who was frequently at court. Bianca bore Frederick two children, Constance and Manfred, who seem to have been the emperor's favourites. It is possible that Frederick married Bianca towards the end of her life. From his numerous mistresses Frederick had at least ten illegitimate children, the most prominent of whom was Enzo, who became king of Sardinia.

Frederick's court made a lasting achievement in the field of poetry. Palermo, which had a tradition from Arab times, became influenced by the Provençal poets, who were writing lyric love poems. These poems, along with the songs of the troubadours, celebrated the sentiments of the chivalrous knight and his idealised love of a lady. They became popular around the courts of Europe at a time when knights went on long pilgrimages to the Holy Land, leaving their women behind.

Around 1233 a group of courtiers began experimenting with poems on the theme of courtly love. They were not professional poets but held other jobs and came from different parts of the *regno*, several from eastern Sicily. The difference was that, using the Arab and Provençal traditions as a starting point, they wrote in the popular local language, the Sicilian dialect. These poets, dubbed the Sicilian school, are credited with the invention of two new forms of poetry; the *canzone*, a lyric poem suited to a musical setting, and the sonnet, a 14-line poem which rhymed to a strict scheme. Both had a major impact upon the literary world, the sonnet going on to be made famous by Petrarch, Dante, Milton and Shakespeare.

Giacomo Da Lentini, a notary from Catania, emerged as the outstanding poet of the group. Admired by Dante, he is considered to have been the inventor of the sonnet. Some 40 poems by Giacomo have survived, including a sonnet to a lady without whom the speaker would not wish to go to paradise. The Sicilian poets occupy an important place in the island's cultural history. They wrote traditional lyric love poetry in a new literary language, a Sicilian version of the Romance vernacular. The language of their poems became a point of reference for Dante and Petrarch as they developed the Tuscan language, which became the basis of modern Italian. An early form of Italian thus first saw the light of day in Palermo and the other cities frequented by the court.

When Dante began to write the *Divine Comedy* in 1308, the first book to be written in the local language, in this case Tuscan, he freely admitted the contribution made by the Sicilian poets. In his work *De vulgari eloquentia* ('On eloquence in the vernacular'), Dante acknowledges it as follows:

> The illustrious heroes Frederick Caesar and his noble son Manfred, followed after elegance and scorned what was mean; so that all the best compositions of the time came from their court. Thus because their royal throne was Sicily, all the poems of our predecessors in the vulgar tongue were called Sicilian.[4]

As well as composing poetry, Frederick wrote a book on one of his great passions, falconry. Written in Latin, entitled *De arte venandi cum avibus* ('The art of hunting with birds') it combined scientific ornithology with a detailed handbook on the best practice for rearing, training and hunting with falcons. Based on years of close observation, it shows how keenly Frederick followed this sport. The scientific elements of the book were influenced by classical works such as *The Zoology of Aristotle*, which was translated at Frederick's court by Michael Scot. It was a book for experts and helped make the sport of falconry more popular. Frederick's original manuscript was lost but a beautifully illustrated edition commissioned by his son Manfred, to whom the book was dedicated, is held at the Vatican Library in Rome.

Frederick enjoyed intellectual disputes at court and in the intimacy of his close circle discussion was open and uninhibited. By not minding what he said in public, however, Frederick came up against the orthodox views of the Church, which was already scandalised by his lifestyle. These factors, combined with the papacy's implacable opposition to a united Germany and Sicily, led to open warfare between popes and the emperor. Frederick was cast in the role of the Antichrist and the papal propaganda machine went into full operation. Many derogatory stories were circulated about Frederick, probably untrue, but illustrating how the emperor was seen in Rome. He was said to have cut off the thumb of a notary who had spelled his name wrong and to have experimented upon a living man, locked into a barrel, to see whether his soul escaped when he died.[5] In 1239 Pope Gregory IX accused Frederick of denying the virgin birth and of claiming that the world had been deceived by three impostors, Moses, Jesus Christ and Muhammad.

Unfazed by such attacks, Frederick entered into an international debate on philosophical issues with Muslims in Egypt, Syria, Iraq and Yemen. He sent their leaders a list, known as the Sicilian Questions, on issues such as the relationship of God with the world. They included: 'How are the words of Muhammad explained?' and 'What proof have we of the immortality of the soul?' While he received a number of thoughtful replies, the debate caused outrage in Christendom. The chronicler Matthew Paris, commenting upon Frederick's relationship with the Church, wrote: 'The whole of Christianity was troubled and the universal church endangered by the wars which arose from the hatred and discord between the Pope and Frederick.'[6]

Germany and northern Italy

Frederick acknowledged the power of the local princes in Germany and relied upon them to rule this part of his empire from when he first accepted the Crown. He gave them increased power to allow himself the freedom to concentrate upon Sicily, something that in the long run undermined the strength of the monarchy. His policy was to keep the princes' loyalty rather than to attempt to unite Germany under central government. According to Geoffrey Barraclough, the historian of medieval Germany, Frederick 'considered himself a Sicilian, spoke of Sicily and its provinces as his own land and of Italy as his inheritance; he had a horror of Germany with its long winters and sombre forests, its muddy towns and rugged castles.'[7]

While Frederick was busy reorganising the government of Sicily, Henry, his eldest son by his first wife Constance, had been resident in Germany. Henry concluded that more central control of the princes was needed and, proud and obstinate, he was determined to get his own way. Frederick, authoritarian as ever, would have none of it. Calling Henry to him, he made it clear that he must obey instructions. Henry, however, stood his ground, until in 1235 he openly challenged his father. He started to build an opposition to Frederick in Germany and called for support from the Lombard cities. Frederick, seeing the tension mounting among the princes, had Henry brought before him, stripped him of his crown and banished him to prison. Seven years went by before Frederick relented and sent for Henry to be brought to him. But rumours had spread of his father's cruelty. Fearing worse punishment to come, Henry seized the opportunity, when travelling under escort, to break away from his guards and commit suicide, riding to his death in a ravine. He was mourned by his father who reconfirmed the powers of the German princes.

The cities of northern Italy had posed a problem for German emperors since the days of Frederick Barbarossa. These cities, ruled by family dynasties and warlords, had become dynamic commercial centres with a growing merchant class. As they developed, they increasingly rebelled against imperial control. Strong local loyalties and a fiercely independent outlook led to infighting and shifting alliances between cities. The battle between Pope and emperor was reflected in two opposing factions: the Guelphs, who were pro-Pope, and the Ghibellines, who were pro-emperor. The rebel cities led by Milan were represented by the Lombard League.

In 1236 Frederick set out to confront the Lombard cities. It was not an easy task for he had only a small army and relied upon mercenaries, while the cities were well supplied and defended. The emperor won an initial victory over the Lombard League but subsequently failed to take Brescia. Campaigning continued further south in Italy, with the emperor taking Ravenna and Faenza and engaging in battles outside Rome.

In 1243 Innocent IV was elected pope. He became Frederick's bitterest enemy, announcing two years later that Frederick was deposed as emperor, citing as his reasons the emperor's harem and Muslim habits. The Pope went on to sponsor an assassination attempt against Frederick, which was discovered and brutally suppressed.

When in 1247 Parma switched allegiance from emperor to the Pope, Frederick put the city under siege. A wooden palisade amounting to a second city was built around it, called Victoria, which contained the treasury, harem and menagerie, for Frederick was travelling with his complete imperial entourage. Parma was cut off and the imperial forces settled down to starve the city into submission. At some stage Frederick left the siege to go hunting. When he returned he found his forces had been defeated. At Parma Frederick lost not only his treasure but also the manuscript of his book on falconry and his trusted adviser, Taddeo da Suessa, who died in prison. It was the worst defeat of the emperor's career and was followed by the loss of two more close associates.

Enzo, Frederick's illegitimate son, had proved to be an energetic and successful commander and had played an important role in the Lombard campaign. During a skirmish Enzo was captured by the Bolognese, strong supporters of the Guelphs. Although well treated by his captors and despite many attempts to free him, Enzo was never released.

A plot to assassinate Frederick was then uncovered. It appears that on the instructions of Pope Innocent IV an attempt was made to poison the emperor by his own doctor. Piero della Vigna, the emperor's chief adviser, was implicated in the plot. It seems that Frederick believed the story for the doctor was executed and Piero was arrested, tried and found guilty. Matthew Paris described what followed:

> Thus certified of the deadly treachery prepared against him, Frederick ordered the doctor to be hanged and Peter, deservedly deprived of his eyes, he had led through many of the cities of Italy and Apulia so that he could publicly confess his crime to everybody. Finally Frederick ordered him to be handed over for execution to

the Pisans, who inexorably loathed this Peter. When he heard this, lest he should suffer death at the will of an enemy – for as Seneca says 'To die at the will of an enemy is to die twice' – Peter struck his head forcibly against the pillar to which he was tied and brained himself.[8]

Whatever the truth behind the doctor's assassination attempt, historians have found it difficult to believe that Piero della Vigna was involved in a plot against the emperor. He had been raised from humble origins and had served Frederick loyally for 20 years. Piero had amassed a personal fortune and was probably guilty of helping himself to imperial funds. The likely explanation of his downfall is that courtiers jealous of Piero's position inflamed Frederick against him. Dante did not think that Piero betrayed the emperor. Piero appears in the *Inferno*, not for betrayal but for committing suicide, and claims his innocence of the plot in the lines: 'I swear to you [...] I never did betray my lord, so worthy of honour, no, nor broke my faith.'[9]

Frederick's death and the aftermath

Frederick fell ill from dysentery while in Apulia in December 1250. In his last days he named Conrad, his son by Yolanda, his second wife and queen of Jerusalem, as his successor in Germany and Sicily. He received the last sacraments from Berardo, archbishop of Palermo, according to Matthew Paris, dressed in the white habit of a Cistercian monk.

> About the same time died Frederick, the greatest of the princes of the earth, wonder of the world and admirable innovator, absolved from the sentence in which he was entangled, having assumed, it is said, the habit of the Cistercians, and amazingly contrite and humbled.[10]

Frederick died on Santa Lucia's Day, 13 December 1250, a few days short of his 56th birthday. He was buried close to his parents and first wife, Constance, in the cathedral at Palermo, where his tomb can be seen today.

Frederick was a man of brilliant personal accomplishment who left behind him little of substance. The result of his policies became apparent after his death when his empire fell apart and his dynasty came to an end.

By granting so many concessions to the German princes, Frederick sacrificed the needs of Germany to the interests of his Sicilian kingdom so that, according to Geoffrey Barraclough:

Germany took a road which differentiated its history for centuries to come, if not for all time, from that of England and France. It passed out of the hands of the monarch into the control of a princely aristocracy, a policy not in the interests of the people.[11]

In Sicily, while successful during his lifetime, Frederick's policy let in the French, who destroyed the remains of the Norman civilisation and began the long domination of the island by foreign powers. The Muslim community, forcibly removed to Lucera, played no further part in the island's history.

German emperors had long wished to add the Sicilian kingdom to their empire. When this was achieved by Frederick, it proved to be a poisoned chalice. The regions of the empire were too diverse and their needs too varied to be ruled as one entity, especially by a mobile court. Vague concepts of empire were losing support, while the momentum was with the rising nation states like England and France.

Above all the long, bitter war between emperor and the papacy was a distraction from government that wasted time and resources and brought both parties into disrepute. It left a poisoned relationship with Rome for Frederick's heirs.

In the words of the historian H. A. L. Fisher, Frederick represents 'the greatest single human force in the Middle Ages which passes in and out like a comet, shines and is gone'.[12]

End of the dynasty

News of the emperor's death was received with jubilation in Rome. It was seen as an opportunity to step up the vendetta with the house of Hohenstaufen. Papal policy became to oust the dynasty from the Crown of Sicily, replacing it with the Pope's own appointed nominee. Frederick's young and inexperienced heirs faced an implacable enemy in Pope Innocent IV.

Conrad, heir to the imperial title, inherited the Sicilian kingdom. Henry, Frederick's son by Isabella of England, inherited Burgundy or Jerusalem,

according to Conrad's wishes, but died aged 18. Manfred, Frederick's son by
Bianca Lancia, received territory in southern Italy.

Conrad soon found himself in difficulties, excommunicated by the Pope
who then declared a Crusade against the Hohenstaufens. While campaigning
in southern Italy, Conrad died of a fever surrounded by his Muslim soldiers,
aged 26. His young son, Conradin, and his mother were sent for their safety to
Bavaria. In the crisis Manfred rose to the occasion, showing many of his father's
dashing qualities. In a dynamic campaign he regained control of southern Italy
and Sicily and, in August 1258, was crowned king of Sicily in Palermo.

In 1261 a new pope was elected, Urban IV, a Frenchman who continued
the anti-Hohenstaufen policy. He chose as his champion Charles of Anjou, a
powerful nobleman from Provence, the youngest brother of Louis IX, king
of France. Charles, who was a capable military commander, had ambitions in
the Mediterranean and saw this as his chance. In 1265 he collected an army of
over 20,000 men and marched into Italy. Early the following year Charles met
Manfred's forces at Benevento in southern Italy in a closely contested battle.
Charles emerged victorious and Manfred, refusing to leave the battlefield,
was killed in action. Charles took over the Sicilian kingdom, imposing a rigid
regime with high taxes to pay for the war. Much of northern Italy also fell to
the French forces.

Conradin, now aged 15, was the rightful king of Sicily. He took up the family
banner and left Bavaria to challenge the invasion of his territories by Charles of
Anjou. As he came south, he attracted troops and supporters as he went, including
from the Ghibelline cities of Italy. His forces met Charles and his army in battle
at Tagliacozzo. While Charles had the advantage of veterans from the Crusades
among his knights, the battle initially went in Conradin's favour. After the early
success Conradin's forces dispersed in search of plunder and were subsequently
annihilated by the French cavalry. Conradin was captured and taken to Naples,
where on Charles' orders and with the agreement of Pope Clement IV, he was
beheaded in a public square. Before his execution, according to legend, Conradin
threw his gauntlet into the crowd as a last gesture of defiance. His execution
came as a shock to the courts of Europe, especially in Germany.

The Hohenstaufen dynasty thus came to an end just 18 years after Frederick's
death. When Enzo, Frederick's only remaining son, imprisoned in Bologna,
died in 1272, the last hope was gone. Charles, with his French army, was now
in full control of Sicily and was ready to develop his Mediterranean plans.

CHAPTER 7

The Sicilian Vespers

On Easter Monday, 30 March 1282, an incident took place at Palermo which had profound consequences not only for Sicily but for the whole of Europe. A crowd had gathered by the church of the Spirito Santo (Holy Spirit), a Norman building located outside the walls of the city to the south-east. Founded in 1177 by the English archbishop of Palermo, Walter of the Mill, the church stood in open countryside near the banks of the river Oreto. The purpose of the gathering was to celebrate evensong, vespers, as was traditional after Easter. Waiting for the service to begin, people were in festive mood, with dancing taking place in the open space in front of the church.

Trouble started with the arrival of French soldiers from Charles of Anjou's military force, then occupying Sicily. The Frenchmen had been drinking and, used to abusing the local population, they began to pay unwelcome attention to the Sicilian women. When murmurs of defiance were heard from the Sicilians, the French retaliated by searching them for weapons. A French sergeant named Drouet went too far in manhandling a young noblewoman. The Sicilians could take it no longer and a cry went up of *'Moranu li Franchiski!'* ('Death to the French!'), a knife was drawn and Drouet was killed, either by the woman's husband or by a youth in the crowd. A short, fierce struggle followed, the Sicilians attacking the fully armed French with sticks, stones and knives, at the end of which all the French and many Sicilians lay dead. Just as the fighting ceased, the church bells for vespers rang out all over Palermo. At this moment a massacre of the French began, leading to the War of the Sicilian Vespers, which consumed the countries of the Mediterranean for the next 20 years.[1]

Sicily has always been fertile ground for conspiracy theories and the story of the Sicilian Vespers is one of the most intriguing examples. From one point of view the revolt of the Sicilians against the French was a spontaneous act of aggression against their oppressors and was praised as such by Italian nationalists in the nineteenth century. On the other hand there is evidence to suggest that the revolt was carefully orchestrated to take place just in time to wreck the Mediterranean ambitions of Charles of Anjou. Bartholomew of Neocastro, a contemporary chronicler, claimed that 'the revolt was long in preparation'.[2] If this was the case, then it was a conspiracy on a grand scale.

Charles of Anjou's Mediterranean plan

The victories of Charles of Anjou over Frederick II's heirs, Manfred and Conradin, placed him in a strong position to further his interests in the Mediterranean. The Angevins, who took their name from their home state of Anjou, now occupied southern Italy and Sicily. Charles had the support of the Pope and the Guelph cities of Italy, and as no emperor had been crowned since the death of Frederick II, there was scope for an ambitious ruler to make his mark. Charles was a tall, commanding figure who had proved himself as a military leader in battle. He was well educated and as the younger brother of Louis IX, king of France, his background and connections were impeccable. However, as a boy he had been starved of family affection and he grew up pious, narrow in outlook, cold and aloof, 'his countenance expressive of pride and never brightened by a smile'.[3] His prime motivation was the acquisition of power and he was feared across Europe as an irresistible force.

Charles went on to take central Italy and then returned south to deal with rebellion. Lucera, the Muslim stronghold established by Frederick II, was besieged by the French army under Charles' personal command and was captured in August 1269. What was left of the Arab community, which had once ruled Sicily, dispersed to Muslim territories in North Africa and the Middle East. When Sicily was pacified, Charles imposed a tax regime which was efficiently implemented by French officials assisted by Italians from the mainland. Charles made only one brief visit to Sicily, having chosen Naples as his capital of the region. This was taken by the Sicilians as an insult.

Charles' Mediterranean plan followed that of the Normans and Hohenstaufens, from Robert Guiscard onwards, which was to use Sicily as the springboard for an attack on the Byzantine Empire. For years Western powers had cast covetous eyes at the crumbling empire in Eastern Europe with its wealth and strategic possessions. During the 1270s, however, Charles was forced to postpone a major expedition firstly to help his brother, King Louis, on a Crusade and then to accommodate the peace plans of Pope Gregory X. Unable to wage outright war on the Byzantine emperor, Michael Palaeologus, Charles used this period to confront him in different ways. Across the Balkans negotiations took place, combined with intrigue and occasional armed intervention as each side sought to strengthen its position.

By 1281 events had turned in Charles' favour and the way was clear for him to prepare the climax to his plans, namely a great expedition to capture Constantinople. The new pope, Martin IV, was a Frenchman who supported Charles' aims in the east. In a prestigious diplomatic move Charles had become king of Jerusalem, acquiring the title from Maria, Princess of Antioch, an inheritance from Norman times. Charles' position in central Italy was secure and he was now ready to fulfil his self-appointed destiny as a great European statesman.

Sicily became the training ground for an invasion fleet, partly supplied by Venice, consisting of 100 galleys, 200 transport vessels, 10,000 cavalry and a large force of infantry. Sicilians complained that they were being forced to make war on their Greek allies for the pleasure of their French oppressors. Charles controlled Sicily through his viceroy, Herbert of Orleans, in Messina, and a justiciar, or magistrate, in Palermo, John of Saint-Rémy. A network of 42 royal castles across the island kept the population under surveillance. During the preparations for the expedition, French officials stepped up their pressure on the Sicilians, increasing taxes to cover the costs and inflicting cruel punishments for acts of defiance. The atmosphere in Sicily, which had been under French rule for 16 years, became very tense.

As Charles' invasion plan developed, the position of Michael Palaeologus in Constantinople looked increasingly desperate. Fighting started on his Turkish border and in Albania and he was excommunicated by the Pope. He was becoming isolated and badly needed allies. Charles in his arrogance, however, underestimated his enemies and made no attempt to conceal his objectives.

The grand conspiracy

After the deaths of Manfred and Conradin, the Hohenstaufen cause became centred in Spain at the court of Peter of Aragon. Peter was married to Constance,

Manfred's daughter, and so together they represented a direct line to the
Hohenstaufen kings. In 1276 Peter succeeded his father to become King
Peter III of Aragon with Constance his queen. As Aragon had amalgamated with
Catalonia, Peter's court was based in Barcelona, a major port whose merchants
were already established in southern Italy. Sicily, which offered both a source
of agricultural produce and a market for Spanish textiles, was of interest to
these merchants. The court at Barcelona, with its pro-Ghibelline, anti-papal
tradition, attracted able men who had served Frederick II and his sons, eager
for revenge. They were welcomed by Constance, who had long been urging
her husband to avenge Manfred's death.

The mastermind behind the conspiracy was John of Procida, a doctor
from Salerno who became a professor of medicine at his hometown's famous
medical school. There he came to the attention of Frederick II, who made him
his personal physician. Impressed with John's abilities, Frederick appointed
him as counsellor, used him on diplomatic missions and as tutor to his son
Manfred. He was given estates near Naples, which included the island of
Procida. John attended the emperor during his final illness and was a witness to his will.

John became Manfred's chancellor and was with him when he lost the
Battle of Benevento. According to the legend, John was present in disguise
when Conradin was beheaded in a public square in Naples, where he recovered
the gauntlet that Conradin threw in defiance into the crowd. Once Charles of
Anjou's army was established in southern Italy, John's estates were confiscated,
and it was alleged that John's daughter was raped and one of his sons killed by
the French officer who came to take over his property. When Peter of Aragon
made John his chancellor, with responsibility for foreign affairs, the campaign
to oppose Charles' grand plan was set in motion.

The work of building an alliance began with a period of intense diplomacy,
with John of Procida, his sons and his agents, criss-crossing the Mediterranean
to recruit supporters. Sometimes disguised in a monk's habit, John made his
way in secret to his meetings. In 1279 he was in Constantinople, but Michael
Paleaologus refused to take part without the Pope's agreement. In Rome Pope
Nicholas III, who mistrusted Charles' ambitions in Italy, was persuaded to give
his consent. By the end of 1280 preparations for an alliance were progressing
well. Constantinople would provide the finance, Aragon the armed forces,
Genoa additional shipping and Sicily the popular backing. As part of the process

an ambassador from Constantinople arrived in Barcelona with a payment of 30,000 ounces of gold.

Visits were made to Sicily to enlist the leading barons, who included Walter of Caltagirone, Alaimo of Lentini and Palmieri Abbate. It is unknown precisely how the conspiracy operated in Sicily as everything was kept secret. What is known is that agents of Aragon were active on the island, arms were brought in and funds arrived from Constantinople.[4]

The crisis point was reached at the beginning of 1282. Charles' armada was being prepared to sail in April. Peter of Aragon's plan was to wait until Charles had left for Constantinople before landing in Sicily. Immediate action was needed to prevent the expedition from sailing. John of Procida, according to the chronicler Brunetto Latini, went to Palermo in January 1282 to see that the island rebelled against Charles. At a crucial meeting he addressed the leading barons as follows:

> My friends, I bring you good news from our lord [Peter of Aragon]. He has prepared a large fleet manned with the best sailors. In Roger Lauria we have the greatest admiral in the world, loyal to the king of Aragon and a true warrior who hates the French for the death of his father. So you need to work out how best to take the island by whatever means you think fit. There is no better time than the present, with King Charles occupied at the pope's court. While he is away you can do what you want in Sicily.[5]

The revolt

After the initial skirmish in front of the church of the Spirito Santo, men covered in blood brandishing weapons taken from the fallen French soldiers ran into the centre of Palermo. To the continuing cry of 'Death to the French!' all the French encountered were slaughtered: soldiers, monks, women and children. If their nationality was in doubt, suspects were shown a chickpea and asked what it was. The correct answer was *ciciru*, a word in the local dialect that was difficult for the French to pronounce. Those who failed the test were killed on the spot. Doors were broken down and households attacked and it is possible that the houses of the French had been previously identified and marked. The Angevin flag was torn down to be replaced by the imperial eagle, the sign given to the city by Frederick II. The justiciar, John of Saint-Rémy, escaped to the

Palazzo dei Normanni, but without the garrison was unable to keep out the mob. When he fled inland to a fortress at Vicari, Palermo was in the hands of the people. Parliament met that same night, declared an independent republic and elected captains to run the city led by a baron named Roger Mastrangelo. Around 2,000 French men and women died that day in Palermo.[6]

The next day the fortress at Vicari, where the justiciar was rallying his troops, was put under siege by the rebels. During negotiations for his release, the justiciar was shot and killed by an archer. The garrison was then massacred. Agents were sent to other cities on the island to spread the news of the revolt. Towns near Palermo were the first to join in, such as Corleone, which sent 3,000 armed men to Palermo, and Calatafimi, where the local justiciar was released unharmed as he was respected for his just administration. By mid-April all western and central Sicily was in rebel hands.

Messina was now the target for the rebels. This was where Charles' governor of Sicily, Herbert of Orleans, resided and where his fleet was anchored. It was Charles' preferred city on the island and had received many benefits from him. Initially Messina supported the Angevins but as the popular revolt spread, the governor's position became untenable. Herbert negotiated a safe passage for himself and his followers to Calabria, where they began to prepare a counter-attack. Messina formally joined the revolt on 30 April, apparently after receiving a payment of funds from Constantinople. A letter of confirmation of Messina's support was sent to the emperor in Constantinople, who received it with relief. When a number of French ships in the harbour at Messina were burned, the rest of the fleet withdrew.

Charles was furious when he heard the news and appealed to the Pope for support. The rebels and Michael Paleaologus found themselves excommunicated. The counter-attack took several months to prepare and in August Charles landed north of Messina with a large force. The Sicilians were urged to surrender by both Charles and the Pope. But the Sicilians had had enough of Angevin rule. The castle in Messina was taken by the rebels and Charles' representatives killed. Alaimo of Lentini, one of the leaders of the revolt, took decisive charge in Messina, repairing the defences and putting together a fleet of Sicilian, Genoese and Venetian ships. Charles launched several attacks on the city but was unable to capture it and after sustaining heavy losses he withdrew his troops.

So far the Sicilians had defeated the Angevins on their own, taking control of the key cities of Palermo and Messina. Charles, however, remained close by with his large army and navy and it was only a matter of time before the next assault came. The Sicilians had already appealed to the Pope, but to no avail. So they turned to Peter of Aragon, who with his fleet was campaigning in North Africa. A delegation was sent to Peter appealing to him to come to their aid and offering him the Crown of Sicily, with his wife Constance the rightful queen. After some discussion Peter accepted, and on 30 August the Aragonese fleet arrived at Trapani. Here Peter was enthusiastically received, according to the chronicler Esclot:

> And forthwith all the high nobles and knights of the land went out in barques to the ship of the King and when they were thereon, they kneeled down at his feet and kissed his hand, greeting him with much honour and beseeching him to descend upon the shore of his own land.

Peter was taken from Trapani to the palace in Palermo.

> Then the people of the land held high festival during four days or more. And they sent precious gifts of gold and silver to the King, likewise cloths of gold and silken stuffs. And the King was well pleased with the people of Trapani and of the regions round about.[7]

When Peter was crowned king of Sicily in Palermo on 4 September, he promised the people that he would reintroduce the just laws of King William the Good.

The war

The arrival of Peter in Sicily turned a local revolt into a wider conflict between the Aragonese and the Angevins for control of the Mediterranean, with Sicily once again the prize for competing powers. As initially both sides were short of resources, neither wanted to risk a pitched battle and once Peter entered Messina, Charles withdrew his forces from Sicily.

Charles then proposed that possession of Sicily be decided by single combat between himself and Peter of Aragon, an event to take place in Bordeaux, then English territory and thus neutral, on 1 June 1283. Both leaders managed to avoid the meeting while claiming moral victory. A trap was laid there for

Peter by the Angevins, which he successfully avoided. At this stage the Pope stepped up the pressure on Peter by declaring his territories forfeit, to be distributed to the Church, requiring Peter to return to Barcelona to defend his crown.

Constance was left in Sicily as regent, supported by John of Procida, now in his eighties, as chancellor and Alaimo of Lentini as justiciar. Palermo was reinstated as the island's capital and parliament was reconvened in the Palazzo dei Normanni. Spaniards began to arrive in Sicily to develop trade and, for the nobility, to be granted land. Their arrival led to tensions and anti-Aragonese feeling, to the extent that some Sicilians went over to the Angevin side. One of these was Walter of Caltagirone, a leading conspirator in the Sicilian Vespers, who was caught negotiating with the Angevins and executed for treason. Alaimo ended his days in a Catalan prison on suspicion of the same offence.

The war took place mostly at sea between the Angevins and the merged Catalan and Sicilian fleets commanded by Roger of Lauria. Roger was a powerful character, part naval commander, part pirate, described by Amari as 'great at once in his virtues and in his vices, of dauntless valour and brutal ferocity'.[8] In July 1283 he won his first major victory in the harbour at Malta, killing the Angevin admiral in single combat.

> And after this combat of the admirals no man made more resistance and the Catalans seized and took captive all the galleys of the Provençals. And they cast the dead into the sea and them that had lived and escaped from the onslaught they bound in chains. And those were in number 860 men and amongst them were many knights and high nobles from Marseilles and from Provence.[9]

Roger went on to defeat the Angevins at Naples and Provence, where Charles' son, Charles of Salerno, was taken prisoner. Roger's battles were won by a combination of close command of his captains and clever use of tactics. When not fighting the French, he was not above carrying out raids on shipping and coastal towns for his own benefit.

In 1285 came the deaths of both Charles of Anjou and Peter of Aragon. The war was continued by their heirs, James of Aragon and Charles of Salerno, who had secured his release from prison. Pope Martin IV died in the same year, and was succeeded by Honorius IV. In December 1295 the younger brother of James of Aragon was elected king of Sicily by the barons and became Frederick III. The

Pope, continuing previous strategy, excommunicated Frederick and announced a Crusade against him.

The Peace of Caltabellotta in 1302 brought an end to the first phase of the war. The Angevins withdrew their troops from Sicily and recognised Aragon's rule of the island during the lifetime of Frederick, who took the title of king of Trinacria, the ancient name for Sicily.

The outcome

The long-term effects of the Sicilian Vespers were very great. Instead of the French becoming a major power in the Mediterranean, as Charles of Anjou had planned, this role fell to the Spanish. The war rumbled on for many years but ultimately Aragon was able to consolidate its position in Sicily. The Spanish then continued to rule Sicily, in one form or another, with some intervals, until the arrival of Garibaldi in 1860. The papacy, in becoming so involved in Sicilian politics, overreached itself and undermined its own authority. Byzantium was saved from invasion and her empire survived until the city fell to the Turks in 1453.

The Sicilian Vespers changed the course of the island's history, cutting the island off from the Italian mainland and the mainstream of Italian life. As a result the Renaissance passed Sicily by. Through becoming linked to Spain, Sicily lost her productive trade with southern Italy and her ties to North Africa and Greece. She also lost the close connections with the University of Naples and the medical school at Salerno, where her civil servants and doctors were trained. The structural problems of Sicily and southern Italy, which led to long-term underdevelopment, began at this point, according to the Italian historian Benedetto Croce:

> As we well know, the Sicilian Vespers, which rhetorical and politically ingenuous persons still extol as a great historical event, [...] in reality [...] marked the beginning of much trouble and little greatness. It was not the Angevin conquest but rather the rebellion and separation of Sicily that broke the unity of the Norman/Swabian monarchy, weakened its power, deprived it of its historical mission and actually gave birth to the Kingdom of Naples.[10]

While the cities of central and northern Italy grew and prospered, developing sophisticated economies based on trading, Palermo lagged far behind. Her population fell to around 50,000, or half what it was under the Norman kings. Trade on the island fell into the hands of the Genoese and Venetians and Sicily's role became entrenched as that of a grain producer.[11] The decline of Sicily was hastened by a lack of strong central government, which allowed the cities to compete with one another. The barons took full advantage of the situation to increase their local power, which eventually led to civil war.

Sicilians gained little from their courageous role in throwing out the French invaders. The island lost its independence and became a pawn in the wider game of power politics for control of the Mediterranean. There followed a long era of colonial rule from Spain.

Epilogue

The Sicilian Vespers became part of the island's legend, referred to in the works of Dante, Petrarch and Boccaccio and commemorated on plaques in Palermo. What began as a brutal massacre became magnified into one of the most glorious events in Sicilian history. While it was accepted that the Sicilian Vespers were part of a wider scheme to foil Charles of Anjou, the precise nature of the conspiracy remained controversial. In Sicily today the word *vespro* is used as shorthand for a popular revolt.

In the nineteenth century the story was taken up in Italy as an example of a successful revolt at a time when much of the country was once again under foreign domination. Michele Amari, the Sicilian historian, published his work on the Sicilian Vespers in 1842 and was soon in trouble with the authorities. He left Palermo for Paris, where he studied Arabic and wrote his history of Muslim Sicily. On the Sicilian Vespers, while Amari acknowledged international involvement before and after the revolt in Sicily, as a liberal politician and supporter of the Risorgimento he could not accept that the revolt itself was orchestrated from abroad. For him it was a spontaneous rising of the Sicilian people, pushed too far by their French oppressors. In his own words:

> But it was God's will that Charles should be humbled, not by the lofty, but by the lowly, and that his overthrow should be accomplished by the means that could least of all have been anticipated – by a popular tumult in Palermo![12]

Verdi, a fervent supporter of Italian nationalism, was also interested in the story of the Sicilian Vespers and composed an opera on the subject for the Opéra de Paris. The libretto was by Eugène Scribe, the most distinguished librettist in Paris. *Les vêpres siciliennes* opened in Paris on 13 June 1855 and was initially a great success. It was a grand opera in five acts and the libretto bears little resemblance to the historical facts. Verdi was unhappy with the way the characters were portrayed and especially with the ending. In Scribe's version the church bells toll for the wedding of the hero and heroine as well as for the start of the revolt. Scribe, however, was too grand to make amendments for Verdi and defended his right to play fast and loose with history. After its early success the opera lost popularity, perhaps because the French appeared as the oppressors. For Italy the location of the story was moved to Portugal, but the opera was never well received by the Italians. None of this was Verdi's fault, for despite the grand-opera format and the limitations of the libretto, it still contained music of the highest quality.

The definitive work on the Sicilian Vespers was published in 1958 by Steven Runciman. In Runciman's view the rebellion could not have taken place without outside help. He admired Amari's scholarship but found that he exaggerated his case for a spontaneous revolt due to his political beliefs. Runciman concluded:

> The actual date of the outbreak may have been fortuitous; but it was so convenient for the Byzantines that the Emperor Michael almost certainly had something to do with it, as his own words and the message sent from Messina suggest. It was a little early for Aragon, and the Aragonese alliance was not at first entirely welcome to the Sicilians; nor, as the sequel showed, were they prepared to maintain it if it threatened their independence.
>
> The main credit, if a massacre deserves credit, should go to the Sicilians themselves, who provided the motive force. The organisation of the conspiracy and the alliances that enabled it to succeed was chiefly due to John of Procida; but the financing and the dating were the work of the Emperor at Constantinople.[13]

So while the story remains shrouded in mystery, on balance it seems likely that when the church bells rang out for the service on Easter Monday 1282 in Palermo, they really did signal the start of the revolt known as the Sicilian Vespers.

CHAPTER 8

The Spanish Domination

The Spanish domination of Sicily lasted for longer than that of any foreign power since the Romans and did much to shape modern Sicily. In different forms, and with some intervals, it stretched from the War of the Sicilian Vespers until the arrival of Garibaldi in 1860. The Arabs and Normans came to Sicily to make new lives for themselves and developed the island to the best of their abilities, creating a thriving economy from which the population at large benefited. For the Spanish, Sicily was a colony to be exploited for its strategic position and supplies of grain. As Spain became united and its empire expanded in Europe as well as in Central and South America, so Sicily took on a diminishing role in international affairs.[1]

Along with Spanish rule came a powerful form of Catholicism promoted by religious orders such as the Jesuits and regulated by the Holy Office of the Inquisition. The importance of religion needed demonstration. This produced on the one hand a flowering of creative art to communicate the Christian message and on the other a deeply oppressive regime to ensure orthodoxy. Palermo became a place of brilliant art but also one of arbitrary arrests and gruesome public executions.

The Spanish were great builders, going in for grandiose, flamboyant architecture with which they transformed the medieval city. Enthusiastic patrons of the arts, they were responsible for much of what we admire today, the baroque piazzas and churches, the monumental city gates, the palaces, paintings and sculptures.

Rule from Aragon

After a long-drawn-out war with the Angevins, Aragon succeeded in consolidating its hold on Sicily. In the chaotic wartime conditions the leading barons increased their power to the extent that by 1390 four of the top families had divided the island up among themselves. The east was governed by the Alagona from Catania, the south by the Peralta from Sciacca and the north coast by the Ventimiglia. The Chiaramonte, the strongest of them all, ruled Palermo and the small but prosperous city of Modica. In 1392 an expedition was sent to reconquer Sicily for the Aragonese. While some of the barons supported the invaders, Palermo held out under siege for a month. When finally the city capitulated, Andrea Chiaramonte was beheaded outside his palace in Piazza Marina and his property seized by the victorious Spanish general. In 1412 envoys were sent to Sicily to consolidate Aragonese rule. From that point, as the historian Denis Mack Smith noted:

> Sicily was no longer a residence of kings, but for four hundred years was to be administered by viceroys, a centre less of politics than of administration, and with none of the perquisites pertaining to a major focus of government.[2]

The majority of the 78 successive viceroys who ruled the island were Spanish. Only a few were Sicilian and none were after the first 50 years. The post was seen as prestigious but not one of the first rank and it was not without its difficulties. Viceroys tended to be criticised for being either too lenient or too authoritarian and received plenty of advice on how to handle the Sicilians, who were apparently slow to spend their own money but quick to spend public funds. One viceroy was advised: 'Governing Sicily is fatal to all rulers. In a short space of time they find themselves besieged with problems.'[3]

The Inquisition and the expulsion of the Jews

When Ferdinand succeeded to the throne in 1479, Aragon was united with Castile through his wife Isabella to form the Spanish state. Due to the large Moorish and Jewish communities in their territories, religious unity was a priority for the sovereigns. Accordingly they set up the Tribunal of the Holy Office of the

Inquisition to ensure that their subjects followed orthodox Catholicism. The Holy Office was led by the formidable Inquisitor General, the Dominican friar Tomás de Torquemada. Torquemada held a privileged position at court, acted as Queen Isabella's personal confessor, and wielded a great deal of influence. From 1487 onwards inquisitors were sent to Sicily to eliminate heresy and exercise control over moral behaviour. Ferdinand and Isabella took Grenada, the last Moorish stronghold in Spain, in 1492. Later that same year came the edict announcing the expulsion of the Jews from all Spanish territory, including Sicily.

Sicily had a well-established Jewish community that went back to Roman times. Fleeing from persecution in the Middle East, many of the Jews had arrived as slaves, later to gain their freedom. Under the Arabs and Normans they were free to practise their religion. They built synagogues and cemeteries and enjoyed full rights of owning property. Under Frederick II Jewish immigration from North Africa was encouraged to offset the departure of the Arabs.

At the time of the edict there were 35,000 Jews living in Sicily, out of a total population of 620,000, in 52 locations around the island. The highest concentration was in Palermo, where out of the city's population of 40,000 some 5,000 were Jews. The Jewish quarter lay outside the Cassaro district, around today's Piazza Meschita. 'Meschita' is the Italian for 'mosque' or 'synagogue'. The Jewish synagogue was located where the church of San Nicola da Tolentino (St Nicholas of Tolentino) stands today on Via Maqueda. The community specialised in the production of fabrics, being expert in the colouring process, and in the working of silk. Sicilian silk was still famous and was one of the island's high-value exports. The Jews were also well known as doctors and merchants. Among themselves they spoke a form of Arabic Hebrew reflecting their connections with North Africa and the Middle East. They were well integrated and made a significant contribution to the city's economic, cultural and intellectual life.

The edict for expulsion, which reached Palermo in June 1492, came as a bolt from the blue. The city was totally unprepared for it and received the news in a state of shock. Administration of the edict lay with the viceroy, Fernando de Acuña, and the inquisitor sent from Madrid, Antonio La Pegna. According to the edict, Jews had to choose between converting to Christianity and leaving Sicily. For those leaving, property had to be sold, with the proceeds going to the Crown, all credit repaid and all personal belongings of value left behind. Money could be sent abroad through a letter of credit from a bank, for those fortunate enough to be able to arrange it. These regulations started a treasure hunt by the authorities to identify Jewish property, consisting of houses, shops, land, livestock and personal possessions. A time limit for departure was set at three months, which was later extended to six months.

The numbers of Jews who left Sicily, compared to those who converted to Christianity and stayed on the island, is unknown. It is probable that, as in the case of Spain, the majority left. The Jews were required to report to Messina for embarkation, where checks were made to see that all the terms of the edict had been fulfilled. Many faced a perilous journey to the coast, for while the authorities had guaranteed their safety, in practice they were subject to attack. Travelling on foot, on horseback, on donkeys and in carts, they left the places of their birth in small groups led by their rabbis.

In August the first group of 350 Jews left Palermo for Messina. The last to leave did so in December, accompanied by the Jewish mayor of Palermo, David Lu Medicu, who had done all he could for his community. It is not known where they went. It is likely that many settled in Calabria and southern Italy, while the Papal States, North Africa, Istanbul and Salonica also received Jewish refugees. Little is known about the journeys that they endured. One eyewitness, who saw a Jewish group arrive at Genoa after expulsion from Castile, recorded the following: 'It was a sad spectacle; most were exhausted by hunger and thirst; they looked like ghosts. Many died on the harbour front at the place reserved for them, not far from the market.'[4]

The exodus marked the end of the Jews in Sicily, for as a community they never returned. For the majority it was a departure without hope and with no future, leaving behind everything they owned. Virtually all traces of their presence were destroyed, including their cemeteries. Gravestones inscribed in Hebrew, looted from Jewish cemeteries, can be seen today incorporated into other buildings. The main relics of a once thriving Jewish community in Sicily are the underground baths in Syracuse, which lay hidden for centuries and are now open to the public.[5]

For the Jews who converted and remained in Sicily worse was to come. In 1500 a royal decree, under the auspices of Diego Deza, the new Inquisitor General, brought in stricter controls on heresy with the approval of the Borgia pope, Alexander VI. It was difficult for the converts, the so-called *marrani*, to hide their cultural differences. As a result many were arrested and accused of continuing to follow the Jewish faith. During interrogation, torture was used to obtain confessions, with instructions not to stop until the truth was told. Favourite methods, which were not supposed to draw blood or cause permanent injury, were the rack, the rope, whereby the victim was suspended by a rope attached to his wrists, hands tied behind his back, and dropped from a height, and simulated drowning. In total 1,890 men and women were accused of heresy by the Inquisition in Sicily between the years 1511 and 1560. Of these 149 were burned at the stake, 55 of them in Palermo. The rest were imprisoned, sent to the galleys or freed. All lost their possessions. Protests against this campaign took place in Palermo, where it was considered unjust and vindictive. Eventually an ambassador was sent from Palermo to Madrid to seek justice for the converts, but with little success.[6]

The Inquisition became established in Sicily, where it exercised a malign influence for nearly 300 years. The violent methods of the inquisitors combined with the encouragement of informers created an atmosphere of fear and intimidation which amounted to a reign of terror. Reporting directly to the king in Madrid, the Inquisition provided another means of control in parallel to that of the viceroys, whose military forces were limited. The Sicilian barons were quick to recognise the importance of the Inquisition and allied themselves to it as associates, a position granting immunity from some of the courts. The viceroys complained that the Inquisition protected 'all the rich nobles and rich criminals of the kingdom' and that lawyers were useless once it got involved.[7]

Society became profoundly affected by an institution which imposed conformity and prevented new ideas from circulating. Books were censored and education was dominated by the Jesuits. Persecution of minorities continued, including the converted Jews and Muslims as well as Greek speakers. Hunts went on to identify witches, bigamists and homosexuals. Sailors who had been held prisoner by the Turks, and had then escaped, were arrested on suspicion of following Islam. In the smaller towns local police enforced the Inquisition's rules and severely punished any behaviour considered deviant. The Holy Office became so wealthy through confiscation of property that the senate in Palermo complained that it was being driven solely by greed.

From 1605 to 1782 the Inquisition was based in the Palazzo Chiaramonte (also known as Lo Steri, from the Latin *hosterium* meaning 'a fortified palace') in Palermo's Piazza Marina. Here prisoners' graffiti and drawings have been found in the prison cells. There are drawings of Christ and the saints, prayers and poems, including some in English and German. They include the words *pazienza, pane e tempo* ('patience, bread and time') and a poem in the Sicilian dialect which begins:

> Open your eyes to this terrible gloom,
> And find yourself alone in fear.

Prisoners suffered prolonged torture as the inquisitors tried to uncover their true beliefs. In 1657 an incident took place in which a prisoner, a deranged monk named Diego La Matina, managed to fight back during interrogation by his inquisitor. According to a contemporary account:

> This Fra Diego, as though possessed by the Devil, broke free of the manacles about his hands and with these same irons repeatedly beat the Inquisitor, wounding him fatally with a blow to the forehead and to the top of the head from which he died.[8]

The monk, who was considered a heretic for consistently refusing to conform to orthodox beliefs, was kept in prison for months, chained to a chair until he was burned at the stake. During his execution a flock of crows screeched around him and flew off at his death. To the assembled crowd they were thought to be demons released from his body.

In 1724 an *auto-da-fé* was staged in the square facing Palermo's cathedral and the Palazzo Arcivescovile (Archbishop's Palace). The scene, captured in a painting by Antonino Mongitore now in the British Museum, shows tiers of seats constructed like a theatre for the barons and churchmen to get a good view. A large crowd gathered to watch the victims dressed in tall dunces' caps being burned alive.

In Sicily the last such execution took place in 1732. The Inquisition was finally abolished on the island by the reforming viceroy Domenico Caracciolo in 1782.

The redesign of Palermo

The Spanish made their mark on Palermo for reasons of defence, religion and prestige and their achievements in town planning were remarkable. Under their rule Palermo took on a whole new look worthy of its position as a seat of the viceroys. The redesign of Palermo coincided with the baroque era and the baroque, with its strong theatrical appeal, became the dominant style of the city. This urban development opened up the heart of the city with new wide roads and surrounded it with monumental city gates. It destroyed much of medieval

Palermo, which was further disrupted by the construction of new palaces for the nobility. Building was forbidden for half a mile outside the city walls for reasons of security. Beyond that limit shanty towns sprung up to accommodate the increasing numbers of the poor who were forced to leave the land. Palermo's population quadrupled during the sixteenth century to 114,000 by 1591.

Late medieval Palermo, as inherited by the Spanish, was a substantial city although much reduced in wealth and population from her peak in Norman times. The chronicler Pietro Ransano, who was in Palermo in 1469, found the city 'prosperous, rich and noble, well populated and decorated with many beautiful things from ancient times'.[9] He recorded his impressions of the city's layout, with its high walls made from huge, squared stones interspersed with four main gates crowned with towers. The Norman castle with its marble floors and gold mosaics he found magnificent. Around the city he saw lush countryside providing rich produce, grapes, fruit and sugar cane, the whole area well supplied with water.

Palermo in this period was a city of great religious ceremonies. These popular rites were encouraged by the viceroys as they brought the people together and gave the poor a chance to join in celebrations. They were also an opportunity for the barons to parade their wealth and the Church its pageantry. Ransano attended the six-day festival in Palermo to celebrate Ferdinand's marriage to Isabella. He witnessed a great procession singing hymns, led by the clergy in their finery, which went down to the sea from the cathedral. The streets were decorated with coloured fabrics hung from the balconies of the houses along the route. In the evening the streets were lit by lanterns, including on the galleys in the port, creating a spectacle which was much admired by residents and the foreign visitors.

The barons, who were fiercely competitive, vied with one another to build the most extravagant palaces in Palermo, designed to demonstrate their wealth and status. Two early examples are the Chiaramonte and Sclafani, both fortress–palaces containing magnificent reception rooms and living quarters. This trend continued under the viceroys, bringing many changes to the city centre. Between the luxurious palaces of the nobility lay the narrow streets and alleyways where the majority of the people lived in abject poverty.

The balance of power in the Mediterranean was radically altered in 1453 when the Turks captured Constantinople, bringing to an end the Byzantine Empire. Renamed Istanbul, the city became the capital of the Ottoman Empire, which in the sixteenth century provided a major challenge to Spain and the Christian states of Western Europe. For Palermo the rise of the Ottoman Empire had two major consequences. Firstly trade with Eastern Europe virtually ceased, further depressing the Sicilian economy. Secondly, as Turkish ambitions in the Mediterranean grew, Sicily became an island fortress, an outpost of Spain in a lengthy maritime war. To finance the war, taxes on the Sicilian population were increased. From being a centre of Mediterranean trade in the early medieval period, by the sixteenth century Palermo was the heavily defended capital of an island under siege conditions.

Palermo's fortifications were radically overhauled during the period 1535–72. A feature of the siege of Constantinople had been the widespread use of gunpowder both by artillery and the infantry. Fortifications needed to be adapted to withstand these weapons. Accordingly huge bastions sloping outwards to deflect cannonballs were incorporated at intervals into Palermo's walls. Defences were deepened, walls were thickened and cannon installed at strategic points. The Castellammare fortress, which dominated the entrance to the port and which also served as a means of subduing revolts in the city, was strengthened. The port was extended by the addition of new quays and larger galleys were built to augment the small Sicilian fleet. This work as well as that carried out on the east coast at Messina, Augusta and Syracuse was done on the orders of Antonio Ferramolino, an expert military engineer from Bergamo in northern Italy, who spent 17 years in Sicily. In a report sent to King Charles V in Madrid, the viceroy Ferrando Gonzaga wrote in July 1546:

> I have surrounded Palermo with bastions in sight of each other, according to a plan of the site, supported by strong if ancient walls. Ditches are difficult to dig there but parapets have been added out of loose stone and in my opinion we can resist any attack.[10]

The Turkish advance was finally halted in 1571 in a sea battle at Lepanto, off the coast of Greece, where the Ottoman fleet was decisively beaten by the combined fleets of Spain, Sicily, the Papal States, Venice, Genoa and the Knights of Malta. While the Turkish threat subsided, Sicily remained vulnerable to raids from pirates based in North Africa.

As work on the fortifications continued, major alterations were made to the centre of the city. The two rivers that flowed down either side, the Kemonia and the Papireto, were diverted underground, improving sanitation and allowing for the development of new districts. The ancient road leading down from the Palazzo dei Normanni past the cathedral, known as the Cassaro, was extended to the sea and was renamed Via Toledo after the viceroy, Don García, Duke of Toledo. At the end of this road, near the Palazzo dei Normanni, a triumphal arch was built, Porta Nuova, commemorating the arrival of King Charles V, the Holy Roman Emperor, in Palermo after his victory in Tunisia.

A new road was opened up in 1600 at right angles to Via Toledo, running roughly north–south, which dramatically changed the centre of the city. This was Via Maqueda, named after the viceroy, the Duke of Maqueda. At the crossroads where they met a complex baroque monument was built called the Quattro Canti (figure 2). It represented the four *mandamenti* or quarters of the city – Albergheria, Seralcadio, Kalsa and Loggia – and featured statues of the four seasons, four Spanish kings of Sicily and four patron saints of the city. At either end of Via Maqueda city gates were built, the Vicario to the south and the Maqueda to the north. Palermo, poised between mountains and the sea, was

2. The Quattro Canti (Four Corners) (Barberis, 1893).

now divided into four quarters by the form of a cross made by the intersection of the two main roads, Toledo and Maqueda.

Santa Rosalia and the plague

From 1624 to 1626 Palermo suffered from an epidemic of plague which killed around a quarter of its population of 130,000. The plague arrived by ship from Tunis in May 1624 and spread slowly at first, with two or three people dying each day. Shortly this rose to over 50 a day, with deaths taking place all over the city, including at the Palazzo dei Normanni, the residence of the viceroy. In an attempt to stem the plague's advance, a crucifix was carried in a procession from the cathedral down to the church of Santa Maria della Catena (St Mary's of the Chain) by the Cala, the old port. It was soon clear, however, that the plague was spreading like wildfire and on 24 June the viceroy declared a state of emergency.

To handle the crisis the senate met in almost permanent session, issuing a series of proclamations to contain the plague. A doctor and an officer responsible for hygiene were assigned to supervise each of the city's four main districts. Movement in and out of the city was severely restricted, people were told to stay in their districts, to report sick people and to isolate their houses. Punishments for not obeying the orders were severe. Palermo became a city under siege with the terrified citizens forced to stay put and wait for the epidemic to run its course. *Lazzaretti*, or emergency hospitals, were set up to cope with the sick and dying, the main one at the Cuba, the old Norman palace located outside the city on the road to Monreale. Volunteers came forward to look after the sick, including doctors who worked for no pay.

In July the viceroy Emanuele Filiberto left the palace to see for himself what was happening. He travelled by carriage down Via Toledo to Porta Felice and by the time he returned to the palace he was already infected. Relics of Santa Cristina and a painting of Santa Rosalia were taken to his bedside to ward off the plague, but despite the efforts of his doctor, Filiberto died on 3 August. A funeral service was held for him at the cathedral at the end of the month. Nothing halted the spread of the plague, which between May and December 1624 was calculated to have claimed 10,000 lives.[11]

At the time four saints, Cristina, Agata, Oliva and Ninfa, were each associated with a specific *mandamento* or quarter of Palermo. The monument known as the Quattro Canti, at the centre of the city, featured the saints, linking them to their quarters. Santa Cristina was recognised as the city's patron saint. On 15 July 1624 bones were found in a cave on Monte Pellegrino, just outside Palermo, believed to be those of Santa Rosalia. Rosalia was another saint favoured in the city, who had been invoked in the past for protection from the plague. There are different versions of how her bones came to be discovered. According to the Church, it was on the advice of a woman named Geronima La Cattuta, to whom Rosalia appeared in a dream, telling her exactly where to dig in the cave. A popular version maintains that that the bones were found by a lone hunter.[12]

Little is known about the life of Rosalia. From the varying accounts, it appears that she was born into a noble family around 1130 in the times of the Norman kings, the daughter of a certain Duke Sinibaldi. She may have been the niece of King William II. At an early age she left her family to live as a religious hermit in caves firstly in the Quisquina, a mountainous region near Agrigento, and then on Monte Pellegrino. She may have served as a nun of the Basilian order at the convent attached to the church of the Martorana, for her image appeared on an icon from the convent, together with the saints Oliva, Elia and Venera. According to the Church, she died on 4 September 1170.[13]

The archbishop of Palermo, Giannettino Doria, who took control of the city following the viceroy's death, set up a commission consisting of church-men and medical experts to examine the bones and to verify their origin. On 22 February 1625 the bones were declared genuine. Vincenzo Auria, who lived through the plague, recorded:

> The cardinal and the theologians, called together for this purpose, declared that the bones found on Monte Pellegrino were indeed those of our glorious Santa Rosalia, our Palermitan. The sacred bones were worshipped and when a cask was ready they were taken from the archbishop's residence to the cathedral in a procession with all the clergy. Great joy was felt by all those present. Lights appeared throughout the city for two days and I put lanterns at my windows. We Christians, followers of the saint, hope that she will intercede on our behalf with the Lord to end this plague.[14]

The archbishop began to use the saint's relics to boost the morale of the people, who were exhausted and demoralised. On 9 June the first *festino* took place. The senate encouraged people to come out onto the streets to honour the saint, bringing flowers and not to be dressed in mourning. A solemn procession went down Via Toledo through triumphal arches from the cathedral to Porta Felice, re-entering the city at Porta dei Greci. It continued along Via Alloro and past the church of San Giuseppe dei Teatini (St Joseph of the Theatines) to turn once more into Via Toledo and arrive back at the cathedral. This event was accompanied by a huge outpouring of popular emotion and adoration for Santa Rosalia. On 15 August she was proclaimed the patron saint of Palermo, becoming known affectionately by the people as the Santuzza ('the little saint'). The *festino* became a hugely popular annual event lasting for five days. A triumphal carriage, carrying a statue of the saint at its peak, was introduced in 1686.[15]

In recognition of the saint and her status in the city a number of works were ordered by the senate. A cask of silver and crystal was made to hold her remains. Chapels for her were ordered to be built in the cathedral and in the cave on Monte Pellegrino. A painting was commissioned from Vincenzo La Barbera in 1624, which set the tone for future images of the saint. La Barbera was devoted to Santa Rosalia, for his daughter was said to have been miraculously cured by her. The picture shows Rosalia interceding with the Holy Trinity and the Virgin Mary for the city of Palermo, as she gestures towards the *lazzaretto*. Behind her can be seen the Cala and Porta Felice, and in the background, Monte Pellegrino.[16]

Pictures of Santa Rosalia were also painted by the Flemish painter Anthony Van Dyck, who found himself in Palermo at the time. Van Dyck arrived in Palermo early in 1624 to carry out an important commission, a portrait of the viceroy, Emanuele Filiberto. Filiberto was a keen patron of the arts and built for himself a picture gallery of 200 paintings at the royal palace in Palermo. Van Dyck, who was 25, had been living in Genoa and found accommodation with the well-established Genoese community in Palermo in the district known as the Loggia, behind the church of San Domenico (St Dominic). Their church of San Giorgio dei Genovesi (St George of the Genoese) is still to be found there. In the portrait of Filiberto Van Dyck produced the perfect image of the seventeenth-century ruler, for it combined personal elegance with military bearing, the viceroy shown wearing his magnificently decorated suit of armour. The portrait, which was finished just before the plague struck, fell down from its place in the Sala di Ruggero in the royal palace, which was taken as an ill omen by Filiberto.[17]

Van Dyck was also commissioned to paint pictures to commemorate Santa Rosalia. His work built on the image created by La Barbera to produce what became the accepted iconography of the saint. In his paintings Rosalia appears

with long, fair hair, dressed in a monastic robe. She is placed beside her cave
on Monte Pellegrino, interceding for her city, which is spread out below. She
is accompanied by a garland of roses, signifying her name; some lilies; a skull,
referring to her life as a hermit or perhaps to the plague; and a book. Five of
the paintings have survived in different cities, from London to New York and
Madrid, though none in Palermo.[18]

By the spring of 1626 the effects of the plague were receding and on 10 June
the city was declared clear of infection. The archbishop in his public announcement stated that 'the malignant disease is dead thanks to the intercession of
our glorious Santa Rosalia'.

In 1647 the senate announced that in recognition of the saint's contribution to the city two dates would be celebrated in perpetuity as festivals in her
honour. The first was 15 July, to commemorate the finding of her bones, and
the second was 4 September, her *dies natalis*, the date of her death and rebirth
to eternal life. The *festino* has continued ever since while the September date is
marked by a procession to the saint's sanctuary on Monte Pellegrino.[19]

International travellers

The grand tour, on which the young aristocrats of Europe completed their
education, was extended in the eighteenth century to include Sicily. Until that
time Italy had played an important part in the tour but only as far as Naples. As
the countries around the Mediterranean became more stable, so Sicily began to
be explored by international travellers. This coincided with a renewed interest
in the ancient world, especially in Greece.

The Sicilians had already made a significant contribution to the rediscovery
of Greek Sicily. The first printed history of Sicily was published in 1558 by the
Dominican friar Tommaso Fazello. Fazello worked in Palermo as the prior
of the church of San Domenico. He spent years exploring Sicily, searching
for remains of the ancient Greek cities, and succeeded in identifying Selinus
(modern Selinunte), Akrai (Palazzolo Acreide), Segesta, Kamarina, Himera
and Akragas (Agrigento). His work was based on the ancient historians, such
as Diodorus Siculus, and combined history with the topography of the cities
and descriptions of the monuments. In 1613 a reconstruction of ancient Greek
Syracuse was published by Vincenzo Mirabella, a Syracusan nobleman. His

work contained descriptions of the ancient city and the monuments illustrated by maps. The work of these two pioneers in the history and archaeology of Sicily inspired others to follow. It was not, however, until the second half of the nineteenth century that the rediscovery of ancient Greek Sicily really took off.

Two travellers from northern Europe, who visited Sicily in the 1770s, encouraged others by publishing accounts of their travels. The first was the Scot Patrick Brydone, whose *Tour through Sicily and Malta*, written as a series of letters to his friend William Beckford, appeared in 1773. Sicily was virtually unknown in England at the time. Brydone described an island filled with ancient Greek monuments, wild countryside, a volcano and picturesque cities whose population was hospitable to foreigners. He also recounted his adventures with brigands in the more remote parts of the island. The combination of classical culture and present-day adventure hit a chord with the public and his book, translated into French and German, was widely read across Europe.

Brydone was much taken with the approach to Palermo, through countryside filled with abundant crops and orchards. Coming into the city, however, he passed with distaste a place of execution where the bodies of robbers were displayed. Once Brydone had explored Palermo, he admired the Spanish plan of the city:

> It is by much the most regular I have seen, and it is built upon that plan, which I think all large cities ought to follow. The two great streets intersect each other in the centre of the city, where they form a handsome square, called the Ottangolo [the Quattro Canti], adorned with elegant uniform buildings. From the centre of this square you see the whole of these noble streets, and the four great gates of the city which terminate them; the symmetry and beauty of which produce a fine effect.[20]

Brydone was in Palermo for the *festino* of Santa Rosalia, which he described with enthusiasm, and was particularly impressed by the huge carriage carrying the statue of the saint:

> About five in the afternoon, the festival began by the triumph of Santa Rosalia, who was drawn with great pomp through the centre of the city, from the Marina to the Porta Nuova. The triumphal car was preceded by a troop of horse, with trumpets and kettledrums; and all the city officers in their gala uniforms. It is indeed a most enormous machine: it measures seventy feet long, thirty wide and upwards of eighty high; and as it passed along, over-topped the loftiest houses of

Palermo. There is a large dome supported by six Corinthian columns, adorned with a number of figures of saints and angels; and on the summit of the dome there is a gigantic silver figure of Santa Rosalia.

When the procession was over a firework display took place at the Marina. Brydone and his companions were guests of the city. 'During this exhibition we had a handsome entertainment of coffee, ices and sweetmeats with a variety of excellent wines in the pavilion on the Marina, at the expense of the Mayor, the Duke of Castellano.'[21]

Goethe reached Sicily in April 1787 after extensive travels through mainland Italy. He was struck with the unique environment of the island, noting: 'To have seen Italy without having seen Sicily is not to have seen Italy at all, for Sicily is the clue to everything.'[22] Like Brydone, whose book he had read, Goethe admired Palermo but found it confusing once away from the main streets.

> We went out first thing to take a closer look at the city, which is easy to grasp in its overall plan, but difficult to get to know in detail. A street a mile long runs from the lower to the upper gate; this is bisected by another street, so that everything which lies along these axes is easy to find. But the inner part of the city is a confusing labyrinth, where a stranger can find his way only with the help of a guide.

Later that same day Goethe, who was staying in Via Butera near Piazza Marina, went down to the seafront.

> Towards evening we watched with great interest the famous carriage parade of the nobility, who at that hour drive out of the town towards the harbour in order to take the air, chat with each other and, above all, flirt with the ladies. Two hours before sunset a full moon rose, bathing the evening in an inexpressible glory. Owing to the mountains behind Palermo to the south, sunlight and moonlight are never seen reflected in the water at these hours. Even on this brightest of days, the sea was dark blue, sombre and, so to speak, intrusive, whereas in Naples, from noon on, it always becomes increasingly serene, brilliant and, so to speak, extensive.[23]

Goethe was unimpressed, however, by the litter he found on the streets of Palermo and asked a shopkeeper: 'By all the saints, why is your city so filthy? Can nothing be done about it?' The shopkeeper replied: 'That is the way things have always been. What we throw out of our homes immediately starts to rot on our doorsteps.' He went on to blame the corruption of the authorities and the nobility, who preferred a soft, elastic surface for their carriages.[24]

Sicily became an established part of the grand tour. More journals were published containing visitors' impressions of the island, in which some found it romantic, others wild and dangerous. Most agreed that it was exotic and different and the number of international visitors to the island steadily increased.

The role of the aristocracy

The Spanish era was the heyday of the Sicilian aristocracy. Through their estates across the island, and their orchards in the Conca d'Oro around Palermo, they controlled the wealth of Sicily. Cheap labour was provided by the peasants. The aristocracy's privileged position was accepted by the viceroys as it was needed to keep the peace, for the number of Spanish troops assigned to Sicily was not very great. In this way the barons managed to maintain their feudal privileges while ignoring their obligations to the state. So at a time when elsewhere in Europe the power of the barons was being curtailed, in Sicily it was given free rein.

The barons' estates, the *latifondi*, were worked by peasants to produce the grain which had long been Sicily's main export. The peasants worked under conditions little better than slavery and were often forced to travel long distances to get to work. Only the men worked in the fields. Women stayed at home looking after the family. As a class peasants were too weak and too downtrodden to seek improvement in their condition. Society became polarised between the wealthy aristocracy on the one hand and the peasants, sunk in poverty, on the other. In Palermo the two classes eyed each other with mutual suspicion, interspersed with periods of armed conflict.

Under the earlier viceroys the barons mostly lived on their estates, which they actively developed. By the late seventeenth century the move to the cities was gaining pace, especially to Palermo where the viceroy and his court were based. Here the barons built their palaces, financed by loans against their estates, and lived a life of conspicuous luxury. They became absentee landlords, delegating the management of their estates to a class of manager known as *gabelloti*, a word derived from *gabella*, meaning 'contract'. The *gabelloti* were middlemen who ran the estates for personal gain with little thought of improving working conditions or production methods. They employed local thugs to keep the peasants under control and blackmailed their employers for higher pay. The aim of a *gabelloto* was to make a quick fortune and join the ranks of the aristocracy. The result was disastrous for agriculture, the mainstay of the economy, and for the peasants who worked on the land.

The senate represented the highest judicial court in Palermo, consisting of a judge and six senators elected annually from the aristocracy. The senate looked after the city's finances, health and public-building programmes. It was a staunch defender of aristocratic privilege. Parliament, which represented the whole island, was made up of three *bracci* or levels: *militare* (aristocracy), *ecclesiastico* (Church) and *demaniale* (communes of the royal domain), the last being the closest to a representative body, but it met only infrequently. On their estates the barons enforced their own form of justice through the *gabelloti*. In Palermo, with the viceroys often absent on diplomatic missions, there was plenty of scope for corruption and the barons were able to buy favours. The rule of law was heavily biased in favour of the rich.

In the seventeenth century this situation led to the formation of a secret society called the Beati Paoli. This organisation's mission was to seek justice for the common man in the face of the barons' control of the legal system. The Beati Poli became one of the legends of Palermo, shadowy figures in dark cloaks making their way across the city to help citizens in need. Their meeting places were below ground, in cellars and caves in the Capo district, where a street has been named after them.

Given the privileged status involved, there was pressure to join the ranks of the aristocracy. The viceroys took advantage of this by selling titles, which became a major source of income. Titles proliferated to such an extent that by the end of the eighteenth century the Sicilian aristocracy included 142 princes, 788 marquises, and 1,500 barons and dukes. The baroque facades of their palaces hid a declining prosperity, for by this time mounting debts were eating away at the wealth of the aristocracy.[25]

Spanish Bourbon rule from Naples

The Spanish rule of Sicily from Madrid ended in 1713 following the Treaty of Utrecht, which brought to a close the War of the Spanish Succession. The island was assigned first to Savoy and then to Austria. An expedition by the Spanish Bourbons took Naples in 1734, establishing Charles, son of Philip V of Spain, as king. When Charles inherited the Spanish Crown, he left Naples and Sicily to his youngest son, who became Ferdinand III of Sicily and Ferdinand IV of Naples.

Sicily suffered badly during the last years of Spanish rule. The economic difficulties which had overwhelmed the Spanish Empire were equally felt in Sicily. Lack of food in Palermo led to a revolt against the Spanish in 1647 which was harshly put down. Strong rivalry between Palermo and Messina led to open warfare between the two cities.

Under the Spanish Bourbons Sicily was ruled from Naples by a viceroy supported by a military garrison. Palermo was now by far the dominant city, Messina having been hit by natural disasters, first an earthquake and then the plague. Palermo's population in the eighteenth century rose to 200,000, making it among the largest cities in Italy. Most of the aristocracy lived in Palermo together with an increasing number of the poor and destitute, peasants who could no longer make a living on the land. Building speculation and illegal construction were rife. Viceroys were mostly content to keep the status quo, placating the nobility with honours and elaborate ceremonies and the poor with cheap bread.[26]

In 1781 a new viceroy arrived in Palermo, a Neapolitan born in Spain named Domenico Caracciolo. Caracciolo is famous for being one of the few governors of Sicily who made a serious attempt at reform and his name is remembered in Palermo in a piazza in the Vucciria market. He was a senior minister of King Ferdinand's, an economist and diplomat, whose previous assignments had been in Paris and London. Caracciolo was independent, with no axe to grind, and was appalled at what he found in Sicily, commenting: 'As well as being badly organised, Sicily is inhabited by great barons and the destitute poor, that is to say by the oppressors and the oppressed, because the courts serve as instruments of oppression.'[27]

The administration that Caracciolo inherited in Palermo was inefficient and corrupt, with a tax burden that fell mostly on the poor and a food market that was dominated by monopolies and rackets. Senators in Palermo enjoyed the best jobs with high salaries. The infrastructure of the island was almost nonexistent with no proper roads joining the coastal cities or those of the interior.

Caracciolo, who was energetic and full of ideas, threw himself into an ambitious reform programme. In Palermo he tackled the abuses in market monopolies and the multiple jobs held by officers in the city's administration. He abolished the Holy Office of the Inquisition in Sicily in March 1782 and the archives took three days to be burned in the courtyard of the Palazzo Chiaramonte. Plans were drawn up for the building of three major roads: Palermo–Messina, Palermo–Sciacca and Palermo–Agrigento. He started work on a major project to evaluate land across the island as the basis for a fairer tax system, using a model from Lombardy in northern Italy.

In all these plans he came up against a wall of opposition from the nobility, who felt their privileges to be under threat. In Caracciolo's view these privileges could only be justified by a corresponding commitment to public service. He complained: 'Tradition is the argument always brought up here by those who intend to feather their nest at the expense of the king and the poor.'[28]

However, the poor, who knew only servitude, were afraid of change and were still locked into a feudal mentality. In Palermo Caracciolo faced a revolt when he tried to limit the annual *festino* for Santa Rosalia from five days to three, as the *festino* had become the major social event of the year with huge popular support. The king had to intervene to countermand the order.

Caracciolo had only partial success with his reforms, which appeared threatening to the barons and unsettling to the poor. Roads were built, the lot of the poor was improved and the Inquisition was abolished. His land reform, however, was not implemented. After five years in Sicily the king brought Caracciolo to Naples to be his first minister. He died there three years later aged 73. In his attempt to modernise Sicily Caracciolo had identified the main problems and had worked out some of the solutions. His efforts were heroic but also to some extent misguided, as the historian Francesco Renda pointed out:

> It was utopian to try to introduce in Sicily a system of land tenure from Lombardy. It was utopian to act in Sicily, the Italian deep south, in the same way as in Lombardy, the Italian far north. And it still remains utopian two centuries later.[29]

In 1789, the year Caracciolo died, the French Revolution broke out, changing the face of Europe and leading to the Napoleonic Wars. During the wars Sicily became the base of operations for the British fleet in the Mediterranean.

CHAPTER 9

Nelson and the British Protectorate

At the start of the Napoleonic Wars William Pitt, the British prime minister, ordered a fleet to be sent into the Mediterranean to protect British interests. There followed a treaty with Ferdinand IV, the Bourbon king of Naples who ruled southern Italy and Sicily, to provide the fleet with harbours and supplies. In September 1793 the thirty-five-year-old Captain Horatio Nelson was sent to Naples on a mission to confirm the treaty, which he successfully accomplished. Later in the war, when the whole of mainland Italy fell to the French, King Ferdinand and his court were taken by the British to Palermo. In return for providing a base for their fleet, the British agreed to defend Sicily from the French, and from 1806 to 1815 the island became a British protectorate.

The British intervention sped up change in Sicily, encouraging the move from a feudal to a more modern society. It interrupted Bourbon rule of the island and demonstrated that a more liberal form of government was possible. Under the British, strong opposition to the Bourbons developed among progressive Sicilians, who began to assert their identity and reform their institutions. A new constitution was introduced, based on the British model, and for four years Sicily experimented with a constitutional regime. After the war, when the Bourbons reasserted their authoritarian rule and abandoned the new constitution, the opposition continued fighting for a better Sicily. The period from 1816 to 1860 in Sicily was one of sustained unrest and repeated revolt against Bourbon rule, paving the way for Garibaldi.

Nelson in the Mediterranean

In March 1798 Nelson, who had been promoted to rear-admiral, sailed from Portsmouth aboard his flagship, the 74-gun *Vanguard*, with orders to track a French expeditionary force which was being prepared in Toulon. It took several months to locate the French, so it was not until 1 August that the two fleets met off the Egyptian coast at Aboukir Bay. By sending a line of ships to the shoreward side, a risky manoeuvre in shallow water, Nelson was able to attack the French on both sides and win a famous victory. The Battle of the Nile had important consequences for the course of the war. It prevented Napoleon from using Egypt as the base from which to attack British India and it established the supremacy of the British fleet in the Mediterranean.

Nelson withdrew in triumph to Naples, where he was feted by the Bourbon king and queen and by the British ambassador, Sir William Hamilton, and his wife, Emma, whom he had already met in 1793. Nelson was suffering from poor health, exacerbated by a flesh wound he had received in the battle. Emma, who was overcome with emotion at Nelson's arrival, helped to look after him during his convalescence. When the French, aided by Neapolitan rebels, threatened Naples, Nelson took the king and queen and the Hamiltons aboard his flagship to Palermo, where they arrived on 26 December 1798. It was in Sicily that Nelson began his love affair with Emma Hamilton.

The Bourbon king and queen, who were to have a close and uneasy relationship with the British in Sicily, were ill suited to their roles as wartime monarchs. When diplomacy and flexibility were called for, they remained autocratic and felt humiliated to be dependent upon the British. Ferdinand, known as *Il Nasone* for his large and ill-shaped nose, preferred hunting and fishing to the hard work of government, which he happily left to his wife. Not particularly bright, his awkward manners and notorious idleness hid a strong determination to preserve his Neapolitan kingdom. The queen, Maria Carolina, was the daughter of Maria Theresa, the Austrian empress and the sister of Marie Antoinette, the French queen executed during the revolution. She was a difficult, contradictory character who never adapted to her role in Palermo and whose scheming caused the government much trouble. Maria Carolina hated Palermo, which she described as: 'Poverty-stricken and peopled by rogues, where the price of everything is exorbitant and the climate depressing.'[1]

The British protectorate

By the time the British arrived in Sicily the island's economy was deeply depressed. The long Spanish rule had been strong on pomp and show but weak on finance. Nelson described what he found as follows:

> The state of Sicily is almost as bad as a civilised country can be. There are no troops fit to be called such, with a scarcity of corn never known, and of course bread so dear that the lower class of people are discontented. The nobles are oppressors and the middle rank wish for change; and although they would prefer us to the French, yet I believe they would receive the French rather than not change from the oppression of the nobles.[2]

Agriculture, still overwhelmingly the main sector of the economy, was concentrated in the hands of the big families to the extent that the richest nobleman, the Prince of Butera, personally accounted for 10 per cent of revenue. The barons still possessed feudal rights and dominated both parliament and the courts while paying very little tax. With no incentive for change, agricultural technology had fallen far behind, so that according to the British, Sicilian estates were producing only about a third of their potential. The rest of the economy consisted of satisfying the consumption needs of the aristocracy, for there was almost no industry or manufacturing on the island. Commercial activity was hampered by the lack of good roads, as it took four days to travel from Palermo to Messina by carriage, and the inland roads were inadequate for the passage of goods. Ownership of property was highly concentrated in the hands of the Crown, the aristocracy and the Church. By contrast the mass of the people, who were either rural peasants or poor city dwellers, owned next to nothing. They were close to starvation and as a class were poorly dressed, badly housed and oppressed by high taxes. Paolo Balsamo, an expert on agriculture, compared the lot of the Sicilian peasants to that of rural tribes in Africa.[3]

Out of a total Sicilian population of 1.5 million, 200,000 were concentrated in Palermo, easily the largest city on the island and the third largest in Italy. Messina and Catania, the next most important cities, had around 60,000 residents between them. The rest of the population was spread out around the island in smaller centres. The concentration in Palermo was due to the continued influx of the poor and destitute from the countryside, who established themselves precariously in shanty towns outside the city walls. The stark difference between rich and poor was a continual source of tension.[4]

So at a time when new industries were becoming established across Europe, Sicily was isolated from these developments. Renda, commenting on the state of the island in 1812, wrote: 'What strikes one in particular about Sicily is its backwardness compared to the developed regions of Western Europe. Sicily seems to be at least a century behind, living in a wild and primitive state.'[5]

The Bourbons were able to return to Naples in 1799 where, with Nelson's help, they exacted brutal revenge upon the revolutionaries who had thrown them out. In gratitude for his support, Ferdinand presented Nelson with a large estate at Bronte in eastern Sicily. Nelson never saw the estate, which passed to his heirs at his death. When hostilities with the French resumed, Messina's defences were strengthened by the British. Malta, which had been taken by Nelson in 1800, was also protected. All of southern Italy was then taken by the French with Joseph, Napoleon's brother, in charge in Naples. The threat of a French invasion in Sicily became very real. In 1806 the Bourbon king and queen were once again transported to Palermo, this time accompanied by their government ministers and a contingent of troops. An agreement was made with the British who undertook to protect Sicily from the French in return for being able to use the island as a base of operations for their fleet. They were also granted freedom from customs duties. The agreement included the payment by the British of an annual subsidy and the provision of at least 10,000 troops. British protection of Sicily proved its worth in 1810 by repelling an attack by Murat, Napoleon's general, who had assumed command in Naples.

The return of the Bourbon royal family was not well received. It was clear that the Bourbons viewed Palermo as a temporary base until they could return to Naples. In the meantime their maintenance was expensive, while the arrogance of their officials angered the Palermitans. The queen, Maria Carolina, ruled through her foreign ministers with scant regard for the interests of the island. She built up a network of spies in Sicily and Naples in the hope of aiding a speedy return to Naples. Though hating the French for executing her sister, Maria Carolina was not above scheming with them and at one stage corresponded directly with Napoleon. Matters came to a head when Ferdinand and Maria Carolina demanded more funds from the Sicilian parliament for their own use. Opposition to Bourbon demands built up in parliament, led by the princes Belmonte, Castelnuovo and Villafranca. The constitution had changed little under the Spanish and the Sicilian parliament, one of the oldest in Europe, maintained a role of advising the Crown on finances. Ferdinand had no intention of accepting this role. He had the princes arrested and sent to prison islands off the Sicilian coast. Supporters of the princes appealed to the British for help.

Bentinck and the Constitution of 1812

At this stage of the war, with all of mainland Italy in the hands of the French, Sicily was seen as vital to British interests in the Mediterranean. Accordingly a British minister, Lord William Bentinck, was appointed to the court in Palermo to resolve matters. Bentinck, who was the second son of the Duke of Portland, was a soldier and politician who had served in the Peninsular War and in India as governor of Madras. From his time in India he brought an eye for development, which he applied in Sicily. He arrived in Palermo in July 1811. When his initial advice was rejected by Ferdinand, Bentinck reacted by recalling the princes from prison, appointing them ministers in the government and calling for constitutional reform. These measures were strongly opposed by the Bourbons, particularly by Maria Carolina, who said of Bentinck: 'This vile sergeant was sent here by the Prince Regent to make bows and not to dictate laws.'[6]

   In the increasingly bitter dispute Bentinck held the whip hand as the Bourbons were dependent upon the British subsidy. In ruling Sicily Ferdinand was persuaded to stand down in favour of his son, the hereditary prince, Francesco. Maria Carolina returned to Austria, as a contemporary commentator noted: 'The queen, who headed a party in opposition to this change (of the ancient constitution) and who had wickedly proposed to Buonaparte to make a second Sicilian Vespers of the British, was then retired.'[7]

   In this period Bentinck travelled across Sicily, listening to the people's grievances and becoming convinced of the island's potential for development. At the peak of his optimism he proposed to Lord Castlereagh, the British foreign minister, that the British permanently take over Sicily. In his opinion, due its great potential, the island would rapidly become a source of wealth and strength in the hands of Great Britain.[8]

Now in charge of the government, Bentinck encouraged the development of a pro-reform party, charging Paolo Balsamo with the task of drafting a new constitution. Balsamo was a priest and economist who had studied abroad, where he became an expert in agricultural science, a subject he taught in Palermo. The constitution, which was completed in July 1812, gave Sicilians a new autonomy with free elections. Government was divided between the executive, in the hands of the Crown; the legislature, to be handled in parliament; and the judiciary, dealt with by the courts. Parliament was to consist of two houses, along British lines, including a House of Commons. Feudal practices were abolished and the king was to remain in Sicily, only leaving with the consent of parliament. Agricultural reforms were also proposed by Balsamo.

This political experiment, which lasted until the end of the Napoleonic Wars, was not a success. Sicily was not ready for such dramatic change. There was no political class capable of governing Sicily, for the princes lacked political experience and were divided among themselves. The population at large neither understood nor cared about the constitution. Their priority was food, which required fundamental land reform. This was something the majority of barons were reluctant to consider, for attitudes formed centuries before had hardened like rock and prevented all attempts at reform. Bentinck realised that his assessment of Sicily's ability to change had been over-optimistic, noting that in Sicily as in India, political compromise was always seen as weakness. In the long term the constitution did, however, help the development of government in Sicily.[9]

As the war came to an end British interest in Sicily ceased, with Malta considered sufficient as a strategic base in the central Mediterranean. The British government viewed Sicily as a complex island with whose internal affairs they did not wish to be further concerned. Bentinck was recalled to London in 1814, to be replaced by a minister less interested in reform, and the last British troops left Sicily in October 1815.

The Congress of Vienna, which established the political settlement after the war, reinstated Ferdinand in his kingdom of Naples, which had been freed from the French by the Austrians. After Palermo's parliament had failed to produce the required taxes, Ferdinand dissolved the two houses and, ignoring the provisions in the constitution, left for Naples without consulting parliament. Here in 1816 he announced the unification of his kingdoms of Naples and Sicily, renaming them the Kingdom of the Two Sicilies, and taking for himself the title of Ferdinand I.

The wartime economy

The ten years of British occupation of Sicily gave a boost to the economy. The British subsidy, £300,000 a year from 1806, rising to £400,000 a year from 1809 to 1815, brought in much-needed capital. The British military contingent, which varied in number from 10,000 to 17,000, provided a market for all kinds of goods, especially meat and other foodstuffs. The British fleet needed to be maintained, producing work for local shipbuilders. As a result skills were revitalised and the Sicilian merchant fleet doubled in size. As the Sicilian ports were declared duty-free for British traders, they became commercial centres for British goods, which became fashionable in Palermo, including British cloth. A thriving trade in smuggled goods built up with ports in mainland Italy. Commercial activity was sufficient to justify the presence of over 30 British consular officials in Sicily by 1812.

The most successful commercial venture was the establishment of a wine trade at Marsala by British entrepreneurs. The first of these was John Woodhouse, who by adding alcohol to Sicilian wine, produced a product that could compete with sherry and port. Fortified wines were in demand in England, where they sold at a premium price, and unlike table wine travelled well. A trial shipment to England in 1773 set Woodhouse on his way. Twenty years later he established his business in Marsala, which took off with the arrival of the British fleet. When Nelson sailed for Egypt before the Battle of the Nile, his fleet carried 40,000 gallons of Sicilian wine on board.

Another Englishman, Benjamin Ingham, opened a winery in Marsala in 1806. Ingham studied wine production in Spain and introduced scientific methods to Sicily. Local landowners were encouraged to produce the grapes while the British built access roads, production plants and arranged the shipping. By 1814 there were four British wineries at Marsala and several more at the nearby port of Mazara. The wine trade in Marsala grew to such an extent that by 1839 1 million gallons were being sent to England and even larger quantities to the Americas.[10] Some of the buildings for the British wineries, known locally as *bagli*, can still be seen today in Marsala.

While some of the economic benefits of the British occupation had a lasting effect, the immediate impact of the British departure was an economic slump. With the armed forces and the subsidy gone, commercial activity declined sharply and unemployment soared.

Opposition to the Bourbons

Sicily entered a turbulent period in the aftermath of the British occupation. For Palermo the new political settlement was a disaster. The city was no longer the capital of a kingdom and was reduced to provincial status. Naples, the centre of power, came to be hated by Sicilians, who felt that they had been betrayed by Ferdinand. Sicilians also felt let down by the British, who now followed a policy of non-intervention. When the Bourbons took up the reins of government in the combined kingdom of Naples and Sicily, they introduced a centralised administration along French lines. This was part of a repressive regime designed to keep control of their territories. Ferdinand was reported as saying that he ruled through the three f's: *forca, farina e feste* ('gallows, bread and festivals'). Public hangings were followed by the distribution of bread during grand festivals.[11] Ferdinand, however, now faced opposition from all sides of society as the social revolution brewing in Sicily came to boiling point. The barons were set on reinstating Sicily's autonomy. The peasants and urban poor were living in desperate conditions. Political reform was called for by middle-class activists, who joined secret societies known as the Carbonari to resist Bourbon rule. Starting in Naples, a popular revolt broke out in Palermo in July 1820, supported by the barons. Squads of peasants took to the streets, joined by armed gangs from the barons' estates, who together fought running battles with the Neapolitan garrison. Order was eventually restored by a Bourbon army of 12,000 troops commanded by General Florestano Pepe.

In 1825 Ferdinand was succeeded by his son, Francis I, who proved to be even less capable than his father. Ferdinand II, who came to the throne in 1830 and ruled until 1859, was more forward-looking and supported the development of both industry and agriculture. Palermo, however, continued in a state of subdued rebellion. To strengthen their hold on the city, the Neapolitan prefects employed increasingly harsh methods, including the use of torture in the prisons. Sicilians were excluded from senior government positions and the press was censored. An alarmingly high crime rate indicated that the social fabric was breaking down. According to a British report: 'From time to time conspiracies on a large scale, either discovered, or which broke out, tempted the government, and as in 1821, gave dozens of victims to the scaffold, and sometimes as in 1837, gave to it a hundred.'[12]

Bourbon repression in this period is demonstrated by the Ucciardone in Palermo, a large prison complex built between 1837 and 1860 to hold the revolutionaries.

In 1848 a well-orchestrated revolt took place in Palermo. It began on 12 January, the king's birthday, and defeated the Neapolitan garrison within a few days. After overcoming a further 5,000 Neapolitan troops, the revolt spread across the island. Parliament was recalled under the leadership of Vincenzo Fardella. A provisional government was established, led by Ruggero Settimo, an ex-admiral and leading member of the anti-Bourbon movement. Members of the government included Michele Amari, the historian of the Sicilian Vespers and Muslim Sicily, who became finance minister, and Giuseppe La Farina, who was minister of war. Francesco Crispi, a young lawyer and journalist, began his political career as a member of parliament. The liberal constitution of 1812 was reintroduced and discussions began on the merits of joining a future federation of Italian states.

Facing defeat in Sicily, King Ferdinand offered concessions, while the Sicilians called on Britain for advice on their future. Britain replied that while Sicilians had a right to their constitution of 1812, they could not expect Britain to interfere on their behalf. In the meantime the Bourbons were preparing an invasion of Sicily. Messina fell first, to the army led by Carlo Filangieri, after heavy bombardments had destroyed much of the city. After Catania fell to similar tactics, Palermo capitulated in May 1849. An amnesty was granted to the majority of those who had opposed the Bourbons, with an exception made for the leadership, so that Fardella, Settimo, Amari, La Farina and others went into exile. Crispi, who was not on the list, nevertheless saw no future for himself under the Bourbons and also left Sicily.[13] Filangieri, the Bourbon general, was made governor of Sicily and Duke of Taormina. Among the Sicilian leadership it became accepted that outside help was now essential to obtain freedom from the Bourbons and in exile the leaders were drawn to the growing movement for a free and independent Italy.

CHAPTER 10

From Garibaldi to Mussolini

N ationalism was a powerful force in nineteenth-century Europe. In Italy the movement for unification, known as the Risorgimento, had its roots in the years following the Napoleonic Wars. It gained momentum from the revolutions of 1848, for as well as in Palermo a revolt had taken place in Milan, where the Austrians were temporarily thrown out of the city. In exile the leaders of the revolts kept in touch with their compatriots back home to stir up opposition to foreign rule by the Austrians in the north and the Spanish Bourbons in the south. Revolutionary groups known as the Carbonari, inspired by the principles of the French Revolution, worked secretly to overthrow the foreign regimes. The Carbonari (whose name means 'charcoal burners') were a secret society linked to the Freemasons. While they lacked a clear agenda, the society provided a vehicle for patriotic young men. Italian patriotism was fanned by the writings of Giuseppe Mazzini, which were spread by the press, and by Verdi's operas. Patriotic references in operas by Verdi were met with tumultuous applause in opera houses across Italy.

Political leadership for unification came from Count Camillo Benso di Cavour, the prime minister of Piedmont, which united with Sardinia made a powerful small state in northern Italy. Mazzini, an original thinker and writer, provided the ideas that inspired support for the movement, while Giuseppe Garibaldi, a soldier with experience as a guerrilla commander in South America, brought military leadership. Vittorio Emanuele, king of Piedmont, acted as the movement's figurehead. Together they succeeded in moulding the disparate states of Italy into a kingdom, against all the odds, in a remarkably short time.

Garibaldi in Sicily

In 1860 Garibaldi, hearing of more uprisings in Sicily, gathered volunteers for an expedition to the island. He nearly reversed his decision when news arrived of a setback. He was persuaded to go ahead by Francesco Crispi, who had taken part in the revolt of 1848, and Nino Bixio, one of his chief lieutenants. The expedition was ready in early May and sailed from Quarto, near Genoa, in two steamships. Successfully avoiding a Neapolitan squadron, it arrived at the port of Marsala on the west coast of Sicily on 11 May. It was a risky venture, for of the 1,089 volunteers known thereafter as the Mille (the Thousand), only a few had any military experience. This core of soldiers included some who had fought in the recent campaign in the Crimea. The Mille were mostly middle-class professionals from northern Italy, of all age groups, caught up in the enthusiasm for Italian unification. There were also about a hundred Sicilians and Neapolitans, plus four Hungarians. Initially opposing them in Sicily were 25,000 regular Bourbon troops.

By good fortune, at Marsala were two British warships sent to look after British interests in the wine trade. When the Bourbon ships reached Marsala they were inhibited in their response by the British presence, for the Bourbons did not want to offend the British, who remained the major naval power in the Mediterranean. The expedition landed without incident and gathered in Marsala for the march to Palermo. The Garibaldini, who were organised into eight companies, displayed a motley array of uniforms, some already wearing the red shirts that would become their hallmark. Crispi was among Garibaldi's staff as political secretary. As they made their way inland towards Salemi on the road to Palermo, the Garibaldini were joined by small bands of peasants armed with scythes, pitchforks and ancient firearms. At a strategic point high in the mountains stood the village of Calatafimi, blocking the way to Palermo. Outside the village General Francesco Landi, with 3,000 Bourbon troops supported by artillery, was well established in a strong defensive position.

The fighting was fierce in the heat of the day and the Garibaldini, outnumbered and carrying old-fashioned rifles, were soon struggling. Their morale and determination, however, carried the day, the decisive action being a bayonet charge uphill led by Garibaldi. The Mille lost 30 men killed and 150 wounded that day but achieved a breakthrough in the campaign for Sicily. Their momentum was maintained and the Bourbons, demoralised by their defeat, withdrew to Palermo.

The battle had been won by the courage of the Garibaldini and the few Sicilians who took part in the fighting, but also by Garibaldi's inspired leadership. In battle he was calm and decisive, appearing wherever there was a crisis, showing complete disregard for his own safety. At a crucial moment Bixio cried: 'General, do you want to die like this?' To which Garibaldi replied: 'How better than in my own country?'[1] He was a theatrical figure, easily recognised, with long hair to his shoulders, wearing the poncho he had adopted in South America. To the Sicilian people he appeared as a prophet who had come to save them, a warrior saint whom they took to their hearts. From the Battle of Calatafimi he began to take on an aura of invincibility that was one of his greatest assets.

In his approach to Palermo Garibaldi found the direct routes blocked by Bourbon troops. Intelligence from the city indicated that the least-guarded gate lay to the south-east. He decided to approach the city by a roundabout route and arranged several feints to confuse the enemy. His aim was to avoid a pitched battle, and thus to annul the Bourbons' advantage in numbers, while once inside the city he relied upon the Palermitans to come to his aid. The Mille, exhausted and down to 750 men, had been joined by 3,000 excitable and ill-disciplined Sicilians.

On 27 May an advance guard led by Lajos Tüköry, a Hungarian with the rank of colonel, set out for Porta Termini, the gate to the south-east. Tüköry led his 50 men quietly as far as the Ponte dell'Ammiraglio (the Admiral's Bridge) before the Sicilians who were following the advance party started firing in the air, excited at the prospect of entering Palermo. This alerted the Bourbon troops; in the words of a participant: 'We advanced rapidly but at the Admiral's Bridge we met ferocious resistance. A fierce fight developed with bayonets, on the street, under the arches of the bridge and in the nearby gardens.'[2] Tüköry fell during the fighting, shot in the leg.[3] Having passed the bridge, further progress was temporarily held up. Finally the Garibaldini fought their way into the city at Porta Termini to the Fieravecchia (the modern Piazza Rivoluzione) and then past Via Maqueda to Piazza Bologni. Garibaldi established himself in Piazza Pretoria in the old senate building.

As the Garibaldini entered the city, General Ferdinando Lanza, who was in charge of the defence, ordered an artillery barrage onto the city's centre. This was fired from ships in the port and from the Castellammare, the heavily fortified castle by the port. Other foreign ships were also present at Palermo, including HMS *Hannibal*, under the command of Rear Admiral Sir Rodney Mundy, who was stationed there to protect British personnel and property. Mundy sent one of his staff, Lieutenant Wilmot, to meet Garibaldi in an attempt to broker a peace deal. Wilmot reported that the general was open to negotiations and made this comment on conditions in the city:

> The damage done [...] is very great, especially in the neighbourhood of Garibaldi's headquarters; but, strangely enough, the vast Pretorio Palace, which he occupied, had not a single shell in it, although a church, convent and other public buildings, which formed the other three sides of the square were riddled, the convent being in flames and completely in ruins. The shells were still falling and several times I had to shelter myself in a doorway till they exploded. It was also very unpleasant crossing the Toledo [the modern Corso Vittorio Emanuele] and streets facing the Palace and Mint, as the troops were constantly firing down them with musketry and field pieces.[4]

The bombardments destroyed sections of the city, with houses and churches burned, causing a considerable loss of life among the civilian population. In the chaotic conditions the Bourbon troops lost their discipline and were seen shooting civilians and looting churches. Their actions ensured support for Garibaldi from the Palermitans, who were described by a British naval officer as 'a turbulent population of 200,000 who are a strange mixture of oriental apathy and spasmodic desperation'.[5] Barricades appeared in the streets and the Bourbons became confined to the area around the cathedral and the Palazzo dei Normanni, with the lower city in the hands of the Garibaldini.

After four days of bombardment and fighting in the streets, a stalemate was reached and General Landi called for a meeting on Mundy's ship to discuss an armistice. Despite an overwhelming superiority in numbers he had lost 200 men killed and 800 wounded and supplies were running low. Morale among his troops was poor as it became clear that the whole city was against them. At discussions aboard HMS *Hannibal*, with Rear Admiral Mundy acting as mediator, the ceasefire was agreed. It eventually held and on 7 June the Bourbon withdrawal began. As the troops marched down to the port they filed past a small detachment of red-shirted Garibaldini led by the general's son, Menotti, a spectacle the British found humiliating. Casualties in the city amounted to between 2,000 and 3,000 killed and wounded, with many still recovering in the hospitals.[6]

When the fighting was over Garibaldi went out to thank the Palermitans for their help in defeating the Bourbons, which was witnessed by one of his men:

> The General made a tour of the city, where he could get through on horseback. The people went down on their knees, touching his stirrups and kissing his hands. I saw babies lifted up to him as to a saint.[7]

Mundy went to visit Garibaldi, who was established in a large suite of apartments in the Palazzo dei Normanni. He noted the general's astuteness and nobility of character, which he found deeply impressive. Before leaving Palermo, Garibaldi wrote to Mundy on 7 July: 'Thanks, Admiral [...] thanks for your magnanimous conduct! [...] thanks in the name of Palermo, of Sicily, of entire Italy!'[8]

Later in July Garibaldi was back in action with a strengthened force including a British regiment under Colonel John Dunne. Along the north coast at Milazzo the Garibaldini won a notable victory. Garibaldi and his troops left for Calabria on 18 August and by early in October they had taken Naples. Bourbon rule of the Two Sicilies was over. Garibaldi ruled Sicily as dictator for only five months. Then, after holding a plebiscite, which showed an overwhelming majority in favour of joining the Italian state, he handed over control of Sicily to Cavour in Turin. The Italian state was established in March 1861 when Vittorio Emanuele II was crowned king of Italy. The additions of Venice and Rome followed and in 1871 the capital was moved to Rome.

Rule from Turin

After the euphoria of Garibaldi's campaign, disillusionment quickly set in. Sicilians supported the revolution for different reasons. All were united in wanting to be rid of the Bourbons. In their place the aristocracy and political activists were looking for some degree of self-government with a link to Italy. The poor simply wanted food, land and social justice. Garibaldi had shown sympathy for all these demands.

Cavour, however, favoured a centralised state. His idea of unification was to bring the regions under the control of Turin. He reneged on autonomy for

Sicily, brought in conscription to the army and sold off Church property, leaving many of the poor in the countryside worse off than ever. He sent his prefect to Palermo, supported by police and tax-collectors, to run the island. Total misunderstanding existed between the Sicilians and the Piedmontese from the start. They found each other's language and behaviour incomprehensible. To the Piedmontese Sicily seemed like a foreign country, more like somewhere in Africa than Italy. To Sicilians the Piedmontese represented just another foreign occupying force. Peasants in the interior of the island had so little understanding of unification that for years some of them mistook *l'Italia* for *La Talia*, whom they thought to be the king's wife.[9]

The mood of Sicilians at this time was caught by Giuseppe Tomasi di Lampedusa in his historical novel *The Leopard*, published in 1958. In it the prince, Fabrizio, discusses the position of Sicily after Garibaldi's departure with Chevalley, an administrator from Piedmont. In Fabrizio's view, no one really cared about Sicilian interests and, for all their sacrifices, Sicilians had just replaced Naples with Turin. 'I must say, between ourselves,' says Fabrizio, 'that I have strong doubts whether the new kingdom will have many gifts for us in its luggage.'[10]

Removal of the Bourbon regime exposed the extreme imbalances in Sicilian society. The wealth of the island remained in the hands of a small elite class of aristocratic families who owned the large estates. The aristocracy was, however, in the process of sinking under the weight of its debts. On the rise were the managers of the estates, the *gabelloti*, who were fast becoming powerful middlemen. Next there came a growing class of smaller property owners whose aim was to join the aristocracy. Then there came the disenfranchised classes, the vast majority of the population, represented by the urban poor and the peasants who worked the land in semi-feudal conditions.

The Sicilian economy now faced open competition, something that its industries were badly placed to handle. As a result, at a time when the economy of northern Italy was taking off, Sicily's traditional industries went into decline. The few profitable industries included the wine trade first established by the British at Marsala, the sulphur industry inland from Agrigento and the citrus production for export. None of these offered employment for the masses. The population faced high tax demands from Turin, and when the monasteries were closed, unemployment increased further. The food supply was also a problem, for while Sicily's population increased by 21 per cent between 1798 and 1861 to reach 2.3 million, there were no major changes in production methods.[11]

The new liberal parliament, based on a restricted electorate, was dominated by the aristocracy. It proved to be corruptible, and in the absence of effective government criminal activity flourished. The *gabelloti* used strong-arm methods to manage the estates. Armed gangs protected crops and livestock while brigands, who preyed upon villages in the interior, were employed to intimidate rivals. Workers at the sulphur mines in the interior were exploited, with women and young boys put to work in dangerous conditions for minimal pay. The urban unemployed joined deserters from the army to swell criminal gangs which engaged in gang warfare. Killings and kidnappings became regular occurrences in Palermo.

General unrest and anger with Turin led to a major rebellion in Palermo in 1866. The leaders were unknown but a plan existed, for armed gangs gathered in Monreale and moved down into the city. The gangs included men who had taken part in the revolts of 1848 and 1860, bandits from the interior, army deserters and working people fearing for their livelihoods. Church bells acted as a rallying call and the gangs went on a rampage in Palermo, looting shops for food and clothing. For a week the city was in a state of anarchy. Order was restored by the Italian navy, which shelled the city, and by a force of 40,000 troops.

The rise of the mafia

Ever since 1816, when the Spanish Bourbons reintroduced their autocratic rule, Sicily had been in a state of ferment. One revolt against the regime followed another with men of violence joining the common cause. Fighting against the Bourbons, these men learned to operate in secret and to spread their net wide, establishing contacts across society. This was the background to the emergence of the Sicilian mafia as a flourishing criminal association, in the lawless environment of the 1860s.

The mafia developed where money was being made and was drawn to Palermo, the island's centre of political and economic activity. The Conca d'Oro, the rich citrus-growing area around the city, was an early target. The export of lemons, on which Sicily temporarily had a world monopoly, was highly profitable. The

1. Santa Rosalia, Palermo's patron saint.

2. The cathedral.

3. Church of San Domenico (St Dominic).

4. Fontana Pretoria (Pretoria Fountain).

5. Mosaic, church of the Martorana.

6. Mosaic, Cappella Palatina (Palatine Chapel).

7. Teatro Politeama (Politeama Theatre).

8. Teatro Massimo (Massimo Theatre), the opera house.

9. Palazzo dei Normanni (Norman Palace).

10. Church of San Cataldo (St Catald).

11. Il Genio di Palermo (the Genius of Palermo), Piazza Garraffo.

12. Il Genio di Palermo (the Genius of Palermo), Piazza Rivoluzione.

13. Il Genio di Palermo (the Genius of Palermo), Villa Giulia.

14. The Cala, as shown in Alexey Bogolyubov, *Palermo* (1850).

15. The Marina and Monte Pellegrino, as shown in George Loring Brown, *Monte Pellegrino at Palermo* (1856).

16. Modern Palermo, as seen from Monte Pellegrino.

17. Palazzina Cinese (Chinese Pavilion).

18. Mondello.

industry needed capital, protection for the lemon groves to mature, a regular water supply and reliable, cheap labour. The mafia stepped in to provide these services and came to dominate the industry. It built a growing network of support in the community through the payment of bribes and the ever-present threat of violence, infiltrating Palermo's food markets as well as local government. In the countryside the *gabelloti* often merged with the mafia and exerted increased control over the large estates.

The origin of the term 'mafia' is uncertain and much debated. It probably lies in Arabic words used in Palermo's dialect meaning 'bold' or 'strong'. Another school of thought maintains that it was not a Sicilian word at all but was brought to Sicily by the Piedmontese. The first record of the name in a criminal context comes from a popular play of 1863 by Giuseppe Rizzotto called *I mafiusi di la Vicaria* (The Mafiosi of the Vicaria). The play's setting among criminals imprisoned in Palermo was entirely appropriate, as the prisons were the mafia's recruitment and training grounds. Two years later, in a document signed by the prefect of Palermo, reference was made to a crime attributable to the *maffia o associazione malandrinesca* ('mafia or criminal association').[12]

Central to mafia operations was the principle of *omertà*, literally 'manliness' (from *uomo* for 'man') but in this context meaning silence. Through *omertà* the mafia built for itself immunity from the law by putting powerful pressure upon people to remain silent. There was moral pressure to support the mafia against the authorities, backed by physical pressure in the form of death threats for anyone who spoke up as a witness to a crime. The mafia's bread and butter operation was the collection of the *pizzo*, or protection money, which was broadly applied to commercial operations, both large and small. By the mid-1870s, according to the historian John Dickie, the most important components of the mafia system were already in place. 'The mafia had the protection rackets and the powerful political friends, and it also had its cellular structure, its name, its rituals, and an untrustworthy state as a competitor.'[13]

A hard-hitting report on conditions in Sicily was published in 1877 by Leopoldo Franchetti and Sidney Sonnino. The authors were well-respected barons from Tuscany, both landowners, but with no axe to grind in Sicily. Theirs was a private report, carefully researched, and based on wide-ranging interviews and visits around the island. The report began by describing the attractions of Palermo: 'Its main streets, the monumental aspect of its palaces, the night time illuminations are among the best in Europe, which present all the signs of a centre of a city which is rich and industrious.'[14] It went on to present conclusions which dramatically highlighted Sicily's unresolved problems.

The report found that little had changed since Bourbon times and that the island remained isolated from the rest of Italy. The government in Rome had a responsibility to Sicilians that it was not fulfilling. Instead of supporting the mass of the population, Sicily was organised for the exclusive benefit of the landowners, who were often hand in glove with criminals.

The aristocracy was backward looking and irresponsible, more interested in power and show than in providing leadership. The rich continued to subdue the poor, often by violent means. As a result the most talented Sicilians left the island. The report stated: 'The lives and the property of citizens are open to the whims of the most powerful [...] who steal nearly always with impunity.'[15]

The attitudes of Sicilians towards authority and the public interest were particularly illuminating. Public authority was seen as negative, a brutal force which was not to be acknowledged. Corruption was rife, even at high levels, with complicity universal. Social and civic values were nonexistent. Not only was no one working for the common good, but the very concept did not seem to exist. 'In Sicilian society,' continued the report, 'all relationships are based on personal interest and on what one individual owes to another, to the exclusion of any social or public interest.'[16]

The mafia was described as a thriving concern whose impunity from the law was taken for granted. Criminals were not arrested, stated the report, for the following reasons:

> Everyone knows who they are, where they are, what they are up to and what they will do in the future, yet no one denounces them and no one will act as a witness against them; not even offended parties, who if they are strong enough will revenge themselves, or if not, resign themselves and keep quiet.[17]

A big difference in the level of crime was found between east and west: the east of Sicily represented by Messina, Catania and Syracuse being a promised land compared to Palermo.

Urgent action was recommended. Sonnino favoured a local solution while Franchetti wanted one imposed from outside. Both found the national government in Rome, which had condoned local corruption, to be responsible for improving conditions in Sicily. Their biggest criticism was reserved for the Sicilian ruling class, which they found to be backward-looking and corrupt. This conclusion ensured that the report got nowhere, as it struck at the heart of the elite's privileges. On the excuse that the report was the product of northern Italian prejudice towards the south, it was archived.[18]

As the mafia expanded it built a network of contacts based on the interweaving of criminal, business and political interests. While the criminal association remained small, hidden support from its network in the community at large was widespread. It was this infiltration and corruption of legitimate sectors of society that gave the mafia both its strength and its longevity. The assassination of the marquis Emanuele Notarbartolo in 1893 demonstrated how the system worked. Against a background of bank scandals, Notarbartolo, who had been mayor of Palermo in the 1870s, was appointed governor of the Banco di Sicilia. Here he imposed a regime of strict regulation. Under his successor, fresh scandals emerged involving loans made on preferential terms together with suspected fraud linked to shares in the Florio shipping company. The word got out that Notarbartolo was to be reinstated as the bank's governor. Shortly afterwards, on a train returning to Palermo, he was brutally stabbed to death. While no witnesses came forward, the crime had all the hallmarks of the mafia, carried out to protect those who had benefited from the fraudulent transactions. A member of parliament with mafia connections was accused of ordering the crime and a worker on his estate of carrying out the murder. The case dragged on for years, becoming a national scandal, but ultimately no one was convicted. Notarbartolo was the first of the so-called *cadaveri eccellenti* ('illustrious corpses'), high-ranking professionals carrying out their normal duties for which they were murdered by the mafia with the complicity of fellow professionals and politicians.[19]

At the turn of the century conditions in Sicily for the mass of the population were harder than ever. The island's population had continued to increase, reaching 3.5 million in 1901. During the next 12 years 1.1 million Sicilians emigrated, 80 per cent of them to the United States.[20] Here they joined communities of southern Italians established in the cities of the east coast, especially New York, where with the expansion of the economy they were able to make themselves a living. Among the immigrants were mafiosi who transplanted their criminal methods to the American continent, initially exploiting Italian communities.

In 1909 the New York Police Department sent a detective to Palermo to get some background on these Sicilian immigrants. Joe Petrosino, whose parents had immigrated to the United States from Salerno, arrived in March and set out for a meeting in the city. He underestimated the dangers, going alone and unarmed, and in Piazza Marina he was shot dead. His murder demonstrated the mafia's growing strength on both sides of the Atlantic.[21]

Palermo's belle époque

During the late nineteenth and early twentieth centuries, the period known as the belle époque, European royalty and other celebrities flocked to Palermo. The term originated in Paris, where residents were enjoying peace and prosperity as the economy boomed and the arts flourished. Palermo's combination of a warm climate, seaside location and exotic environment appealed to northern Europeans, who made the city a fashionable place to visit. The visitors, who arrived by steamship or private yacht, included the Kaiser and his family, members of the Russian royal family, King Edward VII and Queen Alexandra and the Italian king and queen. They were entertained in style by the remaining Sicilian aristocracy, who had been joined, in wealth if not in social status, by a small group of merchant families. The Sicilian aristocracy was so reduced by debt that only 20 palaces were still occupied in Palermo, compared to 200 a century earlier.[22] The merchant families owed their wealth to the wine trade in Marsala, started by John Woodhouse in 1773. A group of British families, led by the Inghams, Whitakers and Woodhouses, was well established in Palermo, running highly profitable businesses. Around these families circulated a thriving British community with its own Anglican church and resident consuls. The Ingham residence in Palermo, a great town house, was converted into a hotel and later restructured by the leading architect of the period, Ernesto Basile. Named the Grand Hotel et des Palmes, it became one of the best hotels in Palermo. The Whitakers built a sumptuous villa named Malfitano, where they entertained guests from all over Europe. Their collection of furniture, paintings and various artefacts from around the world can be seen in the villa today. Also prominent in Palermo was a Sicilian family, the Florios. Ignazio Florio had inherited a business based on the wine trade, enlarged to include interests in shipping and the sulphur

3. Marina and Porta Felice (Gustavo Chiesi, 1892).

industry, which made him one of the wealthiest men in Italy. His wife Franca was a famous beauty and legendary hostess. Basile built the Villa Igiea for the Florios, an example of the Liberty style (art nouveau), which also became a luxury hotel.

The visitors spent their time in lavish entertainment, which included elaborate balls, dinners and amateur theatricals in the palaces and villas of the wealthy families. There were visits to the bathing resort of Mondello and guided tours of the Norman monuments, with concerts and opera performed in the evenings. Carriage rides along the Marina were popular (figure 3), with guests enjoying Sicilian ice creams. Entertaining was hugely expensive and the Florios largely exhausted their fortune in this period.

Among the visitors was Giacomo Puccini, whose *La bohème* was well received in Palermo. After the performance he thanked his hostess at dinner by signing a wooden spoon, on which he transcribed a few notes from the opera. His *Manon Lescaut* was an even greater success. Richard Wagner completed the score of *Parsifal* while staying at the Grand Hotel et des Palmes. Guy de Maupassant, who toured Sicily and spent time in Palermo, recorded his impressions in a journal of his trip. The French artist Jean Houël left an illustrated account of his visit, with drawings of the monuments.[23]

The English travel writer Douglas Sladen knew Sicily well and recommended it as a place to stay in winter. Sladen mixed easily in Palermo society and experienced its generous hospitality. He described an evening out as follows:

> On Shrove Tuesday, when we were in Palermo, we went to a ball given by a very rich Sicilian. He apologised for having supper so early – at eleven, almost directly after the ball had begun – because it would be Lent in an hour. The Sicilians are ardent dancers, and his guests determined to go without supper rather than leave the ballroom so soon. He shrugged his shoulders, and told his steward to have a fresh supper [prepared], all of fish. Now it is not an easy matter to buy fish for 400 people at twelve o'clock at night, so the supper was not ready till seven o'clock in the morning. The guests meanwhile had danced with unabated vigour; there had been light refreshments going, and good whisky and soda, which to the gilded youth of Sicily is the ne plus ultra of drinks. When finally they did sit down to supper, and the smoking fish was brought in, most of them ate the original supper, though they all took fish on their plates.[24]

Great advances were made in the knowledge of ancient Sicily during the belle époque. These were pioneering days for archaeology in Europe, led by men such as Heinrich Schliemann, who discovered Mycenae in 1873, and Arthur Evans, who unearthed the palace of Knossos in Crete in 1900. Both men visited Sicily to examine the ancient sites. International interest was matched by that of Sicilian academics, who began to re-examine their island's ancient past. Most of the sites were readily accessible and archaeology was not yet hampered by excessive regulation. The result was a series of successful digs which brought to light more material from ancient times than ever before. Douglas Sladen wrote enthusiastically in 1901: 'If you want to understand ancient Greece, come to Sicily.'[25]

The pioneers of archaeology in Sicily were Antonio Salinas and Paolo Orsi. Salinas, a professor of archaeology, became director of the museum in Palermo, which was established in the old monastery next to the church of Sant'Ignazio all'Olivella (St Ignatius). There he displayed a collection of Punic and ancient Greek artefacts from Palermo and the sites in western Sicily which he had helped to excavate. Its greatest treasures were the metopes from Selinunte, carved panels from the temples showing scenes from mythology, comparable on a smaller scale to the Elgin marbles. While Salinas took responsibility for western Sicily, Orsi, who came from northern Italy, was his counterpart in Syracuse, responsible for the east of the island, and also developed the museum in Syracuse. These two archaeological museums, in Palermo and Syracuse, soon became recognised as among the best of their kind in Europe.

The second half of the nineteenth century saw major changes to the fabric and orientation of Palermo. Most of the Spanish bastions and gates which had ringed the city, carrying the names of the viceroys, were demolished. For the aristocracy and emerging middle class, focus shifted away from the historic centre to the north of the city along Via della Libertà. Here they built elegant villas in the fashionable Liberty style and smart apartment blocks. This development along the Via della Libertà became the affluent quarter of the city. Between 1867 and 1897 two theatres were added to the city, the Teatro Massimo, the opera house, and the Politeama, designed for more popular productions. The historian of folklore in Palermo, Giuseppe Pitrè, noted in 1904 the huge changes that were being made:

> The city walls crumbled; her bastions gave way to unending public and private housing; her gates remained in name only. The ancient capital city tripled in size outside the historic centre, overflowing the four miles of her circumference to embrace the huge plain filled with gardens and fruit trees, the citizens searching for air, light, greenery, sky and sea.[26]

The belle époque was the last fling of the Sicilian aristocracy. It was a period of high spending when the elite, elegant and thoughtless, threw themselves into an endless social round. It was the expression of a sophisticated but frivolous society which showed no regard for the problems of ordinary citizens. Their priorities were amply demonstrated by the decision to fund the building of theatres rather than to modernise the city's infrastructure or to build housing for the poor. The flow of international visitors was interrupted by the earthquake of 1908, which destroyed most of Messina, and came to an end with the outbreak of World War I.

Mussolini in Sicily

Mussolini rose to power in 1922 in the deeply depressed aftermath of World War I. Despite the fact that the Austrians had been defeated, Italians felt that they had gained little from the war. In the three and a half years of conflict their losses had been 600,000 dead and 500,000 wounded, while the cost of living had more than doubled.[27] The wartime experience had shattered national morale and there was no agreement on the future direction of the country. Mussolini and his Fascist party offered a solution which the democratic politicians were powerless to resist.

The south was unimportant to Mussolini and he gave it little help, his priority being to encourage industry in the north, and thereby to build a strong military nation. As a result the Sicilian economy, devastated by the war, received no stimulus and the island's role became that of providing cheap raw materials. The road-building and modernisation of the railways, which characterised the Fascist era in the north, were not extended to Sicily. 'The quest for national grandeur,' concluded Denis Mack Smith, 'left little money to spare for the backward areas of the fatherland.'[28] With land reform stalled, soldiers returning from the war took matters into their own hands and helped to spur a movement to occupy unused land on the *latifondi*. When the land was set up for use by the cooperatives, the movement was reluctantly accepted by the authorities.

On a visit to Sicily in 1924 Mussolini asked to be taken to Piana dei Greci, a small town in the hills behind Palermo. This posed a problem for his security guards, as the town was known to be a centre of peasant unrest. It was decided that the only way to guarantee the Duce's security on a tour of the town was for him to travel with the local mafia boss, in the boss's car. This brought home to Mussolini the nature of the mafia's threat to authority and, not one to take an insult lightly, when back in Rome he ordered a major crackdown. Cesare Mori was appointed prefect to Sicily, given wide powers to arrest and interrogate suspects, and ordered to obtain quick results. Declaring war on the mafia, Mori rounded up 2,000 suspects and threw them into jail. Legal procedures were ignored. Arrests were arbitrary and torture, with methods dating back to the Inquisition, was freely used by the police. Agreements may have been made with some mafia groups as to where the campaign would be concentrated. Few of the top bosses were held in jail for any length of time, leaving the full force of Mori's campaign to fall upon the mafia's rank and file. In any event the mafia went underground, criminal activity dropped sharply and Mussolini claimed victory. It proved to be primarily a propaganda victory, for in the 1930s the mafia was already reasserting its power.[29]

Some funds were allocated to Palermo for public works in the Fascist era. They were spent in improving the city's infrastructure and public buildings rather than helping the crowded conditions of the poor, who lived in tenements in the alleyways behind the main roads. Via della Libertà was extended to the north of the city, while popular housing was constructed further out of the city. To ease the traffic flow, Via Roma was built linking the central station to the square by the Politeama, cutting through the centre and destroying many old buildings. The post office in Via Roma remains the main memorial to the Fascist era in Palermo. The influx of people from the provinces continued, taking the population up to 412,000 by 1936.[30]

Mussolini returned to Sicily in 1937, making a tour of the island on which he was mostly feted wherever he went. In Palermo he addressed the people at the Foro Italico, the road along the seafront once known as the Marina, in a speech broadcast on radio. He told the audience that Sicily's role was at the centre of the Italian Empire, crucially placed to defend the territories in North Africa. Recalling the island's dramatic history, he promised to solve its problems. Towards the end of the speech the rhetoric became ominously warlike, with warnings to France and Britain on their foreign policies.

In July 1943 the British and Americans invaded Sicily in the first full-scale attack upon Hitler's Europe. The impact of World War II upon his country was Mussolini's disastrous legacy.

CHAPTER 11

Modern Palermo

The story of Palermo from World War II to the present day begins with the invasion of Sicily by the British and Americans in July 1943. It goes on to cover the growing power of the mafia, the mafia's challenge to the Italian state and the rise of the antimafia. In this period Palermo became an epicentre of organised crime, but also an epicentre of the fight against it. The most dramatic confrontations between the mafia and the state, in the history of Italy, took place in Palermo during the 1980s and early 1990s. For the past 20 years life has been quieter in the city. The mafia is still a force to be reckoned with, but the battle is mostly fought behind the scenes.

Recently great improvements have been made to the fabric and culture of Palermo. The ancient Kalsa district has been regenerated and now contains art galleries, refurbished monuments and a seafront once more in popular use. Churches and palaces have been restored and opened to the public. The historic centre has become a popular destination for visitors and Palermitans alike with its monuments, street markets, gardens and restaurants. The Teatro Massimo offers regular seasons of opera, ballet and concerts. Tourism is well established and Palermo is now generally recognised as one of the great historic cities of Italy.

World War II and its aftermath

Sicily's strategic position proved to be of crucial importance in World War II. Once the Allies had defeated the German army in North Africa, Churchill pressed for further military action in the Mediterranean. This was needed to take the pressure off Russia, which was bearing the brunt of German aggression on the eastern front. According to Churchill, Italy was the 'soft underbelly' of Nazi Europe and could be knocked out of the war by decisive action. The invasion of Sicily, agreed between Churchill and Roosevelt at the Casablanca Conference in January 1943, had this objective as well as that of buying time for the preparation of the cross-channel invasion of France.[1]

As the fighting went on in North Africa, Sicily was used as a base for the Luftwaffe from which to attack Allied shipping and the British base in Malta. Sporadic bombing of Sicilian airfields and ports took place from 1940, which intensified as the Allies developed their plans to invade the island. By early 1943 American Boeing B17 Flying Fortresses were making regular sorties to disable Sicilian ports in raids known as 'carpet-bombing'.

The destruction to Palermo from these air raids was worse than anything in the city's previous history. The historic centre was partially destroyed, with the port and Kalsa district reduced to piles of rubble. Among the ruined churches were the Magione, the Casa Professa, Santa Maria della Catena and San Francesco d'Assisi. People able to leave the city fled to the towns inland. Those unable to leave huddled in the buildings that were still habitable, increasingly short of food and basic supplies. During the air raids people took refuge in underground caves and the ancient catacombs. One of these shelters, near the cathedral in Piazza Sette Angeli, took a direct hit which killed all the occupants. A monument stands there today in the piazza. In March 1943 a ship in the port carrying explosives was hit, causing huge damage. A massive bombardment arrived from a fleet of over 200 aircraft in May, which left 1,500 dead and thousands wounded in the city.

The Allied landings in Sicily, the first full-scale invasion of Hitler's Europe, took place on the night of 9–10 July 1943. The British Eighth Army under General Bernard Montgomery landed on the east coast to take the ports of Syracuse, Augusta and Catania before proceeding to Messina. The American Seventh Army under General George S. Patton landed on the south coast at Gela and Licata. Their role was to protect the British advance up the east coast and, after heading north-west, to join the British at Messina. It was an operation involving half a million men, supported by 2,500 ships and an air force providing air superiority. The defence of Sicily lay in the hands of 62,000 German and 200,000 Italian troops.[2]

Despite losses in the British airborne attack, the Allies swiftly established themselves on the island, helped by an intelligence operation which had convinced Hitler that the main invasion would take place in Greece or Sardinia.[3] The British and Canadians subsequently met tough resistance from German paratroops on the plain of Catania while Patton swept across western Sicily to take Palermo unopposed. When the Americans entered the city on 22 July they were welcomed as heroes by the battered population. Patton briefly took up residence in the Palazzo dei Normanni.

Patton's rapid advance was aided by Sicilian Americans. The mafia connection was used by American intelligence officers to create local resistance to the Axis troops. Sicilian Americans with mafia contacts were sent ahead of the main body of troops to alert the local population of their arrival. Mafia bosses seized the opportunity and raised the American flag. The Sicilian Americans in Patton's army, talking to the locals in their own dialect, were able to choose the best routes through the mountains and learn about the location of the enemy. One of their exploits was to capture intact a German map of the minefields. A legend grew up that Lucky Luciano, the American mafia boss, had masterminded these operations, but this is no longer accepted.[4]

Operation Husky, as the Sicilian campaign was called, lasted 38 days and came to an end when the two Allied armies converged on Messina. Despite their overwhelming superiority in numbers and equipment, the Allies were unable to prevent 100,000 German and Italian troops from withdrawing to the mainland, where they continued to hold up the Allies' advance. As a result of the campaign Mussolini fell from power, forced out for his inability to defend his country. Following the armistice signed at Cassibile in Sicily, the announcement was made on 8 September of Italy's capitulation to the Allies.

After the fighting ceased, control of Sicily passed to the Allied Military Government for Occupied Territories (AMGOT) and an administration run by the British and Americans. The priority was to restore some semblance of order and to protect the food supply. The Allies, as they looked for local leaders with anti-Fascist credentials to fill government positions, often chose men with mafia connections. Many were selected as mayors of the cities, including Palermo. The Sicilian mafia, after their suppression by Mussolini, became firmly re-established during the Allied occupation.[5]

The war left Sicily devastated. The port cities had all suffered bomb damage, especially Palermo and Messina. The countryside and small towns where the fighting had taken place were scenes of destruction. Large numbers of mines had been left by the retreating German army. Food was scarce, with prices inflated by the black market, and crime was soaring.

In this environment a separatist movement appeared, encouraged by the relationship with the Americans, which sought some form of independence for Sicily. When the newly formed Italian government drew up plans for the regions this movement was recognised and a substantial degree of autonomy was granted to the island. The Sicilian Regional Government was set up in 1947, and was based in Palermo, an important move for the city, which once again became the centre of government. In the Sala d'Ercole (Room of Hercules) in the Palazzo dei Normanni where the government meets, a plaque on the wall commemorates the dates of the establishment of the first and most recent Sicilian parliaments: 1130 and 1947.

In the 1950s, visitors returned to Sicily and left accounts of their experiences. Some, like the English writers Peter Quennell and Vincent Cronin, were drawn to the ancient monuments, the history and the beauty of the landscape. Others, like Gavin Maxwell, delved into contemporary Sicilian life. He published the story of the bandit Giuliano, who came from Montelepre, a small town in the mountains just outside Palermo. Giuliano supported the separatist movement and liked to be seen as a Robin Hood figure and champion of the people. He became a pawn of the mafia and the landowners and is chiefly remembered for the massacre at Portella della Ginestra. Here in the countryside, on May Day 1947, a workers' festival took place in the aftermath of a left-wing victory in the regional elections. Pressure from peasant workers for land reform and improved working conditions was gaining momentum. The festival, which was attended by a large crowd of workers with their families, was interrupted by machine-gun fire, killing 11 people and wounding 33. The truth behind the massacre was never established. While Giuliano's men carried it out, it was widely thought to have been organised by the mafia. A political motive was suspected, as this was the period when Mario Scelba, minister of the interior in the national government, started his crackdown on communist and trade unionist activity. Giuliano was killed in mysterious circumstances three years later.[6]

Maxwell went on to write about the hard lives and extreme poverty endured by the peasants of western Sicily, for whom land reform remained crucial. The plight of these peasants was brought to the world's attention by Danilo Dolci, described as the Italian Gandhi for his use of non-violent protest. Dolci arrived in western Sicily in 1952 and began to build homes for orphans and abandoned children. He went on to support the construction of a dam near Partinico to irrigate land for the peasants. He was constantly opposed by the mafia and spent time in prison for his protests against the authorities.

Dolci's book, *To Feed the Hungry*, paints a stark picture of Sicily in these postwar years. Half of the island's population lived in conditions described as semi or complete destitution. Half of all Sicilian earners were agricultural workers who were paid by the day and were without any land of their own. Palermo was described by Aldous Huxley, who wrote the introduction to Dolci's book, as follows:

> Palermo is a city of more than half a million inhabitants, of whom well over a hundred thousand live in conditions of what can only be described as Asiatic poverty. In the very heart of the city, behind the handsome buildings that line the principal thoroughfares, lie acre upon acre of slums that rival in squalor the slums of Cairo or Calcutta.[7]

Conditions were such that when the president of the Italian Republic visited Sicily in 1958, he said he had seen things that had 'frozen his ability to smile'.[8]

The postwar reconstruction of Sicily began in the 1950s through the Cassa per il Mezzogiorno, a fund for southern Italy supported by the World Bank, which financed projects in agriculture and industry. A major development was the discovery of oil near Ragusa in 1953 by Gulf Oil. This was followed by a find by the oil company Ente Nazionale Idrocarburi (ENI) off the south coast at Gela. Sicily became the centre of Italy's oil industry, which provided the energy for the industrialisation of northern Italy. Italy's economic miracle, when the northern triangle formed by Milan, Turin and Genoa became one of Europe's dynamic industrial regions, relied significantly upon Sicily for both the oil industry and the supply of emigrant workers.

The rise of the Corleonesi

During the 1950s the mafia changed from a rural to an urban phenomenon. It became well established in the various districts of Palermo, making money from protection rackets, kidnapping, smuggling and cuts from government contracts. In 1957 a conference took place at the Grand Hotel et des Palmes, the building in Via Roma that was originally the town house of Benjamin Ingham, the British wine magnate. Here mafia bosses from Sicily and America met to organise the drugs trade. Lucky Luciano, the mafia boss from New York, was one of those present. He had been expelled from America in 1946 and was living in Naples. It was around this time that the Sicilian mafia began to refer to itself as Cosa Nostra, which means literally 'our thing', the name used by the mafia in America.

As the power of Cosa Nostra increased, so did its ability to influence elections to both the Sicilian and national parliaments. Sicily, with its population of 5 million, had a significant number of seats in the government in Rome, a total of 61 in the chamber of deputies and the senate combined. These seats proved to be of great importance to the national political parties. The leading political party in Italy became the Democrazia Cristiana (DC), or the Christian Democrats, who were strongly supported by the Church and by the Americans, who feared the entry into government of the Partito Comunista Italiano (PCI), the Italian Communist Party. The DC dominated Italian politics for 40 years until the breakup of the Soviet Union and the removal of the communist threat. The party built a strong presence across Sicily and especially in Palermo.[9]

The continued growth of Palermo's population, combined with the war damage done to the city's centre, put severe pressure on housing. The construction industry, which was the largest employer of unskilled labour in the city, was vulnerable to mafia infiltration. Aided by corrupt politicians, this situation resulted in an uncontrolled construction boom. The landscape of Palermo was redefined by rows of cheap apartment blocks built around the city, providing huge profits for a handful of companies. It was in reality a criminal enterprise, which became known as the Sack of Palermo. In the process the historic centre was left semi-abandoned, its population shrinking from 200,000 in 1945 to 125,000 in 1951 and 50,000 by 1974.[10] The outline of the city, which had essentially remained the same as in the belle époque, was changed forever, with the orange and lemon groves of the Conca d'Oro disappearing under a sea of concrete. Nineteenth-century villas built along the Via della Libertà, renowned for their Liberty or art nouveau style, were demolished to make way for more apartments. Visitors cannot help noticing the stark contrast between the modern apartment blocks on the outskirts of the city and the fine architecture of the preceding centuries.

Cosa Nostra's breakthrough came in the early 1970s when President Nixon's war on drugs closed the heroin refineries in Marseilles, which had been run by Corsicans in what was called the French Connection. The role of refining the morphine base, brought to Europe from the Far East by Turkish and Asiatic gangs, was taken over by Cosa Nostra. Specialist laboratories to refine the drug, which was done to a high level of purity, were opened in western Sicily between Palermo and Trapani. Distribution was provided by Cosa Nostra's contacts in America. There they used chains of pizza parlours as the means of reaching retail customers in what became known as the Pizza Connection. In this way Cosa Nostra acquired for a while a near monopoly of the American heroin market. The quantities of heroin produced were industrial in scale and the profits vast. The morphine base bought at $13,000 a kilo was resold as heroin on the American market for $110,000 a kilo. The profits to Cosa Nostra were estimated at hundreds of millions of US dollars a year.[11]

The amounts of money flowing into Palermo were enough to transform the lives of the mafia bosses. The scale was such that on one occasion, when the police were raiding an apartment which turned out to be unoccupied, they found that it was filled with banknotes from floor to ceiling. The flow of money caused Cosa Nostra to move into the world of international finance and to establish links in Milan, Italy's chief financial centre. The Palermo–Milan axis became the conduit for the reinvestment of mafia capital. This was the era of financial scandals surrounding Michele Sindona, the Sicilian banker whose bank crashed and who was poisoned in prison in 1986; Roberto Calvi, chairman of the Banco Ambrosiano, whose faked suicide took place in London in 1982; and Archbishop Paul Marcinkus, governor of the Vatican Bank, who returned to Chicago in disgrace in 1990. These scandals represented the tip of the iceberg of the illicit transactions taking place.

In the wake of the entry into big business came a major change to the structure of Cosa Nostra. Until this point it had consisted of a federation of mafia families, each with its own territory and command structure. Families were grouped into *mandamenti* ('districts') with a *capomandamento* at its head. These *capos* ('bosses') took part in Cosa Nostra's *cupola*, or 'commission', which oversaw strategy and resolved disputes. The *capo dei capi*, the head of the commission, held great prestige but was effectively the first among equals and ruled through consensus. The arrival of the Corleonesi changed all this.

Corleone is a small town in a mountainous region of western Sicily, some

60 kilometres inland from Palermo. In the postwar period a particularly ruthless gang of mafiosi with big ambitions became established there. Led by Luciano Leggio, Salvatore (Totò) Riina and Bernardo Provenzano, they began to challenge the established mafia families in Palermo. After Leggio was arrested in 1974, the campaign was driven by Riina in a single-minded bid for power. In the early 1980s the Corleonesi unleashed their campaign against the rival mafia families. Using teams of trained gunmen, they killed the well-known bosses and their close henchmen. Then the Corleonesi put in their own men to run the families. Anyone suspected of disloyalty, including non-combatants, was eliminated. Total deaths in the war amounted to over a thousand. The mafiosi on the losing side, stunned by the ferocity of the campaign, failed to mount an effective counter-attack. For the next ten years Cosa Nostra became a dictatorship run by Riina, with Provenzano his deputy, a structure which concentrated huge military and financial resources in the hands of the Corleonesi.[12]

The killings were not limited to mafiosi but included senior state officials, the so-called *cadaveri eccellenti*, men who had stood in the way of Cosa Nostra's ambitions. The president of the Regional Government, Piersanti Mattarella, was assassinated in 1980, apparently for his attempts to clean up the awards of government contracts. Two years later it was the turn of the head of the Sicilian PCI and member of the Antimafia Commission, Pio La Torre.

The government in Rome reacted by appointing a prefect to Palermo to address the mafia problem. General Carlo Alberto Dalla Chiesa of the *carabinieri* was Italy's most senior law-enforcement officer. During the 1970s he had successfully led the operation to suppress the left-wing terrorist group the Red Brigades, which carried out a campaign against the state. Their worst crime was the kidnapping and murder of Aldo Moro, a former DC prime minister. When he was kidnapped Moro was building an agreement to include the PCI in government. Dalla Chiesa was only in Palermo for four months in 1982 before he and his wife were gunned down on 3 September by a mafia hit squad. During his short time in Palermo, Dalla Chiesa never received the support or resources he had requested from the government in Rome and was aware of becoming increasingly isolated. In the following year the chief prosecuting magistrate in Palermo, Rocco Chinnici, was also murdered. Palermo began to be compared to Beirut for the number of bombings and shootings that were taking place on the streets.[13]

Antimafia and the maxi-trial

The battle against Cosa Nostra intensified with the formation of a specialised pool of antimafia magistrates. The pool was introduced by Antonino Caponnetto, who took Chinnici's place as the chief prosecutor in Palermo. A method of working developed to deal with terrorists, the pool enabled magistrates to share information on their cases. As a result, the members not only became more efficient but also shared the risks. Among the first members of the pool were Giovanni Falcone and Paolo Borsellino, both of whom had been brought up near the Magione church in Palermo's Kalsa district. New antimafia legislation passed in Rome assisted the pool. Originally promoted by La Torre, the PCI leader, the law made it a crime to belong to an association of the mafia type. This was a breakthrough, for instead of having to prove a case based on a specific crime, with the difficulty of finding witnesses, magistrates now had to prove a broader case of belonging to the mafia. The new law also allowed the assets of convicted mafiosi to be confiscated.[14]

The brutality of the Corleonesi, who did not hesitate in killing women and children, created a reaction that encouraged mafiosi to turn state's evidence. The *pentiti*, as they were called, provided essential information upon which the magistrates began to build a broadly based case against Cosa Nostra. The key witness was Tommaso Buscetta, a member of Cosa Nostra from Palermo who had worked on both sides of the Atlantic. He turned state's evidence after several close relatives were murdered by the Corleonesi in revenge killings that violated the old mafia code. Buscetta, who developed a close relationship with Falcone, provided the magistrates with a detailed picture of the workings of Cosa Nostra and its structure. Particularly enlightening was his description of Cosa Nostra as a single organisation ruled by a central commission with a unified strategy. This piece of evidence, known as the 'Buscetta theorem', was considered highly controversial.

Falcone, Borsellino and the other members of the pool prepared the case for the prosecution of 474 defendants in the greatest assault upon the power of the mafia since Mussolini. The maxi-trial opened in 1986 under siege conditions inside the Ucciardone, Palermo's massive prison dating back to Bourbon times. A special courtroom, known as the bunker, was built there for this purpose. At the end of the trial 360 mafiosi were convicted.[15] Despite this success Falcone failed to be appointed as chief prosecutor in

Palermo. Instead he accepted a job in Rome, where he set about reorganising the government's approach to fighting organised crime. In a short time he set up the first national antimafia unit, based upon the American FBI. In Rome he was also able to ensure that the appeals for the maxi-trial proceeded correctly.

In January 1992 the Supreme Court announced its conclusions. These were to uphold the original verdicts, including acceptance of the Buscetta theorem. It was a historic defeat for Cosa Nostra, which was now officially defined as a unified association running large and valuable businesses. Many of the bosses faced spending the rest of their lives in prison. Crucially, the long-disputed question of mafia impunity had been challenged and defeated.

Cosa Nostra challenges the state

Riina and the other mafia bosses had relied upon the appeals process to reduce the sentences, as had happened so often in the past. When this failed, they launched a campaign of violence in a direct challenge to the Italian state. First to be assassinated was Salvo Lima, representative of the ruling DC in Sicily. Lima had been very influential, both in Sicily and within the DC, and had been the link to Giulio Andreotti, the prime minister. Then on 23 May, when Falcone and his wife were returning to Palermo from Rome, a huge bomb blast killed them and their bodyguards at Capaci, on the way into Palermo from the airport.

Falcone's funeral at the church of San Domenico, which was broadcast live on television, became an occasion of national mourning. Crowds filled central Palermo in a spontaneous outpouring of grief mixed with fury at the authorities' inability to protect its officials. Government ministers and politicians attending the funeral were booed by the crowd.

Rosaria Schifani, the wife of one of Falcone's bodyguards killed in the bomb blast, made a tearful, passionate speech in the church calling on the men of the mafia to change their ways, which was long remembered by those who witnessed it.[16] In the background lurked the suspicion that the mafia, as in so many cases in the past, had acted in collusion with elements of the state. Pino Arlacchi, a sociologist and expert on the mafia, voiced this opinion in a press article on 25 May:

The death of Falcone closes a cycle of history that ends very badly: with the clear and undisputed defeat of the state. The men of Cosa Nostra are strong because they are allied to other, even more dangerous men, who exist amongst us, inside our institutions.[17]

Parliament, which had been undecided on whom to appoint as next president of the Italian Republic, rejected Andreotti and chose instead Oscar Luigi Scalfaro, a member of the DC with sound antimafia credentials.

Then, on 19 July, only two months later, Paolo Borsellino and his bodyguards died in a bomb blast as he was arriving to visit his mother in Via D'Amelio in Palermo. Borsellino had been well aware of the danger that he was in and had been working desperately to uncover those responsible for Falcone's death. Just before he died he confided to his wife that 'The mafia will kill me but at the wishes of others'.[18] At his family's request, Borsellino's funeral was a private affair. At the state funeral held for his bodyguards in the cathedral, the atmosphere was tense. The police, government ministers and even the recently appointed president of the Italian Republic, Scalfaro, were booed and jostled by the crowd. Anti-government feeling ran high against those who were unable, or as some people thought unwilling, to protect their best men.

These events shocked the government in Rome into action. Troops were sent to Palermo to guard the institutions and to protect the magistrates in what was called Operation Sicilian Vespers. New antimafia laws were rushed through, including a harsh prison regime and a witness protection programme. Mafia bosses in prison in Palermo were transferred to remote prison islands including Pianosa in Tuscany, first used by the Romans, with no means of communication with the outside world.

In January 1993 a new chief prosecutor arrived in Palermo, named Gian Carlo Caselli. He came from Turin where he had made his name investigating the Red Brigades, working with Dalla Chiesa. He had strongly supported Falcone. On the day Caselli arrived in Palermo, Riina, the boss of bosses, was arrested while travelling by car in Palermo. He had been in hiding in Sicily since 1970. Despite his arrest, Cosa Nostra's bombing campaign was extended to mainland Italy. In May a car bomb exploded in Rome with no fatalities, but the bombings which followed in Florence and Milan each cost the lives of five people. A larger device which was placed near the stadium in Rome, and timed to go off after a football match, failed to explode.

The state fights back

The arrival of Caselli in Palermo in January 1993 saw the beginning of a new phase in the battle against the mafia. It coincided with a rare moment of national unity when full support was given to the magistrates. The next few years saw significant damage inflicted upon Cosa Nostra by a revitalised pool of magistrates under Caselli's leadership. The combination of a tough prison regime and the benefits offered through a witness protection programme resulted in a wave of mafia collaboration with the authorities. Information from collaborators opened up new avenues of investigation. Technology helped the magistrates' campaign, with telephone tapping and other surveillance techniques being widely used. Following the trail of financial transactions, linked to international markets, also played an important part. This comprehensive intelligence-gathering yielded spectacular results. During Caselli's seven years in Palermo over 300 wanted mafiosi, who had been in hiding in Sicily, were rounded up. Further arrests were made, which led to 650 life sentences being handed out, while millions of dollars in assets were confiscated. Palermo's law enforcement agencies became a skilled antimafia centre, as described by John Dickie:

> Before Giovanni Falcone died, he turned his experience in the Palermo pool of magistrates into a template for Italy's new national organisation for investigating and prosecuting organised crime. After Falcone's death, Palermo continued to be the model for the rest of the country: it became an elite school for teams of mafioso hunters.[19]

Interrogation of mafia collaborators began to uncover information on Cosa Nostra's political connections in Rome. The historic involvement of the mafia in the world of politics was well known. But in the post-World War II years it was ignored by the authorities. In the 1960s the subject was featured in the fiction of Leonardo Sciascia, a prolific writer on Sicily. In his political thrillers, such as *The Day of the Owl*, lone officers of the law apply their reason to solving criminal cases, surrounded by official cover up and political manipulation. In these cases there are no happy endings, society aids the criminals and the truth is never discovered. It was a prophetic view of the nature of organised crime and its link to political corruption in Italy.

Falcone had no illusions as to the political dimension of the mafia problem. Throughout his career he had to contend with interference in the course of his investigations. He faced frequent criticism and humiliation from professional colleagues. Despite the success of the maxi-trial and his obvious qualifications, he was passed over for the post of senior prosecutor in Palermo. In an interview Falcone stated:

> I believe that Cosa Nostra has been involved in all the important events in Sicily beginning with the Allied landing in the Second World War and the election of the Mafia mayors after the Liberation. I would not wish to venture into political analysis myself, but I cannot believe that certain political groups are not allied to Cosa Nostra (due to their shared interests), and are not attempting to manipulate our still young democracy, by eliminating people who cause discomfort to both.[20]

Caselli was convinced that political connections were the key to Cosa Nostra's long-term survival. In his view no group of gangsters, anywhere in the world, lasted for more than a generation. If they were still infesting the country after 130 years, it was due to complicity and infiltration of the legitimate professional world. He also feared that while the whole might of the state had been put behind the campaign to eliminate the terrorist activities of the Red Brigades in the 1970s, the effort to combat the mafia was far less united and depended upon a small group of dedicated officers.[21]

Buscetta, in his discussions with Falcone, referred to the political connection but refused to provide details. After Falcone's death he began to do so, implicating Andreotti, the DC leader and ex-prime minister. Another mafia defector, Gaspare Mutolo, who had been Riina's driver, in talks with Borsellino urged him to pursue the mafia's connections in the professional world. 'But let's do it so as to hit these important people, otherwise you will never destroy the mafia. The mafia is linked to politicians, policemen and magistrates. If you don't cut this umbilical cord you won't get anywhere.'[22]

He went on to provide information on politicians, also implicating Andreotti. Caselli and his team began an investigation that lasted for years. Finally it resulted in Andreotti's acquittal in 2004. The Appeals Court of Palermo did, however, rule that Andreotti had ties with the mafia before 1980, a charge which lapsed due to the statute of limitations, on the basis that it took place too long ago.[23]

Caselli, who noted that support for the magistrates tended to melt away when they tackled political cases, had his own nomination blocked for the senior antimafia position in Italy. In addition to his work as a magistrate in Palermo and Turin, Caselli had served on the Italian Superior Council of Magistrates and in Brussels, where he had represented Italy in the fight against organised crime in Europe. But in 2005 his nomination for the post of national antimafia prosecutor was blocked by a legal amendment introduced by Silvio Berlusconi's government. The amendment was later revoked by the Constitutional Court, but too late for Caselli's nomination.[24]

The antimafia movement

In the 1950s and 1960s popular opposition to the mafia was led by the PCI and the trade unions that supported the rights of peasants and workers. As agricultural work declined, so the opposition became concentrated in Palermo, with the increasing engagement of the professional class. By the 1980s it had become clear that to defeat the mafia a change in the culture of society was needed. For too long the mafia had set the agenda, suppressing the rights of normal citizens. Dalla Chiesa, the *carabinieri* general killed by the mafia in 1982, had understood this. During his short time in Palermo he gave talks in schools for this purpose.

As mayor of Palermo, a major contribution to cultural change has been made by Leoluca Orlando. He saw that people needed to have pride again in their city and set out to regenerate the historic centre of Palermo. A dedicated opponent of the mafia, Orlando's first term as mayor began in 1985, during Falcone's time. In his book *Fighting the Mafia and Renewing Sicilian Culture*, he explains what it was like to be part of the antimafia forces in this period. He was constantly accompanied by bodyguards, and at one stage the personal threat was so imminent that he and his family were forced to flee Sicily and go abroad.

On his return he dedicated himself to the regeneration of the city, introducing a voluntary programme for students called 'Adopt a monument', in which groups of students worked together to clean up public gardens and ancient sites. Orlando's outstanding achievement was the renovation of some of Palermo's most famous monuments. These included the reopening in 1997 of the Teatro Massimo, Palermo's opera house, after 23 years of neglect; the refurbishment of the church of Santa Maria dello Spasimo (St Mary of the Agony) as a venue for public exhibitions and concerts; and the restoration of the Zisa, the summer palace of the Norman kings.[25]

A groundswell of support for the antimafia movement developed in the aftermath of the assassinations of the two judges in 1992. An association named Libera, meaning 'free', was set up in 1995 to involve the wider community in defying the mafia. Founded by Don Luigi Ciotti, a priest in Turin, and Rita Borsellino, the sister of the murdered judge, it began by working in the schools. Educating the young on the true nature of the mafia has long been seen as crucial. Libera went on to promote the use of property confiscated from the mafia in local community projects. Under the law, convicted mafiosi can have their assets confiscated and released for productive purposes. The association now manages 5,000 such properties, including villas, farms and agricultural land on which young volunteers work to create fruit and vegetable gardens or to produce wine and olive oil. The involvement of local residents in these projects helps to break the traditional view of the mafia as the sole provider of jobs. Libera has recently enjoyed a big increase in membership.

One day in 2004 a slogan appeared on stickers, attached to walls and lamp-posts in Palermo, which read: 'A whole people who pay the pizzo are a people without dignity.' It was the work of some young men who had opened a bar but who baulked at the demands of the mafia. Known as Addiopizzo, the association grew to include businesses and consumers united against the payment of the mafia's protection money, believed at the time to be extorted from 80 per cent of Palermo's commercial outlets. A list is published of members, currently around 700, and stickers are displayed on shop windows announcing that the shop is 'pizzo-free'. The association, which is strongest in the more affluent districts of Palermo, is supported by Confindustria Sicilia, the employers' federation. Evidence from collaborators indicates that Addiopizzo is proving to be a problem for the mafia, as collecting the pizzo is considered more difficult and involves an increased risk of arrest.[26]

In recent years the Church has become more outspoken in denouncing the mafia. In May 2013 came the canonisation of Padre Giuseppe (Pino) Puglisi, who defied the mafia in Palermo. Puglisi was a dedicated priest who lived in Brancaccio, a district to the south-east of the city controlled by a powerful mafia family. For his campaign to educate children away from mafia influence, he was shot and killed in 1993, on his 56th birthday. His canonisation was celebrated in the cathedral in Palermo and his sacrifice is now widely recognised. Puglisi wanted suitable premises to carry out his teaching. A new centre for children is currently being built in Brancaccio, on land confiscated from the mafia, in which to continue his work.

The Church's strongest statement to date was made in March 2014 by Pope Francis. He was speaking at a ceremony in Rome, the first of its kind to honour the victims of the various mafia groups in Italy. Families of the victims who attended the ceremony listened while the names of 842 victims were read out, policemen and women, politicians, journalists, trade unionists and magistrates, killed for carrying out their duty. In an uncompromising speech, the Pope directly addressed the men and women of the mafia, urging them to convert while there was still time and to end their lives of crime.

National recognition of the antimafia movement was reinforced on 23 May 2012 when two ships arrived in the port of Palermo carrying 3,000 young people from all over Italy. They came to celebrate the Festa della Legalità (Festival of Legality) on the 20th anniversary of the death of Giovanni Falcone. Led by the president of the Republic, Giorgio Napolitano, and the prime minister, Mario Monti, memorial services were held at key points in the city. These included the courtroom inside the Ucciardone prison, scene of the maxi-trial; Via Carlo Alberto Dalla Chiesa, where the general died; and Via D'Amelio, where Paolo Borsellino was killed. A magnolia tree, which stands outside the apartment block where Falcone lived in Via Notarbartolo, has become a shrine, covered in photographs and messages of support. Here a crowd of more than 10,000 people gathered to honour the sacrifices of the two judges.

The assessment of what has been achieved in the 22 years since the judges' deaths is mixed. On the one hand it is recognised that much has been done to repress the military wing of Cosa Nostra. In 2006 Provenzano, the successor to Riina, was finally arrested after more than 40 years in hiding. There followed the arrests of other prominent bosses. Since 1993 the *cupola*, or commission, which acted as the mafia's ruling body, has not met. No high-profile killings of state officials have taken place in Palermo. Undoubtedly Cosa Nostra's military strength has been much reduced. On the other hand, far less progress has been made to counter the activities of the white-collar mafia, with its great wealth invested in business and finance. Today Cosa Nostra is part of big business, with operations around the world, which is proving much more difficult to investigate. The most elusive and yet crucial element remains the political connection. In the view of the magistrates, while the battles against the mafia go on in Sicily, Calabria and Campania, the war will be won in Rome.[27]

Conditions today

As one enters Palermo today from the north down Via della Libertà, the city gives a confident and prosperous impression. Lined by well-kept apartment blocks with cafes and boutiques at ground level, this broad avenue leads past the Giardino Inglese into the square containing the Politeama, the theatre capped by a four-horse racing chariot recalling ancient Rome. A narrower street continues to the Teatro Massimo, Palermo's opera house, from where Via Maqueda proceeds into the heart of the old city. It is a fitting entrance to a regional capital in Italy's deep south.

But behind this facade lies a troubled city suffering from historic imbalances, which have been exacerbated by the recent recession, the worst in Italy since World War II. The population has risen to 655,000, making Palermo the fifth-largest city in Italy as well as the largest in Sicily. The economy is highly dependent upon local government, which is Palermo's largest employer: perhaps a quarter of the workforce is employed, either full- or part-time, in the public sector. In addition there is a substantial service sector made up of lawyers, accountants and IT specialists engaged in work for local government. The Regional Government's influence on the economy extends to education, healthcare, transport and tourism. It is also the source of contracts and development funds allocated from Rome and Brussels.

As Palermo lacks major industries and significant inward investment, there is a shortage of large companies to absorb the rest of the working population. The commercial sector, which is the second most important in terms of jobs, is fragmented into smaller employers, represented by hotels, restaurants and retail shops. This sector relies largely upon tourism, which over the past five years has attracted some 600,000 visitors annually to Palermo and around 4.2 million to Sicily. There is large potential for growth here, for Sicily, along with the rest of southern Italy, is underperforming in the international tourist market.[28]

Other than tourism, the strength of the economy lies in exports. Here growth is coming from high-quality agricultural products, produced today on a small scale, and in a manufacturing sector which exports goods such as chemicals and electronics to countries around the Mediterranean. The export of petroleum products is also important.

These are testing times for Sicily, a poor region on the periphery of the European Union, as state funding continues to decline. Consumer spending is depressed and commercial initiative is stifled by government bureaucracy. Companies are closing and unemployment is running at twice the national average. In addition Sicily has to deal with boatloads of refugees arriving on her shores from North Africa and the war-torn Middle East.

The European Union is introducing some of the antimafia measures created and tested in Sicily to combat cross-border crime. They include the charge of mafia association, the confiscation of assets of convicted mafiosi and their reuse for the benefit of local communities. These measures are championed by Sonia Alfano, president of the European Antimafia Commission. Alfano, who is Sicilian, took up the antimafia cause after her father, Beppe Alfano, was murdered by the mafia in 1993. She is on record as voicing her concern over conditions prevailing in Italy today, which have similarities to those of 1992. In both periods a breakdown of the established political parties in Rome, with the emergence of new leaders, coincided with a period of economic crisis.[29]

In Sicily, two politicians with strong records for campaigning against the mafia were elected to office in 2012. Voters in Palermo once again chose Leoluca Orlando as mayor of the city to continue his work of urban renewal. Regional elections saw a major change in voting patterns among the Sicilian electorate, with Rosario Crocetta becoming the first left-wing president of the Sicilian region. Crocetta made his name as the antimafia mayor of Gela, an industrial town with a long history of organised crime on the south coast of Sicily. Among his first statements in Palermo was that with his arrival Cosa Nostra would pack their bags, indicating a clean break with the past. While action to date has been encouraging, including close cooperation with the magistrates, the full implications of Crocetta's governorship have still to be seen.[30]

In Palermo magistrates are investigating the events of the 1990s in the wake of the deaths of Falcone and Borsellino. Specifically they are looking at the negotiations between state and mafia that are alleged to have taken place following the mafia's bombing campaign. There seems to be a lot at stake, for death threats have been directed at Antonino Di Matteo, the magistrate handling the case. At the same time, people who were close to Falcone and Borsellino are demanding that the truth behind their murders be established once and for all, in what they see as a crucial test of Italy's democracy.

In January 2015, Italy's parliament elected Sergio Mattarella as the country's president. Mattarella, who is from Palermo, is the first Sicilian to hold this position. His elder brother, Piersanti, was assassinated by the mafia in 1980 when governor of Sicily.

Epilogue

Few cities have experienced such extremes of fortune as Palermo. Few cities have paid so much in the blood of their citizens in the fight for freedom and justice. Few cities have shown such resilience and such a strong spirit of survival.

From the Phoenicians in antiquity to the Americans in the twentieth century, the story of Palermo is one of repeated invasion and rule by foreign powers. As a result the city developed in isolation from the mainstream of European life. Exploitation of the people by a privileged few became the established order, along with corruption and frequent revolts against authority.

Once the domination by foreign powers had gone, instead of at last gaining social justice, the city fell under the sway of a homegrown domination, the mafia. The conditions that made this possible were two campaigns, Garibaldi's in 1860 and that of the British and Americans in 1943, both of which brought abrupt regime change followed by a period of anarchy.

Palermo fought back, demonstrating great powers of endurance. The antimafia campaign, developed in the 1980s, slowly and at high cost made progress. It reached a climax in the confrontation between state and mafia in the early 1990s. Following the assassination of the judges, the campaign went on to achieve notable successes. The work continues as magistrates investigate the mafia's influence at national level. The regeneration of Palermo since the 1980s has been remarkable.

Today the city is at a crossroads, with a new and promising administration in place that is facing tough economic conditions. At the same time there are signs of a wind of change blowing across Sicily, with people determined to reform government. Palermo has been through the fire and is ready to come out the other side.

PART II

The Principal Monuments
A Commentary

CHAPTER 12

The Historic Centre

T he historic centre of Palermo is the scene for this book. This is where most of the events have taken place and where most of the monuments are to be found. It is a well-defined area divided into four quarters by two roads, Corso Vittorio Emanuele, which runs from the mountains towards the seafront, and Via Maqueda, which crosses the Corso at right angles at the centre of the city. It is a compact area measuring about 1.8 kilometres along the Corso by 1.3 kilometres along Via Maqueda. In terms of orientation, the Corso runs north-east towards the sea.

The four quarters are known by names of ancient origin, each one carrying a subsidiary name or names. Starting with the oldest quarter around the Palazzo dei Normanni and proceeding in a clockwise direction, the names are Albergheria (Palazzo Reale), Seralcadio (Capo, Monte di Pietà), Loggia (Castellammare) and Kalsa (Tribunali).

The topography of Palermo has changed substantially over the centuries. In ancient times the sea level was significantly higher than today so that the port reached as high as Via Roma. The Punic settlement stood on a peninsula facing the port, protected on either side by a river. As the sea level subsided so the port reduced in size, with the city expanding to cover the exposed land. By the seventeenth century under the Spanish, the historic centre had taken on its modern aspect with the rivers diverted underground. (See map section for the development of the city.)

The main road, Corso Vittorio Emanuele, has been part of the city's fabric since ancient times. Known as the Cassaro by the Arabs, it became Via Marmorea to the Normans and Via Toledo to the Spanish, who extended it from the centre of the city down to the seafront.[1]

The old city walls, together with the bastions and many of the gates, were demolished in the second half of the nineteenth century, along with the Castellammare, the castle which protected the entrance to the Cala, the old port. The city was then developed to the north down Via della Libertà, which became the affluent district of the modern city.

Unlike many Italian cities, Palermo does not have one central piazza where everyone gathers. Instead there are several piazzas, each representing a different aspect of the city, located both inside and adjoining the historic centre. Piazza Indipendenza, at the far end of Corso Vittorio Emanuele through Porta Nuova (figure 4), represents political power. It contains the seat of Sicily's governor, the Palazzo d'Orleans, as well as access to the Palazzo dei Normanni, where the Regional Government meets. Piazza Cattedrale, further down the Corso heading for the sea, represents the Church and is a gathering point for visitors to the cathedral and the Palazzo Arcivescovile.

At the centre of the city lies Piazza Pretoria, where the mayor has his office, representing a second level of political power. Before the Corso reaches Porta Felice near the seafront lies Piazza Marina, which contains the Palazzo Chiaramonte, representing the historic power of the barons. Located halfway down Via Roma, next to the Vucciria street market, comes Piazza San Domenico, in the heart of the shopping district. Two piazzas built in the nineteenth century are important centres. The first is Piazza Verdi, with the opera house, the Teatro Massimo. The second is Piazza Ruggero Settimo, popularly known as Piazza Politeama, for it holds the Teatro Politeama. Piazza Politeama, a large modern piazza from which Via della Libertà leads out of the city, is the favourite meeting place for the young of Palermo.

The seafront, which was left untouched and run-down for years, is once again coming into popular use. In the belle époque, the sea reached the edge of the road running outside the city walls known as the Marina (today's Foro Italico), as can be seen from prints of the period. After World War II, rubble from bomb damage was dumped in the sea, pushing back the seafront. Today this area is a popular playground for children and a place to fly kites. The Cala has been surrounded by a pedestrian area in which bars and restaurants have been installed from which the yachts and fishing boats can be admired.

4. Porta Nuova (Barberis, nineteenth century).

Visitors cannot fail to notice the extreme contrasts in the fabric of the historic centre. Well-restored palaces and carefully maintained churches stand cheek by jowl with derelict buildings, while weeds grow undisturbed at the base of ancient monuments. A prime example is Piazza Garraffello in the Vucciria, where ruined and abandoned houses make it look more like a war zone than the centre of an Italian city. It seems impossible that such contrasts should exist in one place. But they do: this is Palermo. One of the perennial problems is refuse collection. Rosario La Duca, a historian of Palermo, put it diplomatically when he wrote: 'The city definitely does not constitute a model in terms of urban cleanliness.'

Today the historic centre contains monuments and government offices, street markets, shops, restaurants and tourist infrastructure. It is far less of a residential centre than it used to be, though some repopulation is taking place. Instead the centre has become a destination, not only for visitors from Italy and abroad, but also for Palermitans and residents of the outlying province. People come in to do business or to attend the university, to enjoy walking around the ancient streets and piazzas, and to eat some of their favourite food. Saturday nights are especially lively in central Palermo.

CHAPTER 13

Antiquity

Human habitation around Palermo dates back to prehistoric times. On Monte Pellegrino, in the Addaura caves, opened up by the American army in 1943, an important discovery was made of a series of wall carvings from the Stone Age. They show outline figures of men who may be dancing or taking part in of some kind of ritual. The drawings also feature animals and background scenery. Bones and tools for hunting were also found in separate caves on the mountain. For some time the caves have not been open to the public due to danger from falling rocks. Some of the artefacts may be seen, however, in the Museo Archeologico Regionale. Further evidence from Monte Gallo and Monreale indicates a slow, continuous evolution of human inhabitation of the territory around Palermo, starting at least 10,000 years ago, and leading to the establishment of the first settlement in the eighth century BC.

Panormus, the ancient city of Palermo, was originally a Phoenician settlement situated on a promontory facing a large, natural harbour with a river flowing down either side.[1] The ancient settlement is hard to imagine today as the topography of the city has changed so much. The harbour, which in ancient times reached up to the level of Via Roma, is now reduced to the Cala, where the yachts are moored, and the rivers have been diverted underground. According to Thucydides, Panormus was one of three settlements to which the Phoenicians withdrew when the Greeks arrived in Sicily in large numbers towards the end of the eighth century BC. The other two were Motya (modern Mozia) and Solus. Panormus was fortified with surrounding walls at some time during the seventh century BC. The city later became an important base for the Carthaginians, who absorbed the Phoenician settlements into their empire, until it was captured by the Romans in 254 BC.[2]

Few traces of the ancient city remain. Some fragments of Punic walls can be found in the basement of the Palazzo dei Normanni, in Via Candelai and in Corso Alberto Amedeo. Evidence of an extensive Punic burial ground exists along Corso Calatafimi, the road leading to Monreale. The remains of a Roman villa can be seen in Piazza Vittoria, in the gardens called Villa Bonanno, in front of the Palazzo dei Normanni. The archaeological finds from Panormus have been put together with those from the ancient Greek cities of western Sicily to form a rich collection in the Museo Archeologico Regionale.

MUSEO ARCHEOLOGICO REGIONALE ANTONIO SALINAS
(REGIONAL ARCHAEOLOGICAL MUSEUM ANTONIO SALINAS)

The museum is housed in a seventeenth-century building, once the monastery of the oratory of San Filippo Neri. It is part of the Olivella complex, which includes the nearby church of Sant'Ignazio (St Ignatius). After the suppression of the religious orders in 1866, the building was taken over by the state and was chosen as the location for the museum. The entrance can be found in Piazza Olivella, close to Via Roma.³

The museum was developed around a core of earlier collections by the archaeologist Antonio Salinas, who served as its director from 1873 to 1914. This was the golden age of archaeology, when treasures from the ancient world were being discovered all over the Mediterranean. Sicily was no exception, and Salinas carried out extensive excavations on the island. Under his direction the museum became the main repository of the finds from western Sicily from the Phoenician to the Greek and Roman eras. Comparable work was carried out in eastern Sicily by Paolo Orsi, the director of antiquities for Syracuse, who also developed an archaeological museum.

On entering the museum the visitor is faced with two elegant courtyards, each with its set of cloisters. In the centre of the first courtyard stands a fountain with a statue of Triton from the seventeenth century, which was originally located in the Palazzo dei Normanni. The second courtyard also contains a fountain, together with a bust of Salinas, surrounded by banana trees and papyrus. The cloisters and nearby rooms are filled with statues of Phoenician and Roman origin, ancient anchors, sarcophagi and a famous stone from ancient Egypt with inscriptions. Noteworthy are the statues of Zeus, the emperor Claudius portrayed as Zeus, a Phoenician goddess and Socrates. The mix of fine architecture, statuary and exotic plants makes these courtyards particularly inviting. They were admired by the English traveller Douglas Sladen in 1900, who commented:

> Both the conception and execution of the idea of making these cortili a combination of open-air museum and sub-tropical garden are due to the good taste of Professor Salinas, the accomplished director of the museum, who has made it one of the best in Italy.[4]

The ground-floor rooms contain a collection of inscriptions in Greek and Latin, carved on slabs of stone, followed by a series of lion-head waterspouts from the Greek city of Himera.

The finest pieces in the museum's collection, examples of Sicilian Greek art at its best, can be found in the Selinunte room. They come from Selinus (modern Selinunte), an ancient Greek city on Sicily's southern coast. The temples of Selinus were of the Doric order and carried a decorative frieze above the columns which was composed of alternating metopes (stone panels with carved figures) and triglyphs (panels with vertical bars). Three metopes broken into pieces were found by the Englishmen William Harris and Samuel Angell in 1823. The authorities prevented the metopes from being shipped back to England and the Englishmen had to make do with plaster copies. Harris died of malaria, the curse of ancient Selinus, while in Sicily.

Metopes were used to tell the stories of the ancient Greek gods and heroes, as demonstrated by those found by the Englishmen from 'Temple C', which date from the mid-sixth century BC. In one, Apollo appears in a four-horse chariot; in another, Perseus, helped by Athena, kills the Medusa; and in a third, Heracles carries Libyan thieves tied to a pole. Traces exist of the colours with which the metopes were originally painted. These metopes cover much of the city's lifespan, from the seventh to the fifth centuries BC. The artistic development of the sculptures can be followed, culminating in the metopes from 'Temple E', probably carved around 460 BC. Here we see Athena killing a giant and the marriage of Zeus and Hera. The life of Selinus came to an abrupt end in 409 BC when it was captured and partially destroyed by the Carthaginians.

The first floor contains galleries displaying a variety of items found in the tombs and burial grounds of Palermo and the ancient cities of western Sicily. Their origins are Punic, Greek and Roman. There are terracotta figures, bronzes, funeral shrines, jewellery and stone altars. From the sanctuary of Malaphoros in Selinunte comes a collection of terracotta statuettes, female figures linked to the cult of Demeter and Kore. Demeter, the earth goddess, and her daughter Kore, or Persephone, the goddess of spring, were revered by a people dependent upon the seasons for a good harvest.

In the bronze room are two important exhibits, the bronze ram of Syracuse and the statue of Hercules wrestling with a stag. The bronze ram is one of a pair that once graced the palace of a Greek tyrant in Syracuse, possibly Agathocles or Hiero II, in the third century B C. The statue of Hercules came from a private villa near Pompeii and was donated by the Bourbon king Francis I. Both these bronzes are considered to follow the style of the sculptor Lysippos. Also to be seen is a set of ancient Greek armour with helmet, breastplate and sword.

Other rooms contain Greek and Roman sculptures, including a Roman copy of Praxiteles' *Satyr*, a head of Aristotle and a particularly striking head called *Man from Partinico*.

Mosaics on the second floor include a spectacular scene of Orpheus playing his lyre to a surrounding group of animals and birds, discovered in the Roman villa in Piazza Vittoria.

Outside Palermo

SOLUNTO (ANCIENT SOLUS)

Solunto was one of the smaller coastal cities, ruled in turn by Carthaginians, Greeks and Romans. The substantial archaeological site is located in open countryside, over 200 metres above sea level, on a rocky promontory over-looking the sea. It is to be found near Bagheria, famous for its baroque palaces, some 17 kilometres to the south-east of Palermo.

Known to the ancient writers as Solus, it was founded around 350 B C by Carthaginians to protect Panormus against encroachment by the Greeks, who were established at Himera further down the coast. The city passed to the Greeks in the early third century B C as part of a settlement with Agathocles, the Greek tyrant of Syracuse, following his expedition to North Africa. The Romans took control of Solus in 254 B C after the capture of Panormus.

This site was not the Soloeis referred to by Thucydides as one of the three Phoenician outposts in Sicily (the others being Panormus and Motya). That early settlement was probably sited close by on the bay of Santa Flavia, in an area which has since been built over. The Phoenicians, as a seafaring people, tended to build their settlements close to the shore. The city kept the name of Solus when moved uphill by the Carthaginians to act as a lookout post in the fourth century.[5]

The site, which is rectangular in shape with paths crossing at right angles, is spread over a large expanse of hillside affording views of the coastline from the paved road along the crest of the hill. Above the road are the remains of a theatre, an agora and some Carthaginian sanctuaries. The city's heyday was in the last two centuries BC, with activity ceasing early in the third century AD when the focus moved back again to the coast. A small museum contains a collection of items from the Punic, Greek and Roman eras.

Ancient sites of western Sicily

These are of exceptional interest. Largely abandoned since ancient times, most of these sites are in unspoiled countryside and convey a strong sense of their ancient glory.[6] In order of proximity to Palermo, the sites are as follows.

SEGESTA

Segesta's Greek temple, poised on a hill overlooking the countryside, is one of the most memorable sights in Sicily. It was built to impress the Athenians in the fifth century BC and was never completed. Together with a theatre, this is all that remains of the city that once dominated this corner of Sicily. Originally an Elymian settlement, the city became thoroughly Hellenised and was the enemy of Selinunte, whose territory it bordered. Segesta is to be found off the motorway from Palermo to Trapani, close to the town of Calatafimi, the scene of Garibaldi's first battle with the Bourbon troops.

ERICE (ANCIENT ERYX)

Erice has a special atmosphere due to its isolated position on a hill, some 800 metres above sea level, with spectacular views of the sea. It lies off the motorway close to Trapani. In antiquity Eryx held the most celebrated temple and sanctuary in Sicily, dedicated to the goddess of fertility personified by Astarte for the Phoenicians, Aphrodite for the Greeks and Venus Erycina for the Romans. The temple was visible to sailors at sea and, according to Roman legend, was founded by Aeneas. Only a stretch of Punic wall and artefacts in a small museum are left of the ancient civilisations, while some Norman buildings have survived near the modern village.

MOZIA (ANCIENT MOTYA)

Mozia is a small island off the west coast, situated in a protected bay. First a Phoenician settlement, mentioned by Thucydides, it became the main Carthaginian city in Sicily until destroyed in 397 BC by Dionysius I of Syracuse. Left to the archaeologists, as it was never rebuilt, Mozia provides an insight into the Punic civilisation in Sicily. The outline of the city can be made out and there is a well-stocked museum which contains the famous statue of the *Youth of Motya*. The island is owned by the Whitaker Foundation, as Joseph Whitaker, a British wine magnate and enthusiastic archaeologist, bought the site and began excavating it in 1906. Mozia is to be found on the coast road from Trapani shortly before reaching Marsala. There is a regular boat service to the island.

MARSALA (ANCIENT LILYBAEUM)

The city's name derives from the Arabic 'Marsa-Allah' meaning 'Harbour of God'. The harbour has played a major part in the history of Sicily, as it was from here that Scipio sailed for North Africa with his Roman army to defeat Hannibal, and it was here that Garibaldi landed in 1860. Unlike the other sites, at Marsala a modern city has been built over the ancient settlements. Known as Lilybaeum, 'the town that looks at Libya', the Carthaginians developed it as their main base in Sicily after the destruction of Motya by Dionysius I in 397 BC. Under the Romans it was an important regional centre and in 76–75 BC Cicero served here as quaestor. Punic and Roman remains can be seen in the archaeological park and in the museum. Of special interest are the remains of the Phoenician ship discovered under the sea in 1971. From the late eighteenth century Marsala became the centre of the wine trade run by British traders and their *bagli*, buildings with courtyards that contained the wineries, can be seen there today.

SELINUNTE (ANCIENT SELINUS)

Selinus was the most western of the ancient Greek settlements. It flourished for around 240 years, from its foundation in about 650 BC until its destruction by the Carthaginians in 409 BC.

Situated on the south coast of Sicily not far from Castelvetrano, the large archaeological site is divided into four sections: an acropolis facing the sea containing five temples, one of which has been partially reconstructed; a residential quarter leading uphill; a separate quarter to the east containing three temples, one of which has been reconstructed; and a sanctuary to Demeter Malaphoros, goddess of the harvest, to the west. Harbours were formed by widening the mouths of the rivers that flowed on either side of the city. As much of the city's walls are still in place, together with the outline of streets, this site gives a realistic impression of an ancient city. Near Campobello, about half an hour away, are the quarries that provided the stone to build the temples. Here huge columns can be seen partially cut out of the rock. It is a scene frozen in time, from when the city's temple building came to an end with the arrival of the Carthaginian army in 409 BC.

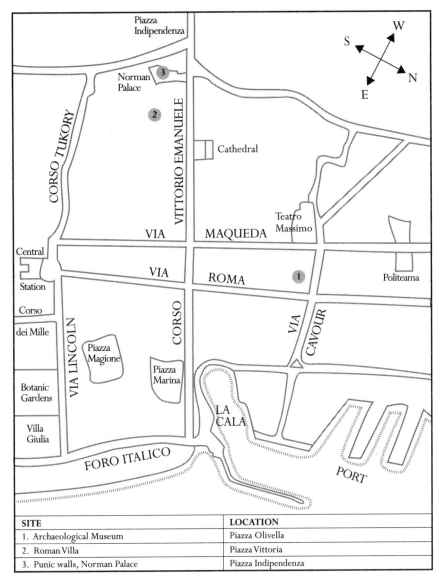

SITE	LOCATION
1. Archaeological Museum	Piazza Olivella
2. Roman Villa	Piazza Vittoria
3. Punic walls, Norman Palace	Piazza Indipendenza

Map 8 Monuments from antiquity.

CHAPTER 14

The Norman Era

The Norman monuments in Palermo, built to glorify Norman power and the Christian religion, include cathedrals, churches, chapels, pavilions and palaces. They are unique for the blend of cultures that they represent: Norman, Arab and Byzantine Greek. The Normans brought their own ideas on architecture from northern Europe and from southern Italy, where they were established prior to arriving in Sicily. The alliance with the Arabs, made after the capture of Palermo in 1072, added a strong Muslim influence to their architecture. The mosaic art of Byzantium was brought to Palermo by the Norman kings and brilliantly incorporated into their buildings.

Outstanding are the Cappella Palatina and Sala di Ruggero (Room of King Roger), both in the Palazzo dei Normanni, the church of the Martorana – full name Santa Maria dell'Ammiraglio (St Mary's of the Admiral) – and the cathedrals at Monreale and Cefalù. They have impressed visitors from Norman times up to the present day and John Julius Norwich, in his history of the Normans in the south, described them as: 'The loveliest and the best. Worth going to Sicily to see.'[1]

The mosaic decoration is the most exciting feature of these monuments. As many of the mosaics in Eastern Europe were destroyed, the Palermo collection is among the finest to have survived from the twelfth century. In Sicily they were first introduced by Roger II and then added to by William I and William II. Once Roger II had established himself as king in 1130 he set about building places of worship suitable for the new monarchy. For decoration he wanted the very best and this came in the form of the mosaic art of Byzantium. So despite the fact that the Hauteville kings were frequently at war with Constantinople, it was from this city that they took inspiration.

These mosaics were initially created by Byzantine craftsmen brought over to Sicily, according to Otto Demus, an authority on the mosaics of Norman Sicily. In considering the import of Byzantine craftsmen, Demus listed the dates when Palermo was at peace with Byzantium, such as in 1143 when Roger II sought the hand of an imperial princess for one of his sons. These dates can be seen to correlate with the periods when the mosaics were set up.[2] Subsequently Sicilian craftsmen learned the technique and made their own contributions.

Mosaic art goes back to the ancient world, when the Romans used it for wall and floor decoration. As the Christian Church expanded in Eastern Europe, new methods of decoration were sought for the glorification of God and to educate a largely illiterate congregation. To meet these needs, a skill was developed using stone and glass cubes to decorate walls and ceilings with religious images. When coloured especially in gold, these images produced a deep, luminous reflection, achieving an effect which made a powerful impact upon the viewer.

As the art progressed, rules were established for the positioning of different religious subjects in an ordered hierarchy. The figure of Christ appeared in the cupola, or on the upper part of the wall above the altar. Scenes from his life were placed one stage lower, with the stories of the saints at a lower level still.

When artists in Constantinople were first called upon to represent Christ they went back to ancient Greek models and produced a figure of youthful beauty recalling Apollo. A second influence appeared, rooted in the Semitic tradition of the Middle East. This depicted Christ in more awesome terms as a mysterious, bearded figure. Over time these influences blended together so that elements of each tradition may be found in the best mosaics. David Talbot Rice, an expert on Byzantine art, summarised this aspect as follows: 'These are the main trends: Hellenic grace, Semitic significance; and the two were blended and attuned to the service of Christianity thanks to Byzantine taste.'[3]

The first full set of religious mosaics depicting the life of Christ was probably set up in Constantinople by Justinian in AD 536–46. The figure of Christ Pantocrator, from the Greek for 'all-powerful' or 'almighty', appeared from the sixth or seventh century onwards, dominating the central domes of churches.

A striking aspect of the Norman monuments is the Muslim influence. As the Normans settled in the city they came to appreciate the Islamic architecture, which was well suited to the climate. The Arabs had ruled Palermo for over 200 years and their builders and craftsmen were well established in the city. Their building methods came directly from Tunisia, from where the Arab emirate had originated, which in turn drew upon architectural principles first established in cities like Cairo and Baghdad. According to these principles an enclosed space was the most important element, putting the emphasis upon the interior rather than the exterior of buildings. A typical Muslim structure consisted of high stone walls with small windows, organised around a central courtyard or garden. Mosques and tombs were among the important buildings on which the crowning glory was the dome. Religious symbolism was strong: 'The dome is, of course, a cosmic symbol in almost every religious tradition, and symbolically, in Islam the dome represents the vault of heaven in the same way as the garden prefigures paradise.'[4]

Intricate decoration using geometric patterns on brightly coloured tiles was used inside buildings on floors and the walls. Ceilings and doors were made in wood that carried detailed carvings. Water was made available for cooling purposes, for washing, for decoration and for irrigating the gardens. These elements, and others common to the Islamic architecture which spread around the Mediterranean and as far afield as India and Afghanistan, became part of Norman Palermo.

While most of the Norman monuments were royal endowments established by Roger II, William I and William II, their first ministers were also represented in the city with their own endowments, in particular George of Antioch, Maio of Bari, Matthew of Ajello and Walter of the Mill.

PALAZZO DEI NORMANNI OR PALAZZO REALE (NORMAN OR ROYAL PALACE)

The entrance to the Palazzo dei Normanni is in Piazza Indipendenza, which lies at the top of Corso Vittorio Emanuele through Porta Nuova. It is at the back of the palace building, the main entrance being on the other side in the modern Piazza del Parlamento. There is not much left of the original Norman exterior due to extensive restructuring over the years. Its position and forbidding walls still demonstrate, however, that it presented a daunting prospect to invaders.

After Palermo was taken by Robert Guiscard and his brother Roger in January 1072, they chose this site as their base. Situated at the highest point of the Cassaro, the ancient city, fortifications had existed here from Phoenician and Carthaginian times, remnants of which can be seen in the basement of the palace. The Arabs built a fort on this site but later their emirs preferred the

Kalsa district down by the port for their palace. Robert Guiscard's successful assault into the Kalsa, which led to the Arab surrender, made it clear that the higher ground offered a stronger defensive position for the Norman headquarters.

Building on the existing Arab fort, the Normans expanded the site until by Roger II's time it had become a fortified palace and residential complex. Inside a walled perimeter were guardhouses, workshops, chapels and living quarters for domestic staff with the royal reception rooms and apartments located on the second floor. There were four towers, the Torre Pisana, Joharia, Kirimbi and Greca. The Torre Pisana, which in Norman times held the treasury, was mentioned in the chronicle of Falcandus in the context of the revolt against William I and must therefore have been built before 1161. The remains of the Torre Pisana, with its solid, square shape, can be seen to the right of the entrance to the palace.

Inside the palace are two famous Norman monuments, the Cappella Palatina and Sala di Ruggero. Access is via a monumental staircase to a loggia overlooking a courtyard, part of the Spanish redesign of the palace. On the wall, near the door into the Cappella Palatina, is a plaque carrying an inscription in Latin, Greek and Arabic, stating that King Roger II ordered a water clock to be made for him in March 1142.

Cappella Palatina (Palatine Chapel)

Upon entering the chapel one is immediately struck by the brilliant colours reflected by the mosaics, the diffused gold light, the myriad figures depicted on the walls and the sheer richness of the decoration. The floor is of marble, inlaid with highly coloured, intricate geometric patterns. The ceiling is of particular note, elaborately carved out of wood, a speciality of Arab craftsmen. It shows scenes from Arab life, including figures from Persian and Indian legend, such as turbaned chess players, soldiers on camels and women riding elephants. It is an intimate setting, built in the form of a small basilica measuring only 32 metres long, with a nave and two aisles separated by fully decorated arches. Maupassant called it 'a jewel of a basilica'.[5]

The Cappella Palatina was built as a private chapel by King Roger II between 1132 and 1140. It was consecrated on Palm Sunday in April 1140 and dedicated to St Peter. The royal apartments were linked to the upper floor of the chapel so that the king had direct access onto the balcony in the north choir.

An inscription on the cupola appears to show that the mosaics at the eastern end were completed in 1143. The mosaics and ornaments of the chapel were later added to by William I, according to the chronicler, Romuald of Salerno.[6] William II was responsible for the decoration of the west wall and for installing the throne. The decorations were thus carried out in three separate stages with magnificent results. As Demus recorded:

> Roger and William I made it a treasure trove of medieval art. Even now, after much spoliation and restoration, its interior is one of the most perfect creations of the Middle Ages, only ceding first rank to the Sainte Chapelle in Paris.[7]

The figure of Christ Pantocrator behind the altar in the main apse has been much restored but still retains its power. The right hand is raised in blessing while the left holds an open Bible showing Christ as the teacher. The letters either side of the figure are symbols for Jesus and Christ, being the Greek first and last letters in these names. The face carries a pensive, melancholy look. Douglas Sladen, an English traveller who wrote extensively on Sicily at the end of the nineteenth century, noted the intensity, concluding that this 'is the face of a founder of a religion'. 'The Christ of the Cappella Reale is exactly the rugged peasant, full of invincible energy, and invincible faith in his mission, with eyes fixed straight on his goal.'[8]

The mosaics in the chapel contain a dense presentation of Bible stories from both the Old and New Testaments interspersed with inscriptions in Greek and Latin. The finest artistic quality is to be found on the east side, for example, in the cupola. Here is another figure of the Pantocrator together with the Archangels Raphael, Michael, Gabriel and Uriel, who are wearing the costumes of the Byzantine court. These mosaics, dating from Roger II's time, were designed and set up by Byzantine craftsmen who may also have worked at Cefalù and the Martorana.[9]

An elaborate marble candlestick carries a portrait of Roger II, in his crown, supporting the seated figure of Christ. It can be found towards the base of the candlestick.

The Cappella Palatina has witnessed many weddings. In 1177 Joanna, daughter of King Henry II of England, was married here to King William II of Sicily by Walter of the Mill, the English archbishop of Palermo. The chapel remains a popular venue for weddings today.

Sala di Ruggero (Room of King Roger)

On the second floor of the palace is another cache of mosaics, this time secular rather than religious in character. They are contained in what is misleadingly called the Sala di Ruggero, for while Roger II appears to have built this part of the palace, known as Joharia, there is no evidence linking him to these mosaics. Indeed nineteenth-century historians like Michele Amari referred to this room as the Sala Normanna ('Norman Room'). The conclusion of Otto Demus was that these mosaics most likely date from between 1160 and 1170, at the end of William I's reign and the beginning of William II's.[10]

The room formed part of the royal apartments and adjoins an impressive hall with a high ceiling, the remains of the Torre Joharia, one of four towers that defended the palace in Norman times. The mosaics appear on the upper half of the walls and over the vaulted ceiling. While more muted in colour than the Cappella Palatina, their impact is nevertheless powerful due to the richness and skill of the designs. They include scenes of huntsmen, hounds and deer amid palm trees, recalling the kings' expeditions into the countryside around Palermo. There are pictures of lions, peacocks and swans, as well as more fanciful, mythological creatures such as griffins. The decoration of the walls and floor is sumptuous with much intricate detail. The style is strongly Muslim, introducing a Persian influence via North Africa. The Sala di Ruggero is one of two sets of secular mosaics in Palermo. The other is in the Palazzo Zisa and stylistically they have much in common.

CHURCH OF SAN GIOVANNI DEGLI EREMITI (ST JOHN OF THE HERMITS)

In Via Benedettini, close to the palace, stands the church of San Giovanni degli Eremiti. Founded by Roger II in 1142 as a Benedictine monastery, it became one of the richest and most important monasteries in the kingdom. The charter of 1148 conferred on the abbot the responsibilities of chaplain and confessor to the court, including to the king himself. There was a cemetery here, of which nothing remains, for members of the court other than the royal family and the top officials.

There is little left of the church's interior, but the building carries on its roof five red cupolas, one of the hallmarks of Norman Sicily. John Julius Norwich describes it as follows:

Of all the Norman churches in Sicily, it is the most characteristic and the most striking, its five vermilion domes – each standing on a cylindrical drum to give it greater height – bursting out from the surrounding greenery like gigantic pomegranates, in almost audible testimony of the Arab craftsmen who built them. They are not beautiful, but they burn themselves into the memory and remain there, stark and vivid, long after many true masterpieces are forgotten."

There are also elegant cloisters and a fountain set in well-kept gardens filled with palm trees and wild flowers. Quiet and peaceful, removed from the bustle of Palermo, the site recalls its monastic origins.

CATTEDRALE (CATHEDRAL)

The cathedral, which at first glance looks more like a fortified Arabian palace than a Christian place of worship, is set back from Corso Vittorio Emanuele, facing a piazza that was once a cemetery. Built in yellow stone with a narrow tower at each corner, it is covered in intricate decoration that continues around the facade to the east side. The west side is joined to the Palazzo Arcivescovile by two Gothic arches. The arcaded porch which surrounds the main entrance was added in the fifteenth century, while the dome, a baroque oddity in this

5. The cathedral – before the dome was added (Bova, eighteenth century).

medieval context, was added in the eighteenth century. A picture in the Palazzo Arcivescovile by an unknown artist shows what the cathedral looked like in its original form (figure 5). Palm trees in the piazza, together with statues of the saints, with Santa Rosalia at the centre, complete the exotic picture. The fact that the cathedral was founded by an Englishman, Walter of the Mill, known in Sicily as Gualtiero Offamilio, makes it all the more remarkable.

Walter came to Palermo as tutor to the royal children and rose up through the ranks to become archbishop and first minister to King William II. He built such a powerful position for himself with the support of leading barons and churchmen that the king, advised by Walter's arch-rival Matthew of Ajello, decided to create a second archbishopric and cathedral at Monreale to curb his power. Not to be outdone, Walter rebuilt the existing one in Palermo making use of Arab builders and craftsmen. Walter was archbishop from 1169 until his death in 1190, when he was succeeded by his brother Bartholomew.

The cathedral was completed in 1185, towards the end of William II's reign, and dedicated to the Assumption of the Virgin Mary. The site had long been used as a place of worship. First there was a Christian church on the site, followed by the Arabs' grand mosque. When the Normans took Palermo in January 1072, the mosque was restored to a Christian church and handed over to the Greek archbishop, Nicodemus. The first cathedral built here by the Normans was linked to the Palazzo dei Normanni by a street with porticoes called Via Coperta.

Taken as a whole, the interior is disappointing, due to alterations carried out in the late eighteenth century, when the Norman structure was replaced with one in a neoclassical style. The interest lies in the individual items on display. Among them from Norman and Hohenstaufen times are the tombs of Roger II, who was crowned king of Sicily in the cathedral in 1130, and his daughter Constance and her husband, the German emperor Henry VI. There is also the tomb of Frederick II, *stupor mundi* ('wonder of the world'), Holy Roman Emperor and king of Sicily (the son of Henry and Constance) and Frederick's first wife, Constance of Aragon. Artefacts discovered in the tombs include Constance of Aragon's crown, made in the royal workshops around 1220. The crypt, which is accessed through the sacristy beyond the treasury, extends for some way below the cathedral. Historic links to the time of the cathedral's foundation include stone tombs, some with elaborate carvings, commemorating the early archbishops. One of these bears the name of Walter of the Mill.

An unusual touch is the inscription of a verse from the Qur'an, in Arabic, carved in the far left-hand column of the porch in front of the main entrance. Presumably this column was part of the material from the Arabs' grand mosque, reused when building the porch.

CHURCH OF SANTA CRISTINA (ST CHRISTINE)

Santa Cristina was the patron saint of Palermo before Santa Rosalia took on this role in 1625. Walter of the Mill founded this church in 1174 upon the site where in 1160 the relics of Santa Cristina were brought into the city down the river Papireto. The simple Norman building is in the form of a square, with solid walls indicating that once they may have supported towers. Internally the church is laid out in a Greek cross, with four pillars and an arched ceiling. The church is to be found at the end of the narrow Strada dei Pellegrini (Street of the Pilgrims), which leads off Via Bonello behind the cathedral. Down the side of the Strada dei Pellegrini runs a stretch of ancient city wall.

CHURCH OF SANTA MARIA DELL'AMMIRAGLIO (ST MARY'S OF THE ADMIRAL), KNOWN AS THE MARTORANA

Close to the Quattro Canti, in the heart of the old city, lies Piazza Bellini. This is an area rich in monuments reflecting many centuries of civic life. On a raised pavement in the piazza stand two Norman churches, the Martorana with its campanile, and San Cataldo (St Catald), identified by its red domes.

The church of St Mary's of the Admiral was founded, built and endowed, the last in 1143, by George of Antioch, Roger II's great admiral. In 1433 it was merged with a nearby Benedictine convent founded by Geoffrey and Eloisa Marturana, from which it took its popular name of the Martorana. George was born of Greek parents in Syria and entered Roger's service in 1112. He rose to become emir of emirs in 1132, a position which combined commander-in-chief with that of first minister. Until his death around 1150 George was the second most powerful man in the kingdom.

The deed of endowment in Greek and Arabic has survived and states that the church was founded by George in honour of the Virgin Mary. Demus tells us that

The founder endowed the church, which he had built and decorated with lavish munificence, according to the wish of the king, with ten Saracen serfs, a village, two fondaca [warehouses], a bakery and a garden in Palermo to provide for the administration of the church and the livings of the future clergy.[12]

The style of the church is Greek, built according to the classic Byzantine ground plan, square in the shape of a cross. It was also influenced by the Islamic building tradition. The nuns and clergy originally appointed to serve there were Greek.

The Martorana dates from the same period as the Cappella Palatina, being built between 1143 and 1151, but is more intimate in style. It contains mosaics of the highest quality, made by craftsmen from Byzantium, the focal point of which is the cupola with the figure of Christ Pantocrator surrounded by the four archangels. Here Christ is shown enthroned and full length. Aspects of the life of the Virgin Mary are displayed, including images of her parents, Joachim and Anna. There are scenes from the Nativity and the lives of the saints, whose names appear in Greek. The vestibule contains Arabic inscriptions and the twelfth-century wooden door is of Arab craftsmanship. The inlaid marble decorations, on the floor and on sections of the walls, are in geometric patterns in the Islamic style.

There are two famous biographical touches in the mosaics. They have been moved from their original positions to either side of the vestibule. On the left the admiral, George, is depicted prostrate before the standing figure of the Virgin Mary. On the right, King Roger is shown being crowned by Christ. Roger wears the ceremonial coat of a Byzantine emperor and receives a Byzantine crown with, above, the Greek inscription *Rogerios Rex*. So while described as king, he was portrayed as an emperor. A similarity between the faces of Christ and Roger has been noted. George and his wife Irene were both buried here.

Ibn Jubayr, an Arab from Spain who visited the church on Christmas Day 1184, when it was at its peak, was most impressed and described it as one of the most wonderful buildings in the world.[13]

After the Greeks left Palermo the church lost its role and came to be used for public meetings. An assembly met here after the Sicilian Vespers to offer the Crown of Sicily to Peter of Aragon. Having been merged with the convent in 1443, the church was abolished as an institution after the unification of Italy.

Additions made to this monument have left it with a mix of styles. While the centre contains the remains of the original church with the mosaics, baroque decoration was placed around the altar and a baroque facade added to the exterior. The campanile dates from the twelfth century.

CHURCH OF SAN CATALDO (ST CATALD)

Next to the Martorana, on the same raised pavement in Piazza Bellini, is the church of San Cataldo. It is named after an Irishman who became bishop of Taranto in the seventh century and who was canonised for his missionary work in southern Italy. Like San Giovanni degli Eremiti, this church, with its three red domes, square shape and pointed windows, is in the Islamic style. It was built in the 1150s by Maio of Bari, emir of emirs to King William I, as the chapel to a sumptuous palace. There is no sign today of the palace. The internal decorations were never completed after Maio's assassination during the barons' revolt in 1160. The interior is simple, Byzantine Greek in shape, with only the floor and altar decorated. On Maio's death it was passed to his successor Silvester and was then granted by William II to Monreale.

CHURCH OF THE SANTISSIMA TRINITÀ (HOLY TRINITY), KNOWN AS THE MAGIONE

The Magione church and monastery complex, which is located in the Kalsa district in Piazza Magione, is approached through a gate and a small formal garden. It was founded by Matthew of Ajello, a senior official under King William I, who became vice chancellor to William II. He was the great rival of Walter of the Mill, the archbishop of Palermo. A late-Norman building, founded around 1150, its construction broadly coincided with that of the Palermo and Monreale cathedrals. Matthew granted the complex to the Cistercian order.

   The church was built in the form of a basilica with three naves divided by columns and a high ceiling in the Gothic style. The facade contains three doorways with the characteristic Norman arches. The church presents another example of the simplicity and purity of Norman design. In the floor can be seen tombs of the Teutonic knights to whom the church was granted by the German emperor, Henry VI, after he captured Palermo in 1194. For the Teutonic knights it became an important staging post for the Crusades. Badly damaged in World War II, the church has been well restored, including the wooden ceiling. To the left of the church is the entrance to a small set of cloisters, one side of which is lined with twin columns and carved capitals showing craftsmanship reminiscent of Monreale.

The well situated in the garden at the centre of the cloisters carries a marble slab with inscriptions in Hebrew. It came from the tomb of a rabbi's son, looted from the Jewish cemetery after the expulsion of the Jews in 1492.

PALAZZO ZISA (ZISA PALACE)

The Palazzo Zisa shows the luxury that the Norman kings created for themselves in their country retreats. It was one of several such buildings in the royal park, known as the Genoard, the others being the Favara, the Cuba, the Cubola and the Cuba Soprana. The Zisa was the greatest of these, built in 1165–7 as a resort in hot weather in the fertile land of the Conca d'Oro. It has been well restored in a garden facing an open space that provides good views of the building. It is to be found outside the historic centre, to the west of the city, at the end of Corso Aprile.

Construction of the Zisa began in the last months of William I's reign and was completed by his son, William II, known for his love of luxury. The contemporary chronicler Romuald of Salerno recorded:

> At that time King William had a large and marvellously designed palace built near Palermo, which he called the Zisa [from the Arabic *al-'Aziz* meaning 'the glorious'] surrounding it with beautiful fruit trees and delightful pleasure gardens, furnished with many streams and splendid fishponds.[14]

Built by Muslim craftsmen, the Zisa is a substantial stone structure on three floors, 25 metres high by 36 metres wide. The simple and somewhat forbidding facade contains small windows, elegant mouldings and doorways. The walls are thick and the whole effect is one of a fortified Arabian palace. The position is superb, facing the sea and with mountains behind, which is reflected in an inscription in the main hall:

> Whenever you wish you can see the most splendid elements in the world, the sea and the mountains, with the great king in residence, magnificent and happy. You are looking at an earthly paradise, the Musta'izz [the eager for glory] and this palace is the Aziz [the glorious].[15]

The grand hall on the ground floor is where the king held court and entertained guests in surroundings of oriental splendour. A fountain in the wall provided a flow of water over marble slabs down the centre over a floor tiled in blue and white. On the wall above the fountain appears a rectangular section of mosaics, featuring palm trees, peacocks and huntsmen with their bows and arrows. These figures are contained within intricate patterns that include illustrations of plants and flowers on a gold background. Around the walls are illustrated panels, one in mosaic, showing blossoms and spreading leaves.

While the mosaics have been much restored, the main features are authentic, according to Demus. Stylistically they stand halfway between the later mosaics of the Cappella Palatina, from the 1150s and 1160s under William I, and those of Monreale in the 1180s. It is likely that at least one of the craftsmen from the Zisa went on to work at Monreale, creating the unique decoration on the north wall. Together with the Sala di Ruggero in the Palazzo dei Normanni, these are the only examples of secular mosaics to have survived in Palermo.[16]

An unusual form of decoration appears above the mosaics, reaching up towards the vaulted ceiling. This is an Islamic device known as a *muqarna*, named after the projecting pieces that resemble stalactites. Developed in the tenth century in Persia and North Africa, the *muqarnas* consist of tiers of pointed niches which were used to decorate domes, cornices and the undersides of arches. While rare in Sicily, a number of examples can be seen in the Zisa. *Muqarnas* also appear in the Cappella Palatina's wooden ceiling.

Among the artefacts on display on the upper floors is a marble tablet with inscriptions in four languages: Greek, Latin, Arabic and Hebrew. The Hebrew is in the form of Arabic Hebrew, as spoken in Palermo, which came from Tunisia. The writing refers to church records of the communities and carries the date of 1148, in the reign of Roger II.

The palace incorporated an early form of air conditioning through a system of terracotta pipes that collected cool breezes on one side of the building and expelled warm air on the other side. Openings in the internal walls ensured a constant flow of air while the thick external walls helped to maintain a steady internal temperature. Water running through the main hall cooled the ground floor while rainwater was collected and stored in marble basins for the rest of the building.

A small chapel of Norman origin dedicated to the Holy Trinity stands next to the Zisa, complete with dome. Simple and unpretentious, it stands in contrast to the opulence of the Palazzo Zisa.

THE CUBA, CUBOLA AND CUBA SOPRANA (ROYAL PAVILIONS)

Corso Calatafimi begins in Piazza Indipendenza and leads to the village of Monreale. About one kilometre along the corso are to be found the remains of royal pavilions that once decorated the royal park in this area. The Cuba, which takes its name from the Arabic for dome, is a kind of mini-palace similar in style to the Zisa. An inscription in Arabic confirms that it was built for William II in 1180. It has the familiar rectangular shape with small windows. Originally it stood on its own in lush countryside facing an artificial lake. The Cuba caught the imagination of Boccaccio, who set one of his stories in *The Decameron* here (day five, tale six). Today the Cuba is surrounded by modern buildings with nothing left inside of note. The Cubola, similar in design but on a small scale, is to be seen nearby, together with the remains of another small pavilion, the Cuba Soprana.

CHURCH OF THE SPIRITO SANTO (HOLY SPIRIT)

The church and convent of the Spirito Santo were built in the reign of King William II between 1173 and 1178 by Walter of the Mill, the English archbishop of Palermo. On the day he laid the foundation stone an eclipse of the sun took place, causing dismay among the superstitious people of Palermo. Being located outside the historic centre, away from the public eye (originally in open countryside, now on Via del Vespro, not far from the central railway station), it escaped the alterations carried out elsewhere in the baroque era. The result is a classic example of Norman architecture, simple and austere in style, with the ground plan designed around three naves. The exterior is noted for its arches and stripes of black lava stone. The church's main claim to fame is that it was here, on 30 March 1282, on open ground facing the church, that the incident took place known as the Sicilian Vespers (see Chapter 7). The public cemetery of Sant'Orsola, which is filled with crowds on popular visiting days, now surrounds the church and contains some domed tombs recalling the city's Muslim past.

PONTE DELL'AMMIRAGLIO (THE ADMIRAL'S BRIDGE)

The Ponte dell'Ammiraglio is to be found not far from the central railway station, heading out of town on the Corso dei Mille. The corso is named after

Garibaldi's Mille (Thousand), as this was the route they took into Palermo. The well-preserved bridge stands out for its fine structure of undressed stone, with seven arches each of a different height, built on the orders of George of Antioch in 1113. Once it spanned the river Oreto, which has since been diverted underground. Apart from its founder, the bridge is famous for being the place where Garibaldi's army first encountered Bourbon troops in the battle for Palermo on 27 May 1860. A solid medieval construction, the bridge stands isolated today amid the ugly modern debris of the city's outskirts.

CHURCH OF SAN GIOVANNI DEI LEBBROSI (ST JOHN OF THE LEPERS)

Just beyond the Ponte dell'Ammiraglio, off Corso dei Mille, stands one of the earliest Norman monuments, the church of San Giovanni dei Lebbrosi. Situated in a small park with palm trees, the church has a simple interior and a Muslim-style exterior with red domes.

It is traditionally thought to have been built by Roger I in 1072 as one of the first Norman buildings in Palermo, based on the conclusions of the Sicilian historian, Tommaso Fazello. According to John Julius Norwich, when the Normans were besieging Palermo in 1071 and Roger was waiting for the arrival of Robert Guiscard's fleet, he captured a small Arab fort at the mouth of the river Oreto. After he had taken Palermo and in thanks for his victory, Roger built this church on the site of the fort, traces of which remain in the garden. A hospital for lepers was later built here, which gave the church its name. The remains of the hospital can be seen nearby. In this setting the church seems to present a direct link to its Norman past.[17]

Outside Palermo

CATTEDRALE DI MONREALE (CATHEDRAL OF MONREALE)

The cathedral and Benedictine monastery built in the village of Monreale, three kilometres above Palermo, is the largest of all the Norman monuments in Sicily. It can be reached by bus from Piazza Indipendenza. In the 1150s Roger II built a park and a castle in the area, which became known as Monte Regali, later shortened to Monreale. The cathedral was founded in 1174 by William II, advised by his vice chancellor Matthew of Ajello, as a means of countering the power of the first minister and archbishop of Palermo, Walter of the Mill. The site was chosen because it was part of the royal domain and for the presence of an old Greek chapel, which provided continuity and paved the way for the new foundation.

The cathedral was dedicated to the Madonna, who, according to the legend, appeared to William in a dream telling him where to find treasure with which to build it. The original endowment of August 1176 conferred on the cathedral possessions that included castles, mills, churches, properties in Palermo and fisheries on the coast. Many of the properties came from the cathedral in Palermo, thus reducing Walter's portfolio. A hundred Benedictine monks arrived in the same year to staff the new monastery. More possessions and privileges followed until the wealth of Monreale was established. In 1183 the Pope made it an archbishopric and a cathedral. The death of King William in November 1189 brought its expansion to an end. William was buried in the cathedral but shortly afterwards the Palermo cathedral reasserted its position as the prime archbishopric in Sicily. A steady decline in Monreale's fortunes followed.

The cathedral was a vast enterprise, motivated by political considerations and, perhaps for that reason, combined with the fact that it lay further from the royal court, lacks the personal appeal of the Cappella Palatina or the Martorana. It is, however, hugely impressive, and together with its cloisters constitutes one of the finest examples of medieval building in Europe. While the exterior has been much restored and altered, the interior is authentic.

The mosaics, which were completed in 1183–9, represent the largest and most important collection from the twelfth century that has come down to us. They cover stories from the Old and New Testaments which taken together constitute a picture gallery in brightly coloured and well-preserved mosaics, carried out by master craftsmen from Byzantium. In the central apse is the huge figure of Christ Pantocrator, above the image of the Madonna, surrounded by the archangels, prophets and apostles. Some personal touches are included. Among the saints is Thomas Becket, portrayed not long after his martyrdom in 1170, and featured for the English connection through William's wife, Joanna, daughter of Henry II. There is a scene of William dedicating a model of the cathedral to the Madonna.

In contrast to the richness and colour of the cathedral's interior, the Benedictine cloisters next door, also commissioned by William, provide an atmosphere of peace and tranquillity. Below a row of Norman–Arab arches, elegant twin columns carry capitals with a fanciful variety of carvings, human heads, animals and birds, the work of expert craftsmen. The columns in both the cloisters and the cathedral come from ancient buildings in mainland Italy. In one corner of the cloisters stands an unusual, Muslim-style fountain. On the capital of a column next to the fountain can be seen a carving of a Norman knight, complete with characteristic helmet and shield.

CATTEDRALE DI CEFALÙ (CATHEDRAL OF CEFALÙ)

Cefalù is a small town occupying a point of land stretching out to sea, located some 70 kilometres from Palermo along the north coast of Sicily. The cathedral was built here on the orders of Roger II, with work starting in summer 1131. It was richly endowed by the king to ensure its complete independence. Building took place in stages, with the basis completed in Roger's time and additions made by William I and William II. The front towers were added in 1240.

In common with other medieval churches there is a founding legend, according to which Roger found himself in a storm at sea, in danger of his life, when returning from southern Italy. He took an oath that if he survived he would found a cathedral at the place where he landed and dedicate it to the Saviour and saints Peter and Paul. When the storm subsided the ship came ashore at Cefalù. The legend hides the true motive for founding the church and a bishopric at Cefalù. This was probably to please Pope Anacletus. It may have been part of the 1130 settlement when Roger was crowned king by the Pope.

The interior has received many additions, especially in the baroque era, but remains exceptional for its mosaics. Carried out by craftsmen brought over by Roger from Byzantium, the decoration in the main apse is of the highest quality. The same craftsmen probably worked on the mosaics in the Cappella Palatina and at the Martorana. The figure of the Pantocrator, which, according to an inscription, was complete by 1148, is especially memorable.

Roger was fond of his cathedral at Cefalù and had a sarcophagus prepared for himself there. He was, however, buried in the cathedral in Palermo. In later Norman times Cefalù fell out of favour, with precedence going to Monreale.

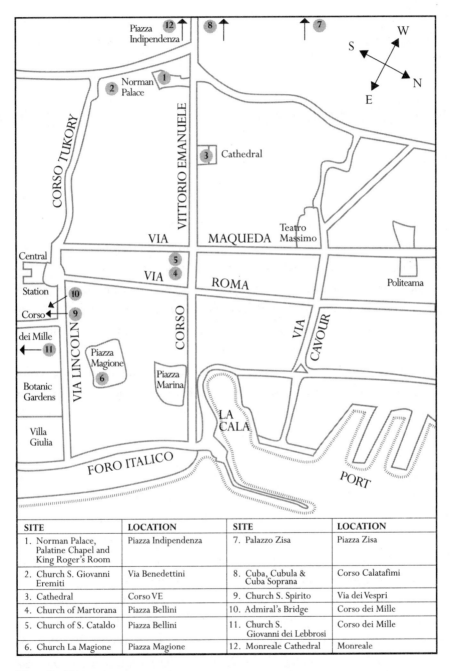

SITE	LOCATION	SITE	LOCATION
1. Norman Palace, Palatine Chapel and King Roger's Room	Piazza Indipendenza	7. Palazzo Zisa	Piazza Zisa
2. Church S. Giovanni Eremiti	Via Benedettini	8. Cuba, Cubula & Cuba Soprana	Corso Calatafimi
3. Cathedral	Corso VE	9. Church S. Spirito	Via dei Vespri
4. Church of Martorana	Piazza Bellini	10. Admiral's Bridge	Corso dei Mille
5. Church of S. Cataldo	Piazza Bellini	11. Church S. Giovanni dei Lebbrosi	Corso dei Mille
6. Church La Magione	Piazza Magione	12. Monreale Cathedral	Monreale

Map 9 Norman monuments.

CHAPTER 15

Baroque Palermo

The baroque art movement that emerged in Rome around 1600 changed the face of cities with its theatrical style. It was adopted by the Catholic Church, for baroque art with its strongly emotional appeal could deliver a religious message to a wide audience. The power of art to impress was also recognised by the aristocracy, who welcomed the new style with open arms.

Conditions in Sicily were particularly conducive to the introduction of the baroque style through the presence of wealthy patrons. The viceroys spent lavishly on their redesign of the city's centre. The Church, controlled by the Inquisition, became wealthy through the confiscation of property from citizens under arrest. Generous resources were available to build chapels and to commission works of art, for example in honour of Santa Rosalia. Another level of Church patronage came from the religious orders, of which there were many in Sicily, led by the Dominicans and Franciscans. The orders raised funds by selling places at their monasteries and convents. These places were in demand by the aristocracy who, rather than break up the inheritance of their estates, sent their younger sons and daughters into the Church.

Under the Spanish, the aristocracy was at the peak of its power and dominated the economy through its ownership of large estates. A trend developed in the second half of the seventeenth century for the barons to move to Palermo, the seat of the viceroy and his court, where they built sumptuous palaces. By 1800 there were more than 300 palaces in the city. Baroque art, in its different forms, suited these patrons and became the dominant style of Palermo.

Sicilian baroque developed through an early provincial phase to a more sophisticated approach led by architects trained in Rome, to arrive at a distinctive creativity all of its own.

The Sicilian architects were professionals, as described by the art historian Anthony Blunt:

> Most of them were experts in mathematics, perspective, astronomy or the art of fortification, and wrote treatises on these subjects, more indeed than their contemporaries on the mainland; but they were also Sicilian, and they used their intellect to produce buildings in which the energy and imagination of the south attained full and mature expression.[1]

Sicilian baroque reached its peak in eastern Sicily, where whole city centres were rebuilt following the earthquake of 1693. It is to be seen at its best in Noto, Ragusa and Modica, in the churches designed by the architect Rosario Gagliardi, and in Andrea Palma's facade for the cathedral in Syracuse.

The outstanding baroque monuments in Palermo, those not to be missed, are to be found in the interiors of churches and oratories. In the churches, work with inlaid and coloured marble was taken to a fine art, which, according to Blunt, 'must be classed amongst the most important and original creations of baroque art on the island'.[2] The finest interiors are those in the churches of San Giuseppe dei Teatini, the Casa Professa, Santa Caterina and the Immacolata Concezione. In the three oratories decorated by Giacomo Serpotta, the use of stucco to portray life-size and smaller human figures represents one of the artistic highlights of Palermo. These are the oratories of Santa Cita, San Lorenzo and San Domenico.

The artistic talent that developed in Palermo was inspired by work done in Rome and Naples and was influenced by artists from Italy and northern Europe who were attracted to the city. Caravaggio stayed in Palermo for a short while in 1609 and left his *Nativity with Saints Lawrence and Francis* in the oratory of San Lorenzo, from where it was stolen in 1969. Van Dyck was in Palermo during the plague in 1624–5, and after leaving the city painted an altarpiece, the *Madonna of the Rosary*, for the oratory of San Domenico. In the early eighteenth century the Flemish painter Guglielmo Borremans worked in Palermo in churches and the palaces of the aristocracy.

The most prominent architects of the baroque era in Palermo were Paolo Amato and Giacomo Amato, who were not related. Paolo made his name with designs for Santa Rosalia's *festino* and was made official architect to the senate in 1686. Giacomo, who began his career as Paolo's pupil, worked in Rome for over ten years before returning to Palermo to make a major contribution to the regeneration of the city. Pietro Novelli of Monreale, who trained in Naples and visited Rome, was the outstanding painter of the period. He supplied many works of art to the churches and palaces of Palermo before becoming court painter to Philip IV of Spain. His daughter, Rosalia, was also a talented artist. Other painters of note, whose frescoes and altarpieces adorn the churches, include Filippo Randazzo, known as 'Il Monocolo' because he had only one eye; Filippo Paladini, of Tuscan origin; Giacomo Lo Verde, who studied under Novelli; and Giuseppe Velasco, born in Palermo of Spanish parents, who became one of the city's most popular artists. The Sicilians worked in family groups and established workshops, some of which became schools which continued for generations.

The Serpotta family, in particular Giacomo and his son Procopio, represented the peak of the local tradition in sculpture. Working in stucco, Giacomo developed a distinctive style of natural, richly decorated figures. Less expensive and lighter than marble, stucco enabled a profusion of figures to be displayed on chapel walls and ceilings. A high degree of skill and dexterity was needed, for stucco dried quickly, leaving only a short time to complete the modelling. A shine was given to the surface of the Serpotta statues by the addition of marble dust to the stucco. In his designs Giacomo Serpotta learned from the work of the Gagini family, the most prominent sculptors in fifteenth- and sixteenth-century Palermo. The Gagini imported white marble from Carrara, in Tuscany, and produced exceptional work. From the Gagini Giacomo Serpotta took the idea of combining full-size figures with smaller, inset reliefs to tell a story. This technique has its origins in the metopes, carved stone panels with which the ancient Greeks decorated their temples. Other notable sculptors at work in the city were Gregorio Tedeschi, born in Florence, who produced statues of the saints, and Ignazio Marabitti, who became well known in the eighteenth century for his fountains.

As well as in the churches and palaces around the city, work by these artists and many others can be seen in the art galleries, the Museo Diocesano (Diocesan Museum) in the Palazzo Arcivescovile next to the cathedral, and the Palazzo Abatellis in Via Alloro (see Chapter 17).

Supplying the architects in the building of these monuments were the craftsmen who developed high-level skills in a range of disciplines. Decorative ironwork was produced for balconies, intricate silverware to contain holy relics, carved woodwork for ceilings and furniture and ceramics for flooring. In addition there was work in marble, glass and fabrics. Workshops were spread across the city, employing a large number of craftsmen who were quick to adapt new techniques learned from abroad.

The baroque style became so accepted that it was considered suitable for additions to older monuments. Interiors of medieval churches received baroque alterations and additions were made to the exteriors of Norman buildings, such as the Martorana church, which was given a new facade, and the cathedral, which had a dome placed on its roof.

Palermo shares something with one of its most famous churches, the Casa Professa – whose name literally means 'the house where you come to profess your faith' – in which not an inch is left undecorated. Similarly, the centre of Palermo is literally crammed with historic buildings, a treasure trove for visitors. One estimate suggests that it contains 150 churches, 28 oratories and more than 200 palaces, the majority from the baroque era.[3] What follows is an introduction to some of the most important. There are many more monuments of interest and one of the pleasures of visiting Palermo is that there is always something new to discover.

The city as theatre

Baroque was much more than a design style for churches and palaces. It embraced the concept of the city as theatre, a place for people to gather and to take part in great ceremonies and festivals. The baroque style with its flamboyant decoration was applied to the city's open spaces, its streets and squares, as well as to the facades of its buildings, to be enjoyed by just walking around.

QUATTRO CANTI (FOUR CORNERS)

When the Spanish redesigned Palermo at the beginning of the seventeenth century, the monument known as Quattro Canti was built at the heart of the city at the intersection of the two main roads, Toledo and Maqueda. Via Toledo, the ancient Cassaro, was extended to the sea and Via Maqueda was built at right angles, dividing the city into four quarters. In the nineteenth century Via Toledo was renamed Corso Vittorio Emanuele. The monument, which was built between

1608 and 1621 on the orders of the viceroy, the Duke of Vigliena, was designed by Giulio Lasso. Octagonal in shape, it consists of four separate, curved facades, each containing a fountain and statues at three levels. Above are a coat of arms and an eagle, the symbol of the city. Each section represents a quarter of the city (Albergheria, Seralcadio, Kalsa and Loggia) and is decorated with statues of the seasons, the Spanish kings of Sicily and the quarters' patron saints (Cristina, Agata, Oliva and Ninfa). It is a complex monument that bears close scrutiny, not made easy by the restricted size of the busy piazza. At the Quattro Canti, looking up and down Corso Vittorio Emanuele, can be seen the two monumental gates that enclose the city, with the sea at one end and the mountains at the other.

PORTA NUOVA

At the far end of Corso Vittorio Emanuele, the entrance to the historic centre is through the Porta Nuova. It stands next to the Palazzo dei Normanni and has an unusual mix of styles, an imposing gate beneath an elegant loggia capped by a pyramid-shaped roof. It was built in 1583 to celebrate the entrance of Charles V to the city after his victory in Tunisia.

Four huge figures on the far side of the gate represent his African prisoners. Another monument to Charles V stands in Piazza Bologni, further down the corso, a bronze statue from 1631 by Scipione Li Volsi.

PORTA FELICE

Porta Felice closes the city at the other end down by the sea. It was built after the ancient road, the Cassaro, was continued to the sea and renamed Via Toledo. The viceroy, Marcantonio Colonna, had the gate built and named after his wife, Felice Orsini. Work began in 1582 but was not completed until 1637 due to the viceroy's departure from Sicily. During the *festino* of Santa Rosalia on 15 July her huge, highly decorated carriage with the saint's statue on top passes through the gate. Colonna's project included creating a seaside promenade along the Marina, which in the eighteenth century became the favourite place for the aristocracy to spend the evening. Pavilions were placed here to accommodate spectators, who enjoyed musical recitals and firework displays. International visitors like Brydone and Goethe commented on the pleasant nature of such evenings by the sea. Through the gate, just inside the city, lies the Fontana del Cavallo Marino (Sea Horse Fountain) by Marabitti. To the right of Porta Felice, when facing the sea, are steps leading up through iron gates to a raised terrace that runs parallel to the seafront. On the right is the garden and long facade of the Palazzo Butera, one of the largest palaces in Palermo, built in the eighteenth century, when the power of the princes of Butera was at its peak.

Churches

CATTEDRALE (CATHEDRAL)

The cathedral was radically altered between 1781 and 1801 by a disastrous project, designed in 1767 by Ferdinando Fuga, on the orders of the Bourbon king of Naples, Ferdinand IV. The dome, totally out of keeping with the original design, was added in this period. Internally the basilica design was changed into that of a Latin cross with the addition of new columns. The decoration was redone in neoclassical style, resulting in the characterless effect we find today. The interest lies in the chapels and the items on display. Important for the baroque era is the chapel of Santa Rosalia, situated to the right of the main altar. Here can be seen the silver urn from 1631 containing the saint's relics and the ornate silver statue of the saint, standing upon a large silver casket. In the nave are statues of the saints by Antonello Gagini, as well as two decorative stoups, vessels containing holy water, one attributed to Gagini. In the chapel to the right of the main entrance can be seen an altarpiece by Pietro Novelli. Much of the sculpture that was removed from the cathedral by Fuga, including some of Antonello Gagini's finest work, is on display in the Museo Diocesano in the Palazzo Arcivescovile (see Chapter 17). The statue of Santa Rosalia defeating the plague, in front of the cathedral, is by Vincenzo Vitagliano from 1744.

CHURCH OF SAN DOMENICO (ST DOMINIC)

The church of San Domenico, with its baroque yellow-and-white facade and twin towers, is one of the famous sights of Palermo. Facing it, in the piazza off Via Roma, stands the column and monument to the Immaculate Virgin. The church is located in the Loggia quarter of the city and behind the church, going down towards the sea, is where the Genoese merchants were once established. The

Dominicans made this site their base for a church and a monastery from 1300. The current church was built in 1640 by the architect and Dominican Andrea Cirrincione. The facade, which was completed in 1726, contains niches with statues of the saints and popes by Giacomo Serpotta's grandson, Giovanni Maria. The interior is vast and austere and is laid out in classic style with three naves. Deep chapels line each side. The notable works of art include an altarpiece of San Domenico by Filippo Paladini and paintings of San Vincenzo, by Giuseppe Velasco, and of Sant'Anna, attributed to Rosalia Novelli. San Domenico is Palermo's second church, coming after the cathedral, and contains the tombs of many famous Sicilians, including Francesco Crispi, Michele Amari and Pietro Novelli. Adjoining the church, with access from the nave to the left of the altar, stand the fourteenth-century cloisters (figure 6). Built with twin columns and decorated capitals, they demonstrate the early style of the San Domenico complex.

6. Cloisters of the church of San Domenico (St Dominic)
(William Leighton Leitch, 1841).

CHURCH OF SAN GIUSEPPE DEI TEATINI (ST JOSEPH OF THE
THEATINES)

This church is among the best expressions of baroque in Palermo, considered
by Blunt to be the most impressive of the seventeenth-century churches in the
city. It was founded by the Theatine order in 1612, with the support of the viceroy, and was built by the Genoese architect Giacomo Besio. The structure was
completed by 1645, while internal decoration continued for another 150 years.
The walls and chapels carry marble decorations and the high ceiling contains
frescoes as well as full-sized figures in stucco. The floor is of coloured marble
and there is some fine woodwork. With its grandiose interior, gold decoration
and massive columns, it gives the impression of great wealth. There are many
fine works of art. There are paintings by Pietro Novelli, Guglielmo Borremans
and Giuseppe Velasco, sculpture by Ignazio Marabitti, stucco figures by Procopio
Serpotta and an altar by Andrea Palma. The church is capped by a majestic
cupola, while the south-east corner carries a curious, unfinished campanile by
Paolo Amato, both of which can be admired from Piazza Pretoria on the other
side of Via Maqueda.

CHURCH OF THE GESÙ (JESUS), ALSO KNOWN AS THE CASA
PROFESSA

In the interior of the Casa Professa – literally meaning 'the house where you
come to profess your faith' – decoration is taken to extremes with no space
left untouched. The sheer profusion of brightly coloured marble and stucco
figures is both fascinating and overwhelming. The church was founded by the
Jesuit order in 1564 on ground once filled with caves made by the Kemonia
river. It is thought that there were early Christian catacombs here. The Jesuit
order, founded in Spain by Ignatius Loyola, was invited to Sicily in 1547 by the
viceroy Juan Vega. Building of the church went on until 1683, with decoration
continuing into the eighteenth century. It is a masterpiece of complex baroque
design. Patrick Brydone, the Scottish traveller, marvelled at it on his visit to
Palermo in 1770, commenting: 'The Jesuit church is equal in magnificence to
anything I have seen in Italy. The genius of these fathers appears strong in all
their works; one is never at a loss to find them out.'[4]

The church is covered with colourful inlaid marble and stucco figures by

Giacomo and Procopio Serpotta. There are paintings by Pietro Novelli, his daughter Rosalia and Filippo Randazzo, and a statue of the Madonna from the Gagini school. The pictures down the right side show the life of Mary, and down the left the Passion of Christ. There are scenes from the Bible in painted glass while semi-precious stone was used on some of the altars.

In the crypt are the remains of an early Christian chapel, a simple white-washed cave carved out of the rock. A faded picture of the Madonna and child and two Christian symbols can be made out on the walls. The symbols are IHS and INRI. The IHS monogram is a shortening of Jesus' name in Greek to the first three letters and was used by the Jesuits on their emblem. INRI stands for the initials, in Latin, of 'Jesus of Nazareth. King of the Jews', which was the sign placed above Christ's head on the cross.

CHURCH OF SANTA CATERINA (ST CATHERINE)

Another example of a sumptuously decorated church, Santa Caterina was built between 1580 and 1596 for the Dominican order, next to their monastery. The church's large cupola was added in the eighteenth century. Near the entrance two Solomonic columns in red marble support the nun's choir, their twisted shape recalling Gian Lorenzo Bernini's work in Rome.[5] Over the arches leading to the chapels, stucco reliefs are displayed illustrating the life of Santa Caterina of Alexandria, to whom is dedicated the altar in the right transept, designed by Andrea Palma. The four figures of saints below the cupola are by Giambattista Ragusa and the statue of Caterina is by Antonello Gagini. To be noted are the scenes from the Old Testament created with inlaid marble. In one scene, 'Jonah Thrown into the Sea', a huge whale is ready to swallow the prophet, with a ship nearby riding the storm, all in vivid colours. Blunt described it as follows:

> The richness and brilliance of the marbling is astonishing, and yet the whole effect is consistent and in no way vulgar. The main lines of the architecture are left so clearly visible and so sharply defined that they impose an order on the exuberant colour and carving. This is indeed Sicilian Baroque in one of its most typical manifestations.[6]

CHURCH OF THE IMMACOLATA CONCEZIONE (IMMACULATE CONCEPTION)

This church, to be found in the Capo market, is one of the most beautiful in the city. It was built between 1604 and 1612, with work on the decoration going on for over a century, creating a fanciful interior filled with stucco, marble, frescoes, precious stone and ornate metalwork. It represented an extraordinary display of wealth in this poor quarter of the city. Notable works of art include an altarpiece by Pietro Novelli honouring the Immaculate Conception; a dramatic painting of the *Miracle of St Benedict* by Giuseppe Velasco; and a statue of Santa Rosalia, flanked by two red Solomonic columns, by Nicola Viviano. The statue was sculpted in 1630, only five years after Santa Rosalia became the city's patron saint. The walls of the church are covered with intricate decoration in stucco and marble, including figures of the saints. There are some especially fine examples of multicoloured marble inlays telling stories from the Bible. On either side of the altar appear statues of popes from Palermo.

CHURCH OF SANTA TERESA ALLA KALSA (ST TERESA AT THE KALSA)

The tall facade of this church dominates Piazza Kalsa down by the sea. A good example of Sicilian baroque with a Roman influence, the church was built for the Carmelite order, who had a convent nearby, by Giacomo Amato between 1686 and 1706. The sculptures of the Holy Family which occupy niches in the facade are by Cristoforo Milanti. The interior contains statues by Giuseppe and Procopio Serpotta from the early 1700s, and in a chapel is a painting of St Teresa by Borremans. The fine marble floor with its geometric designs was made to a design by Giacomo Amato.

Oratories

ROSARIO DI SANTA CITA (ROSARY OF ST CITA)

An oratory was a confraternity established by an order of the Church. It constituted a kind of rich man's club, with strict rules, where members could

attend ceremonies and services in a private chapel. This oratory, established by
Dominicans, was devoted to the rosary, the Catholic prayer ritual, and to the
veneration of the Madonna. Access to the building is by an attractive garden
and loggia and through a reception room containing portraits of the oratory's
superiors. The chapel has kept its original baroque aspect as decorated by
Giacomo Serpotta in 1685–8 and Michele Rosciano in 1707. The altarpiece,
The Madonna of the Rosary, is by Carlo Maratta. The walls are covered in life-
size, allegorical figures and narrative panels illustrating themes such as the
mysteries of the rosary. On the end wall is a panel recording the victory at
Lepanto, a naval battle in 1571 in which the Christian fleet with a Sicilian
contingent defeated the Turks. The divine intervention of the Madonna of
the Rosary in gaining the victory is acknowledged in the scene above the
battle. In his use of stucco Serpotta created a new art form, according to
Sacheverell Sitwell,

> Giacomo Serpotta being one of those sculptors who lifted a minor art quite out
> of itself into an eminence of its own where it can exist apart from architecture,
> and indeed for no other reason. His facility is astonishing; flowers and fruits
> of stucco grow and burgeon from his hand, and there are full length female
> figures by him that are tall and graceful as women's portraits by Thomas
> Gainsborough.[7]

SAN LORENZO (ST LAWRENCE)

Located near the church of San Francesco d'Assisi (St Francis of Assisi), this
elegant oratory was built by the Company of St Francis and decorated by
Giacomo Serpotta between 1699 and 1706. This is Serpotta once again at
his imaginative best, representing a high point of Sicilian sculpture. Eight
life-size figures represent the Virtues such as Faith and Humility, one of
them suckling her baby. Panels tell the story of the lives of St Francis and
St Lawrence. A full panel at the far end is dedicated to the martyrdom of St
Lawrence. All around are dozens of *putti*, lively cherubs enjoying themselves
in a variety of ways. The altar is the work of Serpotta from a design by the
architect Giacomo Amato. The wooden seating down the sides of the oratory carries engravings and inlays in mother-of-pearl. The floor in coloured
marble recalls the Norman chapels.

ROSARIO DI SAN DOMENICO (ROSARY OF ST DOMINIC)

The oratory of San Domenico, which stands behind the church of the same name, contains some of the outstanding works of art in Palermo. It was established in the late sixteenth century by the Company of the Rosary, which represented leading merchants and artists and counted Novelli and Serpotta among its members. The chapel is dominated by Anthony Van Dyck's altarpiece, the *Madonna of the Rosary*. Commissioned before Van Dyck left Palermo in 1625, it was painted in Genoa and delivered in 1628. The Madonna is shown offering a rosary to St Dominic, whose hand is raised to accept it. Two other Dominican saints are depicted, Vincent and Catherine of Siena, as well as the five female saints of Palermo: Rosalia, Ninfa, Cristina, Agata and Oliva. Around the walls are important works by Pietro Novelli and his school, the school of Van Dyck, Giacomo Lo Verde and Guglielmo Borremans.

Giacomo Serpotta was given the task of adding his stucco decoration to the oratory in the early 1700s and he responded with his usual virtuosity. Among the statues are 12 life-size figures representing the Virtues (Charity, Humility, Peace, and so on), aristocratic-looking young women modelled with great skill. They demonstrate a familiarity with Roman baroque sculpture, implying that as a young man Giacomo spent time in Rome.[8] He left his trademark in the shape of a lizard on the right-hand side of the chapel. It appears on a gold column next to the Virtue Fortitude. The dialect name for lizard was *sirpuzza*, a play on Serpotta's own name.

Palaces

Unlike the churches, which for the most part have been maintained and are open to the public, many of the palaces have fallen into disrepair. The financial crisis of the aristocracy led to the number of inhabited palaces falling from around 200 in 1800 to 20 in 1900. The fate of the individual palaces since then has varied greatly. Some have been restored as art galleries and museums (for example, the Palazzo Abatellis and the Palazzo Arcivescovile – see Chapter 17) or are used by local government. Others have been divided into apartments and sold as private residences. Many have just been left abandoned, their magnificent facades the only reminder of their original status. Enough are accessible

to demonstrate the amazing wealth and splendour of Palermo's aristocracy in
the baroque era.

PALAZZO DEI NORMANNI OR PALAZZO REALE (NORMAN OR ROYAL PALACE)

The Palazzo dei Normanni became the seat of the Spanish viceroys in the mid
1550s. Before that, they were based in the Palazzo Chiaramonte in Piazza
Marina, which was taken over by the Inquisition. The radical rebuilding of the
Palazzo dei Normanni, which had fallen into disrepair, went on at the same
time as the redesign of the city centre. It was all part of turning Palermo into
a prestigious city worthy of the viceroys. The Norman towers of the palace
were taken down, the front facade was refurbished and courtyards, loggias,
reception rooms and apartments were added. The palace from Spanish times
is best viewed from the front in Piazza Vittoria, with its grandiose monument
to the Bourbon king Philip V, known as the 'the marble theatre'.

For visitors, the entrance is at the back in Piazza Indipendenza, where a
ramp leads to a gate and then up a monumental staircase to the first floor.
Here can be seen the magnificent courtyard, with its three stories of elegant
loggias, created by the viceroy Maqueda in 1600. Entrance to the Cappella
Palatina (described in Chapter 14) is on this floor. On the second floor is the
Sala d'Ercole (Room of Hercules), started in 1560 and decorated in 1799 with
paintings of the labours of Hercules by Giuseppe Velasco. Today this room is
where the Sicilian government meets. There follows a ballroom, private apartments and the Sala dei Viceré (Room of the Viceroys), which contains portraits
of viceroys, including Caracciolo, from 1754 to 1837. The Sala di Ruggero is
also on this floor (see Chapter 14). The designs of the Spanish were on a grand
scale and the rooms look worthy of royalty.

The palace passed from the Spanish viceroys to the viceroys of the Bourbon
kings of Naples, with a short period in between. In 1947 it became the seat of
Sicily's Regional Government.

PALAZZO BRANCIFORTE

This enormous palace was built in the seventeenth century by Nicolo Branciforte
and enlarged by his son Giuseppe. It was one of the sumptuous residences,

typical of the Sicilian barons, built in the centre of the city alongside the houses of the poor. Its two entrances led to three internal courtyards. The palace is to be found in Via Bara all'Olivella between Via Roma and Via Cavour. Damaged during World War II, it was acquired by the Banco di Sicilia, which has recently completed an outstanding work of renovation. The palace can now be seen once more in all its glory, with its vast halls, reception rooms and courtyards restored to prime condition.

It contains a number of exhibitions, featuring collections owned by the bank's charitable foundation. These include a large number of ancient Greek artefacts from western Sicily, originally owned by the archaeologist Vincenzo Tusa; a library; some modern paintings and a collection of prints, drawings, coins and stamps.

PALAZZO MIRTO

Here one can see how the aristocracy actually lived, for this palace was donated intact to the Regional Government in 1982, complete with furniture and personal bric-a-brac. It was the property of the Filangieri family, counts of San Marco, from the seventeenth century and is located in Via Merlo. Note the decorative eighteenth-century gateway and iron balconies curved outwards to accommodate the skirts of the ladies. This was the Filangieri town residence. In the summer they retired to a villa in the countryside at Bagheria.

The well-kept interior is approached by a marble staircase leading to reception rooms on the first floor, the *piano nobile*. The living rooms are on the second floor. There is a dining room for 24 people, a large ballroom, a 'Chinese' room, all the rage in nineteenth-century Palermo, a bathroom with a family crest, sitting rooms and bedrooms. It is an authentic residence filled with period furniture, pictures, books, Capodimonte porcelain and Murano glass. Some of the family were evidently keen travellers and brought back many souvenirs. On the ground floor are the stables, still complete with horseboxes and carriages, which originally had gates onto two different streets.

PALAZZO COMITINI

This huge palace was built by the architect Nicola Palma, in 1766–71, as the residence of the Prince of Comitini, mayor of Palermo. Today it houses local government offices. The entrance is through two large courtyards that open onto Via Maqueda. A grand staircase in red and white marble leads to reception rooms on the first floor, which include a vast ballroom with a chandelier in Murano glass and an elegant salon lined with mirrors. The second floor, which contained the private apartments, includes a small room lined in ceramics, belonging to the princess. There are decorative ironwork balconies and coloured marble floors, as well as a floor covered in painted tiles.

PALAZZO VALGUARNERA-GANGI

This palace first belonged to the princes of Valguarnera and then to the Gangi. It was built in stages during the eighteenth century and was completed in 1780. It occupies a whole block, with its entrance through a decorative portal in Piazzetta Croce dei Vespri. Its long facade with its balconies runs down Via Teatro Santa Cecilia, while a terrace overlooks Piazza Sant'Anna. In 1750 the interior was decorated in Sicilian baroque style by Marianna Valguarnera, who filled it with ornate furniture by local craftsmen. The *piano nobile*, on the first floor, contains a famous gallery of mirrors; a salon decorated with the fresco called *Triumph of Virtues Necessary for a Prince* by Gaspare Serenario and a dining room containing panels painted by Giuseppe Velasco. The director Luchino Visconti used the palace as the setting for the famous ballroom scene in his 1963 film of *The Leopard*.

PALAZZO LANZA TOMASI

Giuseppe Tomasi di Lampedusa, Duke of Palma and Prince of Lampedusa, was brought up in the family palace next to the oratory of Santa Cita. In April 1943 the palace was destroyed by Allied bombing and is currently being restored. In 1948 Lampedusa bought an eighteenth-century property facing the seafront at 28 Via Butera, where he lived until his death in 1957. It was here that he wrote his historical novel, *The Leopard*. The property, which has a magnificent view overlooking a terrace towards the sea, has been fully restored by Lampedusa's adopted son, Gioacchino Lanza Tomasi. A number of elegant reception rooms, filled with sunlight, are decorated with furnishings from the belle époque. Much of the library came from the original family palace. Next to the palace is the building that once housed the Trinacria Hotel, where in the novel the prince ends his days.

Outside Palermo

Once established in Palermo, the aristocracy began to build elaborate villas for themselves in the surrounding countryside. There they could escape from the heat of the city, *in villeggiatura* ('on holiday'), surrounded by ornamental gardens, vineyards, orange and lemon groves. Two areas were preferred: the Piana dei Colli, the valley running from Palermo to Mondello, and the village of Bagheria, around 15 kilometres from the city. A new style of elaborate country retreat appeared, typically with a central building flanked by curved wings containing stables. A characteristic feature was a double outside staircase leading to the main entrance. There are many such villas, in varying states of repair, dotted around what was once the countryside. Two examples, both normally open to the public, are the villas Cattolica and Palagonia in Bagheria. Bagheria, which was a village in the eighteenth century, is now a busy town with an elegant centre surrounded by sprawling suburbs. It was the birthplace of the painter Renato Guttuso.

VILLA CATTOLICA AND VILLA PALAGONIA, BAGHERIA

The Villa Cattolica, constructed around a central block in 1737, is enclosed by a range of low buildings that create an oval forecourt. Built on raised ground, from an upstairs terrace there is a clear view of the bay of Palermo. The villa contains a large exhibition of Guttuso's work and is worth visiting for this alone. Its architecture and layout demonstrate how the aristocracy continued their grand lifestyle out of the city.

The Villa Palagonia, which was begun in 1705 for Francesco Gravina, Prince of Palagonia, was designed by the assistant architect to the senate of Palermo, Tommaso Napoli. It is an outstanding design, which stands in an attractive garden surrounded by low walls. The main entrance with its twin staircases is a classic of baroque style. The interior is more formal and contains a hall with frescoes and a gallery of mirrors, as well as private apartments. The garden is famous for the bizarre statues, the work of Francesco's grandson Ferdinando, decorating the walls around the villa. They include animals, knights and ladies, dwarves and various grotesque creatures. According to Anthony Blunt: 'They shocked Goethe and delighted the Sitwells, and were recently visited by the wife of Salvador Dalí; but these sculptures have tended to distract attention from the remarkable architectural qualities of the villa itself.'[9]

SANTUARIO DI SANTA ROSALIA (SANCTUARY OF ST ROSALIA),
MONTE PELLEGRINO

Monte Pellegrino, whose rocky outline overlooks the city, has played an
important part in the history of Palermo. Signs of human habitation going back
to the Stone Age have been found here in caves with wall carvings of human
and animal figures. These caves are not currently open to the public. During
the Punic Wars in the third century BC, the Carthaginians camped on Monte
Pellegrino while besieging the Romans. As the name implies (*pellegrino* meaning
'pilgrim') this area has long had sacred connotations.

In Norman times, Rosalia, a young noblewoman, lived as a hermit on the
mountain, dedicating herself to a life of prayer and meditation. She died in 1170
and was subsequently canonised, becoming one of several favoured saints in
the city. On 15 July 1624, when Palermo was being ravaged by the plague, her
bones were discovered in a cave on the mountain. They were recovered, taken
to Palermo, and used as relics to raise the morale of the people in combating
the plague. Rosalia became the hugely popular patron saint of Palermo, known
affectionately as the Santuzza, or 'little saint'. When in 1626 the plague came to

7. The Santuario di Santa Rosalia (Sanctuary of St Rosalia) (William
Leighton Leitch, 1841).

an end, it was due, according to the archbishop of Palermo, to the intervention of Santa Rosalia (see Chapter 8).

The sanctuary, whose origins date back to 1624, consists of a deep cave under the rock covered by a simple baroque facade (figure 7). It has been a place of popular pilgrimage from the beginning and a procession, traditionally barefoot, comes here from Palermo each year on 4 September, the date of the saint's death and rebirth to eternal life, known as her *dies natalis*. Inside the cave the atmosphere is kept cool by dripping water, which is said to have miraculous properties. In the first part of the cave is a baroque altar with Solomonic columns and the remains of a Punic altar. Deeper inside is Gregorio Tedeschi's statue of the reclining saint from 1625, which carries a golden cape provided by the Bourbon king Charles III.

It was the sanctuary's simplicity which impressed Goethe during his visit in 1787:

The shrine itself is more appropriate to the humility of the saint who took refuge there than the pomp of the festival which is celebrated in honour of her renunciation of the world. In all Christendom, which for eighteen hundred years has founded its wealth, its splendours, its solemn festivities upon the poverty of its first founders and most fervent confessors, there may well be no other sacred spot as naively decorated and touchingly venerated as this.[10]

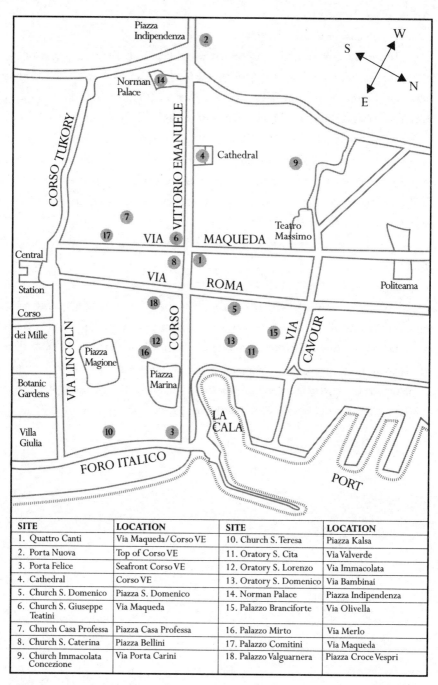

SITE	LOCATION	SITE	LOCATION
1. Quattro Canti	Via Maqueda/Corso VE	10. Church S. Teresa	Piazza Kalsa
2. Porta Nuova	Top of Corso VE	11. Oratory S. Cita	Via Valverde
3. Porta Felice	Seafront Corso VE	12. Oratory S. Lorenzo	Via Immacolata
4. Cathedral	Corso VE	13. Oratory S. Domenico	Via Bambinai
5. Church S. Domenico	Piazza S. Domenico	14. Norman Palace	Piazza Indipendenza
6. Church S. Giuseppe Teatini	Via Maqueda	15. Palazzo Branciforte	Via Olivella
7. Church Casa Professa	Piazza Casa Professa	16. Palazzo Mirto	Via Merlo
8. Church S. Caterina	Piazza Bellini	17. Palazzo Comitini	Via Maqueda
9. Church Immacolata Concezione	Via Porta Carini	18. Palazzo Valguarnera	Piazza Croce Vespri

Map 10 Baroque monuments.

CHAPTER 16

The Nineteenth Century

After Garibaldi freed Palermo from the Bourbons in 1860, the city set in motion an ambitious plan of urban renewal. The immediate priority was to repair the war damage caused by the bombardment of the city's centre. Next was the removal of the fortifications imposed by the long Spanish occupation. Most of the old city walls, bastions and gates were demolished in this period. The Castellammare, the castle protecting the Cala and symbol of Bourbon power, was already being taken apart while Garibaldi was still in Palermo.

A period of construction followed with new districts being developed outside the historic centre. New streets and apartment blocks were built beyond Via Cavour in the district down to the port, while Via della Libertà was extended to the north. The railway station was built to the south. This expansion fundamentally changed the focus of the city, with the aristocracy and the emerging middle class abandoning the historic centre for new properties to the north of the city. Via della Libertà, with its adjoining villas and smart apartment blocks, became the new, affluent district of the city. The old centre was left to the churches, the crumbling palaces and the poor.

The opportunity to modernise the decaying infrastructure was missed by the city's administration, which was still dominated by the aristocracy. Overcrowding, bad sanitation and an inadequate water supply, accompanied by outbreaks of cholera, were the lot of the poor. But the administration had other priorities. The bulk of the funds were spent on public buildings, especially on two grandiose projects. The aristocracy, who travelled widely, wanted to see Palermo take its place among the great cities of Europe. What the city lacked, in their view, were theatres capable of playing to large audiences. The results were the Teatro Massimo, the opera house, and the Politeama, a theatre for popular productions, both built between 1867 and 1897. New public gardens were also established.

Palermo's population grew rapidly in the second half of the nineteenth century, putting more pressure on resources. From 197,000 in 1861, the population reached 306,000 in 1901, an increase of 55 per cent in 40 years.[1]

This was the belle époque, when Palermo hosted royalty from northern Europe and showed off its new look. The contemporary fashion which dominated everything from architecture to painting and furniture design was the Liberty style, so named after the London store which popularised it, owned by Arthur Liberty. Originally the style came from Paris, where it was known as art nouveau. The style was spread to Italy by Arthur Liberty through international fairs and, arriving in Palermo, it was taken up by leading families such as the Florios. The foremost exponent of the Liberty style was the architect Ernesto Basile. The belle époque saw a flowering of the arts that left its mark upon the city.

TEATRO POLITEAMA (POLITEAMA THEATRE)

The Teatro Politeama Garibaldi dominates the large piazza situated at the beginning of Via della Libertà. The piazza's official name is Ruggero Settimo, after the patriot who led the revolutionary government in 1848, but is popularly known as Piazza Politeama. Politeama means 'multi-spectacle' and the theatre, which has seats for 950, was designed as a popular venue for a variety of different productions. The architecture was inspired by ancient Rome, with an entrance through a triumphal arch crowned by a bronze quadriga, a four-horse racing chariot, by Mario Rutelli. The body of the theatre is semicircular, and is supported by columns reminiscent of an ancient circus. It was built to a design by Giuseppe Damiani Almeyda between 1867 and 1874. Almeyda also designed the statue of Ruggero Settimo which stands in front of the Politeama.

Initially intended for daytime performances, the theatre was at first left open to the elements. The roof and the last decorations were finally completed by 1891 in time for the Esposizione Nazionale, the national exhibition put on by Palermo.

The Politeama was inaugurated in 1874 with a performance of Vincenzo Bellini's opera *I Capuleti e i Montecchi* (The Capulets and the Montagues) and, as the Massimo was not yet completed, continued to be used for opera productions. Puccini's *Manon Lescaut* and *La bohème* were both performed here in the 1890s. Today the Politeama puts on popular plays and concerts and represents an important part of the city's cultural life.

TEATRO MASSIMO (MASSIMO THEATRE)

The full name of Palermo's opera house is the Teatro Massimo Vittorio Emanuele, named after the king of Italy, crowned in 1861. Designed on a monumental scale, it combines elements of Greek and Roman architecture with a strongly Sicilian identity, achieved through the use of yellow sandstone. The entrance lies at the top of a broad staircase flanked on either side by a large bronze lion. The lion on the left, when facing the entrance, is by Mario Rutelli and represents lyric opera. The one on the right, by Benedetto Civiletti, represents tragedy. At the top of the stairs are six columns supporting a heavy pediment in the classical style. When it was built, the richly decorated auditorium contained seating for 3,200, making it the third-largest opera house in Europe after Paris and Vienna. Due to modern regulations, today it has seating for 1,350.

A message on the pediment, the origin of which remains a mystery, reads: *L'arte rinnova i popoli e ne rivela la vita. Vano delle scene il diletto ove non miri a preparar l'avvenire.* ('Art renews people and reveals their life. Love of art is useless where it does not seek to prepare the future.')

Opera had long been popular in Palermo. Patrick Brydone, the Scottish traveller who was in Palermo in the summer of 1770, noted the city's fondness for opera and praised the quality of the singers. Alessandro Scarlatti, considered to be the founder of the Neapolitan school of opera, was born in Palermo in 1660. He spent his career on the Italian mainland, mostly in Naples and Rome. His son, Domenico, also composed operas.

To make way for the Massimo many old buildings were demolished, including Porta Maqueda, the gate which had closed the city at the north end of Via Maqueda. According to the legend, a nun whose convent was among the buildings destroyed continues to haunt the corridors of the house. Piazza Verdi, in which the Massimo stands, marks the limit of the historic centre (which lies to the left when facing the Massimo) and the start of the district developed in the nineteenth century.

Building began in 1874, supervised by the Palermitan architect Giovanni

Battista Filippo Basile, but was halted by his death in 1891. His son Ernesto continued the work, which was completed in 1897. That same year, the Massimo was inaugurated on 16 May with a performance of Verdi's *Falstaff*. The first season continued with Puccini's *La bohème* and Amilcare Ponchielli's *La Gioconda* and featured the young tenor Enrico Caruso. Mascagni conducted his *Il piccolo Marat* in the house in 1923. Bellini's operas have always been popular in Palermo as the composer was Sicilian. He came from Catania but made his career in Naples, Milan and Paris during the years from 1825 to 1835. He died in Paris at the age of 33.[2]

Basile also designed two kiosks in Piazza Verdi in the Liberty style, intended for the sale of tobacco and other items to operagoers.

In 1974 the Massimo was closed for repairs for what should have been a short period. Funds were allocated for the work but nothing happened and mafia connections were suspected. The Massimo subsequently remained closed in deteriorating conditions until 1997, only reopening briefly for the filming of *The Godfather Part III* during which Michael Corleone's daughter, played by Sofia Coppola, is shot on the steps outside the entrance.

Palermo's current mayor, Leoluca Orlando, who saw the Massimo as a symbol in his struggle for civic renewal, initiated a legal battle to gain control of the opera house. Eventually he succeeded, and on 12 May 1997, 100 years after its inauguration, the Massimo reopened with a concert played by the Berlin Philharmonic Orchestra. After the performance the audience came down the steps into the square, which was full of cheering people who had come to celebrate the Massimo's rebirth.[3]

Today, fully back in action, the Massimo puts on lively productions from the international operatic repertoire featuring young Italian singers. There are programmes of ballets and concerts and regular tours of the opera house for visitors.

MUSEO RISORGIMENTO (RISORGIMENTO MUSEUM)

This small, atmospheric museum is full of portraits, pictures and memorabilia from the nineteenth-century struggles against the Bourbons. Down the left-hand side is material from 1848–9 and down the right-hand side material from Garibaldi's campaign in 1860. Garibaldi is portrayed as the warrior saint in a large equestrian statue by Mario Rutelli. One of the general's mottoes is repeated here: *Libertà non tradisce i volenti* ('Liberty does not betray the willing'). There is a bust of Lord William Bentinck and portraits of Vittorio Emanuele, the first king of united Italy, and Ruggero Settimo, president of Sicily in 1848–9. A large collection of items from the period includes helmets, uniforms, rifles, pistols, swords, letters and drawings. There are pictures of aristocratic ladies bringing food to Garibaldi's soldiers during the fighting in the city. Entrance to the museum is to the left of the church of San Domenico via the old cloisters of the monastery.

GRAND HOTEL ET DES PALMES

This large, sombre building, which dates from 1856, was the town house of Benjamin Ingham, one of the English magnates in the wine trade. It stands on the corner of Via Roma and Via Mariano Stabile. The Anglican church, which is on the opposite corner, was built at Ingham's expense for the English community. Converted into a hotel in 1872, it was restructured by Ernesto Basile in the fashionable Liberty style in 1907. Famous guests have included Richard Wagner, Oscar Wilde and Francesco Crispi when prime minister. In October 1957 the hotel was the scene of a famous meeting to discuss the drugs trade between members of the Sicilian and American mafias. Among those present was Lucky Luciano, who had been released from prison in America at the end of the war. Today the hotel continues to represent the height of luxury with its marble floors and tropical garden in the centre of the building. The bar on the ground floor is a favourite meeting place.

VILLA MALFITANO

Set in a large park stocked with rare trees on Via Dante, this large property was built in 1886–9 for Joseph (Pip) and Tina Whitaker, the inheritors of the family's wine business in Marsala. The architect was Ignazio Greco. By the early twentieth century, at the peak of the belle époque, this was the hub of English society in Palermo. Among the visitors were King Edward VII in 1907 and George V and Queen Mary in 1925. The Italian king and queen were also entertained here. The property, which contains reception rooms in the style of Louis XV, a ballroom, a huge dining room, a billiard room and a conservatory, is filled with elaborate furnishings from Sicily, England and France. There are landscape paintings by Francesco Lojacono, tapestries from Brussels and a Russian sledge sent by the czar. It demonstrates the extraordinary wealth and social position achieved by the British in Sicily.

Pip Whitaker was interested in archaeology and bought the island of Mozia on the west coast. It is one of the most important Punic sites in the Mediterranean, which was excavated by Whitaker, and is now owned by the Whitaker Foundation.[4]

VILLINO FLORIO (VILLA FLORIO)

Not far from the Villa Malfitano, on Viale Regina Margherita, stands the Villino Florio. This was where Ignazio and Franca Florio entertained royalty, heads of state and European high society. Originally the villa stood in a large park, now built over, and was a masterpiece of Palermo's Liberty style. Designed by Ernesto Basile in 1899–1902, it was furnished by Vittorio Ducrot. The architecture, furnishings, fabrics and wrought ironwork are all typical of the height of the belle époque. Badly damaged by fire in 1962, the villa has been well restored and is currently used by the Regional Government.

PALAZZINA CINESE (CHINESE PAVILION)

This was built for the Bourbon king, Ferdinand of Naples, after he and his wife Maria Carolina were forced to seek refuge in Palermo during the Napoleonic Wars. It was designed and built in 1799 by the architect Giuseppe Venanzio Marvuglia. Among the guests who stayed here was Nelson, who brought the king and queen to Palermo aboard his flagship, and the Hamiltons. Ferdinand left the business of government to his wife and spent his time hunting and fishing. The Favorita park, in which the pavilion is situated at the foot of Monte Pellegrino, was established for this purpose. The pavilion contains an unusual mix of styles, using neoclassical columns, Gothic arches and Chinese motifs, which were popular at the time. Towers at each end of the building lead to a terrace with views over the park. The interior has colourful murals decorated with designs of birds and animals. There is a table with place settings that can be lowered down to the kitchen for replenishment. The setting of the pavilion is spectacular, in an Italianate garden, with views of the nearby mountains.

Close by is the Museo Etnografico Siciliano (Sicilian Ethnographic Museum), which holds the collection of Giuseppe Pitrè, a student of folklore. The collection, which dates from 1909, illustrates traditional Sicilian domestic life.

Outside Palermo

MONDELLO

Mondello lies 11 kilometres north of Palermo beyond the Favorita park, on an inlet of the sea, set between Monte Pellegrino and Monte Gallo. Here a sandy beach stretches around the bay protected by the two mountains. Once the marshes were drained in the nineteenth century it was developed into a fashionable bathing resort with Liberty-style villas by Ernesto Basile built close to the beach. Today Mondello is a small town with a church and a piazza and a variety of fish restaurants. An ornate bathing establishment dominates the beach, called the Kursaal a Mare. It remains Palermo's smart beach resort.

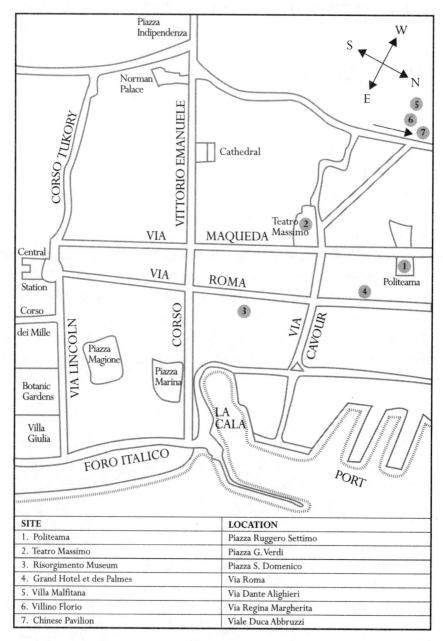

SITE	LOCATION
1. Politeama	Piazza Ruggero Settimo
2. Teatro Massimo	Piazza G. Verdi
3. Risorgimento Museum	Piazza S. Domenico
4. Grand Hotel et des Palmes	Via Roma
5. Villa Malfitana	Via Dante Alighieri
6. Villino Florio	Via Regina Margherita
7. Chinese Pavilion	Viale Duca Abbruzzi

Map 11 Nineteenth-century monuments.

CHAPTER 17

Other Important Monuments

Palermo's monuments are varied and rich in content, with the city's centre densely packed with buildings of historical interest. The works of art have been partly collected into museums and galleries while others remain in their original locations in churches and palaces or in the streets and squares of the city. In the galleries they are displayed in fine old buildings, for renovation to house art collections is something that Palermo does particularly well. The city's multicultural past has left a profusion of architectural styles jostling with one another in a small area, Islamic and Norman overlapping with Gothic and Catalan, together with the dominant baroque. The impact of the Renaissance was limited, apart from the work of some individual artists, as Sicily was isolated from mainland Italy. The artists who worked in Palermo are mostly unknown outside Sicily, as the full history of Sicilian art has still to be written.

MUSEO DIOCESANO, PALAZZO ARCIVESCOVILE (DIOCESAN MUSEUM, ARCHBISHOP'S PALACE)

The Palazzo Arcivescovile faces the square in front of the cathedral to which it is attached by two arches. Its sheer size and imposing facade reflect the status of the archbishop who was one of the most powerful men in Palermo. The road between the palace and the cathedral, Via Matteo Bonello, is named after the baron who assassinated Maio of Bari, chancellor to King William I, in 1160.

The Museo Diocesano, the entrance to which is through a courtyard in the palace, contains a large and important collection of paintings and sculptures from the eleventh to the eighteenth centuries. The collection comes from churches damaged in World War II and from the cathedral, including pieces removed during the restructuring in 1781–1801, on the new design by Ferdinando Fuga. During the restructuring the cathedral was fundamentally changed, the interior losing its original basilica form while the exterior was crowned by a dome.

The collection demonstrates the abilities of the artists who worked in Palermo, not only in painting and sculpture, but also in decorative pieces made in silver and inlaid marble. There is a particularly fine statue of Sant'Agata by Paolo Amato, mounted on a decorative base for parading through the streets. There is much to admire in the museum, including the palace itself, with its elegant reception rooms overlooking the cathedral square. A highlight is the Borremans chapel, a colourful and ornate chapel decorated in 1733–4 with frescoes by Guglielmo Borremans.

Much of the sculpture is by the Gagini, a family represented here by three generations. Domenico, originally from the Ticino area in what is now Switzerland, studied in Florence and worked in Naples before settling in Palermo in 1463. His son, Antonello, generally considered the most accomplished of the family, developed the workshop by employing apprentices from Carrara and handling commissions from all over Sicily. His crowning achievement was a large tribune decorating the far end of the cathedral, behind the altar, built on three levels containing 45 statues. The work was completed by his sons, Antonino, Giacomo and Vincenzo. The tribune was demolished in the restructuring of the cathedral. A number of statues and panels survived in storage below the cathedral and can be seen in the museum together with a model of the original structure. The Gagini were prolific sculptors whose work appears all over Palermo and around Sicily.

There are many pictures of historical significance to Palermo in the collection. The most important is Vincenzo La Barbera's *Santa Rosalia Interceding for Palermo*, painted in 1624. It was paraded through the city in September of that year to assist in combating the plague, which was still active. In it the saint is portrayed appealing to the Holy Trinity and the Virgin Mary above, while gesturing towards the *lazzaretto* in the city below where the victims of the plague were held. The Cala and the main port are both visible with Monte Pellegrino in the background. In this painting La Barbera established the style and iconography to be associated with Santa Rosalia. She wears long hair and a brown monastic habit, associated with the Dominicans, while an angel brings her a garland of roses. Close by are some objects: a skull, representing the transitory nature of life, a book (study and learning) and a lily (purity). Her habit and these objects became the established symbols of Santa Rosalia, developed and made famous by Anthony Van Dyck in his paintings of the saint. Another painting of Santa Rosalia by La Barbera can be seen in the church of Sant'Anna.[1]

Other paintings of historical significance include Mario di Laurito's *Madonna with Child and the Saints of Palermo*, from 1530, and Simon de Wobreck's *Palermo Freed from the Plague*, from 1576. A painting of the cathedral by an unknown artist shows the exterior of the building with its four pointed towers before the addition of the dome. In the room dedicated to Pietro Novelli, Sicily's finest painter of the baroque era, can be found his *Pietà* (1646) and *St Francis* (1635).

PALAZZO ABATELLIS, GALLERIA REGIONALE (ABATELLIS PALACE, REGIONAL GALLERY)

This art gallery, which is more intimate than the Museo Diocesano, contains some of Palermo's best sculptures and paintings from the Middle Ages. They are displayed in a well-restored late fifteenth-century palace built for Francesco Abatellis, who was the port master. After his death it passed to the Benedictine order. The palace, in which Renaissance and Catalan Gothic styles are mixed, is well worth a visit in its own right. It is situated close to Piazza Marina in Via Alloro.

Among the outstanding works of sculpture are Domenico Gagini's *Virgin and Child*; Antonello Gagini's *Portrait of a Young Man* and *Annunciation*; and the bust of Eleonora of Aragon by Francesco Laurana. Laurana, who came from Dalmatia and who worked in France and Naples before coming to Sicily, developed an individual style of portrait busts, of which this is one of his best.

Among the paintings in the gallery are two that have become closely identified with the city. The first is the *Trionfo della Morte* (Triumph of Death) in which a skeleton riding a horse has fired arrows into a number of well-dressed and prosperous-looking people who have collapsed on the ground. To the left, among the more simply dressed people, according to tradition, are portraits of the artist and his assistant. To the right, the action is watched by a group of nobles. It is a powerful depiction of the Apocalypse, a common theme in the Middle Ages, with death striking down the rich and the poor, lay and clergy, young and old. It is a large fresco covering an entire wall, rescued from a courtyard in the Palazzo Sclafani and restored in the 1950s. It dates from the 1440s and is by an unknown artist in a late Gothic style that has been compared to Pisanello. Some commentators have seen the painting as representing Palermo's violent history, during which the city's elite was often cut down by invaders. More likely it reflects the horrors inflicted on Palermo by the frequent bouts of plague.[2]

The second is Antonello da Messina's panel painting from 1476–7, the *Annunziata*, a portrait of the Virgin Mary, said to be Palermo's *Mona Lisa*. The serenity of the figure, with her hand raised, leaves a lasting impression. Antonello, who was Sicily's greatest painter, studied in Rome and worked in Naples and Venice. He was much influenced by the Flemish school of the Van Eycks, where he learned the technique of painting in oils. According to Giorgio Vasari it was Antonello who first introduced this technique to Venice. His *Annunziata*, painted towards the end of his life, was possibly done in Venice and brought to Palermo. Bernard Berenson considered that Antonello's 'latest works are Venetian in spirit and between his and Giovanni Bellini's portraits the differences are slight.'[3]

GALLERIA D'ARTE MODERNA (GALLERY OF MODERN ART)

The gallery is housed in the well-restored convent attached to the church of Sant'Anna, just off Via Roma. It contains a collection of paintings and sculptures from the nineteenth and twentieth centuries with emphasis upon Sicilian, especially Palermitan, artists. With religious subjects no longer dominant, artists were able to express themselves freely in portraits, landscapes and historical scenes. Highlights of the works of art include the neoclassical paintings by Giuseppe Velasco, portraits by Salvatore Lo Forte, a self-portrait by Renato Guttuso and sculpture by Mario Rutelli and Benedetto Civiletti. The landscapes by Francesco Lojacono and Antonino Leto that are displayed here helped to change the popular image of Sicily. Rooms are organised by themes, including Mediterranean landscapes and scenes of Palermo street life. Historical scenes depicted include the Sicilian Vespers and Garibaldi's campaign.

PALAZZO CHIARAMONTE (CHIARAMONTE PALACE)

The Chiaramonte emerged as the most powerful family in Palermo in the period following the Sicilian Vespers. They bought tracts of land in the city and between 1307 and 1380 completed the palace on the site of a Norman glass factory. It stands in a corner of Piazza Marina facing a huge *Ficus macrophylla*, also known as a Moreton Bay Fig tree. A vast, imposing fortress–palace (it is also known as Lo Steri, from *hosterium*, meaning 'a fortified place') with no windows on the ground floor, it was designed for security and to impress rival families. It did not remain long in the hands of the Chiaramonte, for in 1392, having unsuccessfully defied the Aragonese, Andrea Chiaramonte was executed in front of his palace and his property confiscated. In 1535 it became the palace of the Spanish viceroys and from 1605 to 1782 the seat of the Inquisition. Today it holds the rectorate of the university.

The palace is in the Catalan Gothic style, with some Islamic touches in the windows and door frames. Of particular note is the Great Hall on the first floor with its intricately carved wooden ceiling and colourful scenes of chivalry. The second floor holds some important paintings, including Renato Guttuso's *Vucciria*, one of Palermo's most celebrated pictures. Painted in 1974 during one month's intense work, this large canvas captures the spirit of Palermo's street markets with their piles of fruit, slabs covered with fish, rich colours and patterns of sunlight. Guttuso knew the Vucciria from boyhood, when he would make a detour to get there, going down the steps in Via Roma to Piazza Caracciolo and coming out into Piazza San Domenico. 'This blast of local life,' he recalled, 'the cries of the stall holders, the lights and the colours, was enough to clear my mind.'[4]

Behind the palace lies the prison of the Spanish Inquisition where suspects were held for long periods and tortured to reveal their true beliefs. Here prisoners lived on for years with little light or food, often broken in spirit. Many of them were writers and intellectuals who left their own memorials, for recent work has uncovered extensive graffiti on the cell walls, in the form of writings and drawings. There is also a memorial to the monk Diego La Matina, who killed his inquisitor in 1635 before being burned at the stake (see Chapter 8).

PALAZZO DELLE AQUILE (PALACE OF THE EAGLES)

Occupying the southern side of Piazza Pretoria, this palace takes it name from the eagles that decorate its facade. On top of the building stands a statue of Santa Rosalia, from 1661, by Carlo d'Aprile. The facade contains plaques commemorating the revolutions of 1282 and 1848 as well as the arrival of Garibaldi.

The palace is the old Senate House, from where the city was ruled from the fourteenth century to 1816. The current structure dates from 1470; it was extended in the baroque era and restored in the nineteenth century. Today it is the town hall where the mayor has his office.

On the internal staircase is a curious statue of the Genio di Palermo (Genius of Palermo) – see the description below. The first floor contains an assembly room, a sumptuous dining room and reception rooms containing inscriptions and historical memorabilia including objects associated with Napoleon and Garibaldi.

FONTANA PRETORIA, PIAZZA PRETORIA (PRETORIA FOUNTAIN, PIAZZA PRETORIA)

This complex Renaissance fountain, with its array of sculptured figures in white Carrara marble, dominates Piazza Pretoria at the centre of the city, close to the Quattro Canti. It faces the Palazzo delle Aquile. The senate bought the fountain when engaged in the large-scale rebuilding programme for the city centre. In 1550 Don Pedro di Toledo, viceroy of Naples, bought a magnificent Florentine villa and commissioned a fountain for the park from Francesco Camilliani and Michelangelo Naccherino. After Toledo's death, the fountain was sold to Palermo and brought here in 1575 where it was reassembled. After Francesco's death, it was completed and enlarged by his son, Camillo. The fountain's four basins represent the four rivers of Palermo while the statues depict mythological figures, animals and dolphins. The fountain, however, could be seen from the nearby convent of Santa Caterina (St Catherine). The naked figures shocked the nuns so that it became known as the Fontana della Vergogna (Fountain of Shame). In 1655 some of the figures were mutilated, with their noses being cut off. The iron balustrade, designed by Giovanni Battista Filippo Basile, was added in 1858. The fountain is the most visible Renaissance work of art in Palermo.

IL GENIO DI PALERMO (THE GENIUS OF PALERMO)

The Genius of Palermo is a curious and enigmatic figure, portrayed in statues and pictures around the city. Also known as Il Vecchio (the Old Man), he became an official symbol of the city in 1489 with the king's approval. He represents the spirit of the city, sometimes seen as its mythical founder and link to classical origins. While details of the image vary, common elements consist of a seated man with a beard wearing a crown and holding a serpent to his breast. This bizarre and unusually striking image probably dates back to pre-Roman times. Its origins are unknown, though Tommaso Fazello, whose history of ancient Sicily was published in 1558, thought it may have been adapted from an ancient coin. 'I have in my possession,' he wrote, 'an ancient bronze coin of Palermo from which this image of a man may have come. It shows a man in Greek costume with the word *Panormitanon* and on the reverse a phoenix holding a thunderbolt.'[5] The Genius is thus a mythical, pagan figure who personifies Palermo, linked to the ancient gods. In ancient times the serpent occurred in many religions, representing fertility and the creative life force, sexual desire, the spirit of the dead and renewal. Ancient gods who appear in statues holding a serpent include Priapus and Saturn. The unique character of the Genius can be seen from statues at the following locations.

Palazzo delle Aquile (Palace of the Eagles), Piazza Pretoria

On the main staircase inside the palace stands a column some four metres high, on top of which sits the statue of the Genius known as *Palermu u Nicu* (Little Palermo). He sits with his forked beard, a crown on his head, his feet immersed in a large bowl, holding a serpent to his breast. The statue is thought to have come from the workshop of Domenico Gagini and probably dates from the 1470s when the palace was being built by the prefect, Pietro Speciale. Speciale, an intellectual and humanist who initiated much new building in Sicily, selected the figure of the Genius as an emblem to be placed in the palace and elsewhere in the city. Around the bowl appear the words *Panormus conca aurea suos devorat alienos nutrit* ('Palermo, golden shell, devours its own and nourishes foreigners'). In the early days of Spanish rule Palermo was thus seen as a place that enriched foreigners at the expense of its own people.[6]

Piazza Garraffo

Hidden away in this tiny square in the Vucciria district is the regal figure of the Genius known as *Palermu lu Grandi* (Big Palermo). The piazza takes its name from

the Arabic for 'abundant water', with which the district was well supplied by a
nearby river. The full impact of the mythical figure of the Genius, set in a niche
on the wall, is apparent here. The statue was carved in 1483 by the Lombard
sculptor Pietro de Bonitate, a contemporary of Domenico Gagini, and one of
ten master sculptors in Palermo. The Genius is seated on a rock looking straight
ahead with steady gaze, wearing a crown and royal cloak, his beard forked,
holding a large serpent to him. The niches on either side once held statues of
female saints, which added a Christian element to the essentially pagan figure
of the Genius. This monument has been vandalised over the years, and no trace
remains of the coats of arms and other embellishments that were originally here,
while the statues of the female saints were stolen in 1992. Recent restoration
work, however, has improved the monument's appearance.[7]

Piazza Rivoluzione

This Genius appears on top of a fountain wearing a crown and a conventional
beard, displaying a muscular body while gazing at the sky and holding his
serpent. The statue was made in 1589 for the port district, which was being
extended. In 1687 it was moved to the old Arab market square of Piazza
Fieravecchia, where in 1848 it became a rallying point for protestors against
the Bourbon regime. The authorities subsequently removed the statue, which
was returned amid rejoicing on the arrival of Garibaldi, when the piazza was
renamed Rivoluzione. These events are commemorated on the monument by
the following words: *Questo marmo simbolo temuto di libertà sottratto agli occhi
del popolo dalla inquieta tirannide il popolo vincitore ripose nel 1860.* ('This feared
marble symbol of freedom, removed from the eyes of the people by a troubled
tyranny, was replaced by the victorious people in 1860.')

Villa Giulia

A grander version of the Genius can be seen in the garden named Villa Giulia,
next to the Orto Botanico di Palermo (Palermo Botanical Garden). Here he
dominates the centre of an elegant fountain, the work of Ignazio Marabitti
in 1778. The majestic figure of the Genius, dressed in Roman attire, wears
a crown and a long beard and holds in one hand a sceptre and in the other a
serpent. He is surrounded by articles full of classical significance: a dog for

fidelity; the trisceles sign for Sicily; an eagle, emblem of Palermo; a bunch of fruit and grain for abundance, recalling the goddess Ceres (Demeter to the Greeks); and the *fasces lictoriae*, a bundle of rods with an axe that was a symbol of power in ancient Rome.[8]

CHURCH OF SAN FRANCESCO D'ASSISI (ST FRANCIS OF ASSISI)

Frederick II banished the Franciscan order from Sicily as part of his vendetta with the papacy. It was only after the emperor's death that the Franciscans were able to re-establish themselves in Palermo. The nave of the church was built in 1255–77, and the simple facade, with its decorative doorway and rose window, was added in 1302. It stands in a small piazza off Via Paternostro, not far from Corso Vittorio Emanuele. While the facade retains its original aspect, internally almost all traces of Gothic decoration have disappeared. Chapels were added in the fourteenth and fifteenth centuries and many of Palermo's leading artists contributed to the splendour of this church. Some of the first Renaissance sculptures in Sicily were introduced here in the 1460s, in the arch to the Mastrantonio chapel, by Francesco Laurana and Pietro de Bonitate. There are figures of eight Sicilian saints by Giovanni Ragusa; statues of the Virtues by Pietro de Bonitate; a *Pietà* by Ignazio Marabitti and a sarcophagus by Domenico Gagini. Pietro Novelli is represented by his *Vision of St Francis* and, by the entrance, his fresco of *St Francis and the Saints*. To the right is a statue of St George and the Dragon with panels by Antonello Gagini. In 1723 Giacomo Serpotta decorated the nave with statues of the Virtues in stucco. Despite all the additions, the style of the interior has remained simple, with its bare columns and high wooden ceiling.[9]

CHURCH OF SANTA MARIA DELLA CATENA (ST MARY'S OF THE CHAIN)

The elegant porch of this church with its three arches is among the characteristic sights along the south side of the Cala (figure 8). The church was built in 1500–20 by Matteo Carnelivari, who was also responsible for the Palazzo Abatellis. In style it represents a high point in Sicilian Gothic with some Spanish influences, among them the design of the porch. Built on a raised spur of land, this was the point where a chain was attached to close the entrance to the port. On the

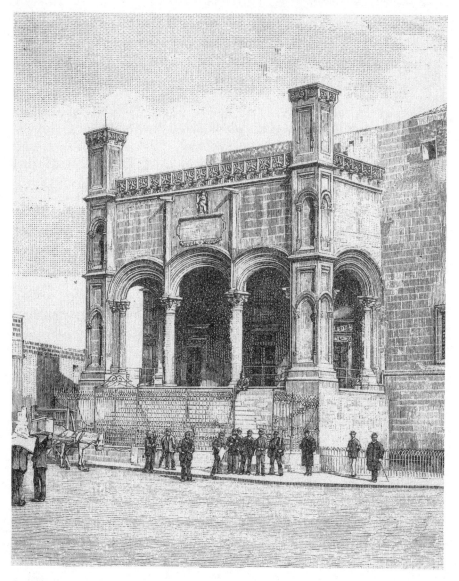

8. The church of Santa Maria della Catena (St Mary's of the Chain) (Gustavo Chiesi, 1892).

far side the chain reached the Castellammare, remnants of which can be seen today. Steps lead up to the porch and to the three highly decorative doorways attributed to Vincenzo Gagini. The simple interior has an arched ceiling and a beautiful sanctuary. On the right-hand side are frescoes from 1743 illustrating the lives of Mary and Jesus by Olivio Sozzi.

CHURCH OF SANTA MARIA DELLO SPASIMO (ST MARY OF THE AGONY)

The ruins of this old church and convent, situated in gardens on Via dello Spasimo, not far from Piazza Kalsa, have been converted into a cultural centre for concerts, plays and exhibitions. Building of the church began in the early 1500s by the monks of the order of Santa Maria di Monte Oliveto but was never finished. Instead the Spanish chose this spot on which to build bastions for the city's defences. During the plague of 1624–5 the convent served as a hospital while the church fell into disrepair. Today the remains of a cloister, some vaulted ceilings and a roofless church, provide an atmospheric backdrop to popular cultural events.

There is a story attached to the church concerning a painting known as *Lo Spasimo di Sicilia*. It was commissioned by the monks from Raphael, who completed it around 1516. The subject is Christ falling under the weight of his cross, when his mother suffered a spasm of agony known as *lo spasimo*. In his *Lives of the Artists*, Giorgio Vasari tells us:

> Raffaello painted for the Brothers of Monte Oliveto, in the monastery called S. Maria dello Spasimo of Palermo, a picture of Christ bearing his cross, which when it was finished nearly came to a bad end. For as it was being borne by sea to Palermo, a great tempest cast the ship upon a rock, and it was broken to pieces, and the crew lost, and all the cargo, except this picture, which was carried in its case by sea to Genoa.

With the Pope's help the monks in Palermo finally received the picture where, according to Vasari, 'it has a greater reputation than the volcano itself.'[10] The painting did not, however, remain in Palermo but was bought by Philip IV of Spain in 1622. During the Napoleonic Wars it was taken as booty to Paris and later returned to Spain where it resides today in the Prado in Madrid.

CASTELLAMMARE

Little remains today of the massive castle that once dominated the north side of the Cala. Entry to the site can be made from Via dei Barilai, the dual carriage-way that runs along the seafront from the north side of the Cala to Piazza XIII Vittime, to an area near the modern port. Here fragments of fortifications from the ninth to the fifteenth centuries can be found, including the remnants of a circular tower, some huge foundation stones, sections of a moat and a stretch of ancient wall. These relics lie abandoned among the buildings and cranes of the modern port.

The Castellammare was built by the Arabs, possibly on Roman foundations, to protect the entrance of the port. A chain was drawn across the entrance to prevent ships from entering, linking the castle to the point now occupied by the church of Santa Maria della Catena. The Castellammare was enlarged by the Normans to contain apartments as well as a prison. During a German invasion Frederick II took refuge here when he was still a boy. The Spanish extended the castle, adding bastions to the central keep, with the aim of using it as a defence against civil unrest within the city. When Garibaldi entered the city in May 1860, the Bourbons turned the guns of the castle onto the city centre, causing great damage. A hated symbol of Bourbon power, the Castellammare was already being destroyed when Garibaldi was in Palermo.

CONVENTO DEI CAPPUCCINI (CAPUCHIN CONVENT)

The convent, to be found near the Norman building of the Cuba in the direction of Monreale, is famous for its catacombs, which contain hundreds of skeletons suspended in long corridors. The bodies are fully dressed, suspended in niches on the walls, their heads hanging down with gaping mouths. The effect is grotesque and macabre but not frightening, as the corridors are painted white and brightly lit. The skeletons are divided into separate sections for priests, professional people, women and children. The catacombs appear to have been used from the seventeenth to the late nineteenth centuries. They are an oddity, for there is no apparent reason or historical precedent for this display. They have been taken as an example of the Sicilians' peculiarly close relationship with death.

OPERA DEI PUPI (PUPPET THEATRE)

Stories of medieval chivalry enacted in puppet shows are an old Sicilian tradition, drawing upon the Norman and Arab past. Similar subjects appear on Sicily's brightly coloured carts. Before the age of mass communication, storytellers recounted long sequences of medieval adventures to enthralled crowds. Some of the stories were centred on the court of Charlemagne in France and his knights, who were engaged in fighting the Saracens and rescuing damsels in distress. Today performances are for visitors and, lasting about an hour, give a flavour of what the theatre was once like. Features include dramatic action scenes of battles with sword and lance, attacks by dragons and knights riding on horseback. All this is accompanied by a commentary, the dialogue of the protagonists, loud sound effects and a barrel organ. The puppets themselves are the most interesting part of the show. Large figures in armour, each one different, with their helmets and shields they are works of art. Although the commentary is in Italian, the act is so full of action that it is not difficult to follow.

Run since 1977 by the Cuticchio family, the small theatre is to be found in Via Bara all'Olivella, a narrow street leading up to Via Maqueda from Via Roma. Antique puppets from the eighteenth century can be admired close up in the small museum near the theatre. A more complete museum of puppets can be found in Via Butera.

MONUMENTS TO VICTIMS OF THE MAFIA

Monuments and memorial plaques to victims of the mafia appear all over Palermo.

In 1983, after the murders of General Dalla Chiesa and the PCI leader Pio La Torre, a monument was built in Piazza XIII Vittime, at the end of Via Cavour near the port. It is a stark piece of sculpture consisting of three tall steel plates simply entitled: 'To the Victims of the Mafia'. The judges Giovanni Falcone and Paolo Borsellino are commemorated in a number of places. Palermo's airport was renamed in their honour, while a monument to Falcone stands on the motorway at Capaci where the bomb was exploded that killed him, his wife and bodyguards on 23 May 1992. Outside the apartment block in Via Notarbartolo, where Falcone lived, stands a magnolia tree that has become a shrine to the two judges. Known as the Albero Falcone (Falcone's Tree), it is covered in photos, letters and messages of support for the two judges. In Piazza della Memoria near the law courts are other monuments to the judges. Dalla Chiesa is remembered in a street named after him that runs down the side of the Giardino Inglese (English Garden). This is where he was murdered, with his wife and his bodyguard, on 3 September 1982. Numerous plaques around the city commemorate magistrates and policemen killed in the course of their duty, including Gaetano Costa (Via Cavour), Joe Petrosino (Piazza Marina),

Calogero Zucchetto (Giardino Inglese) and Emanuele Basile (Monreale). A
garden of remembrance for the victims was created in 2005 at Ciaculli, an
outlying suburb to the south of Palermo. On land famous for mandarin oranges,
confiscated from the mafia, a memorial was created with each tree carrying
the name of an individual victim. A museum is due to be opened there. Public
access to the garden is reserved for special occasions.

PUBLIC GARDENS

Palermo has long been famous for its gardens. Since the late eighteenth century
public gardens have been established in a number of locations.

Villa Bonanno, Piazza Vittoria

In 1905 the space in front of the Palazzo dei Normanni that runs alongside
Corso Vittorio Emanuele was redesigned as a garden by Giuseppe Almeyda,
the architect of the Politeama. It was named after the mayor at the time, Pietro
Bonanno. It is filled with palm trees and other exotic plants. The remains of
a Roman villa can be seen in the gardens, on the side furthest from the corso.
Close to the gardens, towards the palace, stands a celebrated statue to Philip V
of Spain, known as the *Teatro Marmoreo* (Theatre of Marble) for its complex
composition and decoration.

Villa Garibaldi, Piazza Marina

These gardens were established in this ancient piazza by the architect Giovanni
Battista Filippo Basile in 1861–4 to commemorate the campaign of Giuseppe
Garibaldi. They are surrounded by iron railings decorated with figures of animals from hunting scenes, including wild boar. Spaciously laid out, the gardens
contain some spectacular trees, in particular the giant *Ficus macrophylla* which
stands in the corner of the piazza facing the Palazzo Chiaramonte. This tree
is reputed to be 150 years old. The *Ficus macrophylla* (sometimes referred to as
the *Ficus magnolioides*) is one of the features of Palermo also to be found in the
Orto Botanico, the Giardino Inglese and some squares of the city. It originates
from New South Wales in Australia where it is known as the Moreton Bay Fig.
Its aerial roots grow rapidly and once anchored in the ground become massive

props to the branches overhead so that some specimens reach an extraordinary age and spread.

As well as a bust of Garibaldi, the gardens contain memorials to leaders of the revolts against the Bourbons, including Giuseppe La Masa, Francesco Riso and the Hungarian, Lajos Tüköry, who fought with Garibaldi. A plaque to commemorate the New York policeman Joe Petrosino, who was killed by the mafia in the piazza in 1909, appears on the side facing the Palazzo Chiaramonte.

In the past Piazza Marina was the scene of tournaments, jousts, bull-running, artificial hunts, firework displays and weddings. Being close to both the prisons of the Inquisition in Palazzo Chiaramonte and the Vicaria, which stood in Via Toledo (now Corso Vittorio Emanuele), it was also used for public executions.

On Sundays it is now the location for a popular market in bric-a-brac, with stalls put up on the pavements all round the gardens, selling everything from second-hand books to furniture, old prints of the city, glassware, cutlery, pictures and souvenirs of many descriptions.

Orto Botanico (Botanic Garden)

The Orto Botanico is to be found on Via Lincoln, which leads down to the seafront from the central railway station. The gardens were founded in 1785, in the time of Caracciolo the reforming viceroy, and soon achieved international fame. The studies carried out here included the use of plants for medicinal purposes. Today the Orto Botanico forms part of Palermo's university and contains a range of trees and plants from Sicily and the Mediterranean as well as from South Africa, South America and Australia. Among the species are ficus trees, some of which have a vast spread, cotton, papyrus, banana, coffee and sugar cane. A long pathway is bordered by bottle trees, which produce a form of kapok. The citrus fruit trees are a special feature with their prolific crops of oranges, lemons and mandarins. In spring the orange blossom is a particular delight. The Gymnasium, a central building with a neoclassical facade, originally housed the director's office and the laboratories. There remains a large collection of seeds, fruit and wood, which is exchanged around the world. Also to be found is a herb garden, a collection of cacti, a greenhouse with tropical plants and an aquarium divided into 24 basins to hold water lilies and other aquatic species.

Villa Giulia

Situated next to the Orto Botanico, this is a formal, Italianate garden laid out
with wide paths in strict geometric patterns. It dates from the 1780s, while
memorials to famous Palermitans and pavilions, one by Giuseppe Damiani
Almeyda, were added in the nineteenth century. To the west of the garden
can be found the fountain with the statue of the Genius of Palermo by Ignazio
Marabitti.

Giardino Inglese (English Garden)

This garden, established on a design by Giovanni Battista Filippo Basile in
1851–3, is a ten-minute bus ride down Via della Libertà from the Politeama. It
was planned as an informal garden in the English style and is today a favourite
among families with young children for its open spaces, safe paths and quantity
of shade. There is a central bar with outdoor tables. It is well stocked with
Mediterranean trees and plants, including specimens of the giant *Ficus macrophylla*. There are several busts and memorials to famous Sicilians such as the
dramatist Luigi Pirandello.

   Opposite the entrance in Via Libertà is another, smaller garden which contains a majestic equestrian statue of Garibaldi from 1892 by Vincenzo Ragusa.
At its base stands a lion by Mario Rutelli. An inset panel below the statue shows
the landing of the Mille at Marsala.

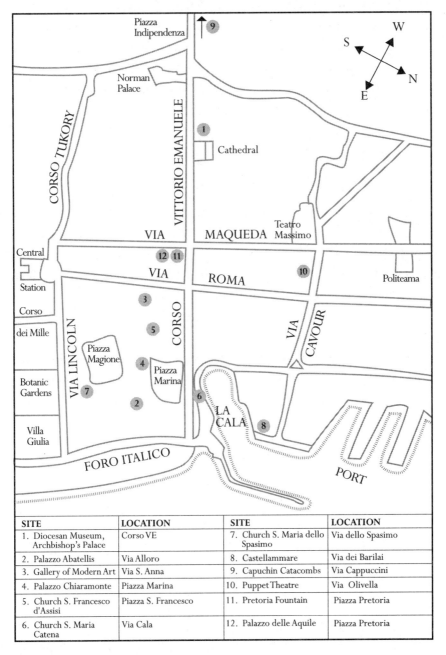

SITE	LOCATION	SITE	LOCATION
1. Diocesan Museum, Archbishop's Palace	Corso VE	7. Church S. Maria dello Spasimo	Via dello Spasimo
2. Palazzo Abatellis	Via Alloro	8. Castellammare	Via dei Barilai
3. Gallery of Modern Art	Via S. Anna	9. Capuchin Catacombs	Via Cappuccini
4. Palazzo Chiaramonte	Piazza Marina	10. Puppet Theatre	Via Olivella
5. Church S. Francesco d'Assisi	Piazza S. Francesco	11. Pretoria Fountain	Piazza Pretoria
6. Church S. Maria Catena	Via Cala	12. Palazzo delle Aquile	Piazza Pretoria

Map 12 Other important monuments.

Notes

Preface

1. Patrick Brydone, *A Tour through Sicily and Malta* (1773; London: H. D. Symonds, 1807), p. 237 [letter xxii].

Prologue

1. Edward Freeman, 'Sicilian cycles', in Edward Freeman, *Historical Essays* (London: Macmillan, 1879), p. 431. Freeman, the historian of ancient Sicily, compared Sicily to Ireland. Both are large islands located near a more developed country with which they have had a troubled relationship; both are former colonies; both have a history of revolt against oppressors; both had poor agricultural workers producing a commodity crop; both were sources of emigration on a large scale; both have a strongly religious culture; both are creative, with a high literary output; and both have their dark side.
2. Leonardo Sciascia, *La corda pazza* (Milan: Adelphi Edizioni, 1991), p. 12 [author's English translation].
3. al-Edrisi, *L'Italia descritta nel 'Libro del Re Ruggero'*, trans. into Italian by M. Amari and C. Schiaparelli (Rome: Coi tipi del Salviucci, 1883), pp. 25, 26 [author's English translation].
4. Statistics taken from the website *Commini-Italiani*. Available at http://www.comuni-italiani. it/082/index.html (accessed 19 September 2014). After Palermo, the largest cities in Sicily are Catania (291,000), Messina (242,000) and Syracuse (119,000).
5. The major mafia groups consist of Cosa Nostra in Sicily, the Camorra in Campania based in Naples, and the Calabrian 'Ndrangheta. The situation in the south was referred to in a speech by Mario Draghi, when he was governor of the Bank of Italy, which was covered by the press including the *Giornale di Sicilia* of 1 June 2010. Growth in the private sector in Sicily, Campania and Calabria is only 45 per cent of that in the centre and north of the country. See the study entitled *Le mani della criminalità sulle imprese: XIII rapporto di Sos Impresa* (Rome: Aliberti, 2011). See also Saverio Lodato and Roberto Scarpinato, *Il ritorno del principe* (Milan: Chiarelettere, 2008), p. 106.
6. This concept, as with Sciascia's other pet ideas, appears in several places in his work. See: a book of interviews and articles entitled *La palma va a nord* (Milan: Edizioni Quaderni Radicali, 1982), p. 9; *The Day of the Owl*, trans. Archibald Colquhoun and Arthur Oliver (London: Granta, 2001), p. 117; and *Sicily as Metaphor: Conversations Presented by Marcelle Padovani*, trans. James Marcus (Marlboro, VT: Marlboro Press, 1994), p. 43.
7. Vincenzo Consolo, *Lo spasimo di Palermo* (Milan: Mondadori, 1998), p. 128 [author's English translation].

Chapter 1: Panormus, Palermo in Antiquity

1. Diodorus Siculus, *Library of History*, ed. Jeffrey Henderson, trans. Francis R. Walton, Loeb Classical Library 409 (Cambridge, MA: Harvard University Press, © 1957), p. 67 [book xxii].

2. Maria Eugenia Aubet, *The Phoenicians and the West* (Cambridge: Cambridge University Press, 1993), p. 138. It is likely, therefore, that Panormus grew progressively from an early Phoenician outpost, enlarged when the Greeks began their expansion in Sicily, to become a full settlement in the seventh century.

3. Edward Freeman, *The History of Sicily* (Oxford: Clarendon Press, 1891), p. 258.

4. Thucydides, *History of the Peloponnesian War*, trans. Rex Warner (1954; rev. edn, London: Penguin, 1972), p. 410 [book vi].

5. On the foundation of Syracuse and the growth of the Sicilian Greek cities, see Jeremy Dummett, *Syracuse, City of Legends: A Glory of Sicily* (London: I.B. Tauris, 2010), p. 5.

6. For ancient Motya, see Aubet, *The Phoenicians and the West*, p. 200.

7. Diodorus Siculus, *Library of History*, ed. Jeffrey Henderson, trans. Francis R. Walton, Loeb Classical Library 409 (Cambridge, MA: Harvard University Press, © 1957), pp. 65–71 [book xxii].

8. Ibid., pp. 113–15 [book xxiii]. A mina was an ancient Greek money value equal to 100 drachmas. Two minas per head represented a substantial payment, possibly the equivalent of five months' pay for a craftsman or soldier. On Greek money, see Paul Cartledge, *Ancient Greece* (Oxford: Oxford University Press, 2009), p. xiv.

9. Livy, *Hannibal's War*, trans. J. C. Yardley (Oxford: Oxford World's Classics, 2006), p. 172 [book xxiii].

10. Virgil, *The Aeneid*, trans. J. W. Mackail (London: Collector's Library, 2004), p. 129 [book v]. The term 'Idalian' refers to Idalium, an ancient city in Cyprus, the birthplace of Venus.

11. Procopius, *History of the Wars*, vol. 3, ed. Jeffrey Henderson, trans. H. B. Dewing, Loeb Classical Library 107 (Cambridge, MA: Harvard University Press, © 1919), p. 47 [book v].

Chapter 2: Arab Palermo

1. Michele Amari, *Storia dei musulmani di Sicilia* (1854; Catania: Romeo Prampolini, 1933), vol. 1, p. 423. Amari, born in Palermo in 1806, was a historian and politician who sought autonomy for Sicily. He served in the provisional government of 1848–9 under Ruggero Settimo and then campaigned for the unification of Italy. He was Italy's first minister of education in the national government in Rome. A distinguished historian of Sicily, he taught himself Arabic, and his book on the Muslims in Sicily, published in 1854, is a classic on the subject. The revised edition of 1933 is widely considered to be the most useful.

2. For the Arab siege of Syracuse, see Jeremy Dummett, *Syracuse, City of Legends: A Glory of Sicily* (London: I.B. Tauris, 2010), p. 124.

3. Theodosius, *Epistola Theodosii monachi ad Leonem archidiaconum de expugnatione Syracusarum*. This letter, written in jail in Palermo sometime between 878 and 885, is quoted in full in Domenico Gaspare Lancia di Brolo, *Storia della Chiesa in Sicilia* (Palermo: Stabilimento tipografico Lao, 1880), vol. 2, p. 250 [author's English translation].

4. Denis Mack Smith, *A History of Sicily: Medieval Sicily 800–1713* (London: Chatto & Windus, 1968), p. 7. Mack Smith's two-volume history of Sicily is an important work of reference on the island.

5. Muhammad Ibn Hawqal, *Description de Palerme*, trans. into Italian by Michele Amari (Paris: Imprimerie Royale, 1865), pp. 21–30 [author's English translation and paraphrase]. Estimates of Palermo's population, based on Ibn Hawqal's figures for the number of butchers, amount to 300,000. Modern historians, including Mack Smith, consider 100,000 to be more realistic.

6. Ibn al-'Awwam, *Le livre de l'agriculture*, trans. into French by J. J. Clément-Mullet (Paris: Albert L. Herold, 1864).

7. William of Apulia, *The Deeds of Robert Guiscard*, trans. Graham A. Loud, p. 13 [book i]. Available at http://www.leeds.ac.uk/arts/downloads/file/1049/the_deeds_of_robert_guiscard_by_

william_of_apulia (accessed 17 September 2014). A chronicle written in the form of a poem in Latin between 1096 and 1099.

Chapter 3: Roger I, Norman Conqueror of Sicily

1. Geoffrey Malaterra, *The Deeds of Count Roger of Calabria and Sicily and of His Brother Duke Robert Guiscard*, trans. Kenneth Baxter Wolf (Ann Arbor, MI: University of Michigan Press, 2005), p. 42. Malaterra was a monk at the Benedictine monastery in Catania who wrote his chronicle in Latin around 1100. Medieval chroniclers, as their name suggests, recorded events with descriptions of the people who took part in them.
2. William of Apulia, *The Deeds of Robert Guiscard*, trans. Graham A. Loud, p. 22 [book i]. Available at http://www.leeds.ac.uk/arts/downloads/file/1049/the_deeds_of_robert_guiscard_by_william_of_apulia (accessed 17 September 2014).
3. Christopher Gravett, *Norman Knight* (Oxford: Osprey, 1993), p. 29. In the cloisters at Monreale, next to the fountain, there is a carving of a knight on the capital of a column wearing the familiar helmet and carrying the long shield characteristic of the Normans.
4. Matthew Bennett, 'Norman Naval activity in the Mediterranean *c*.1060–1108', in Marjorie Chibnall, ed., *Anglo-Norman Studies XV: Proceedings of the Battle Conference 1992* (Woodbridge: Boydell Press, 1993), pp. 41–50.
5. Denis Mack Smith, *A History of Sicily: Medieval Sicily 800–1713* (London: Chatto & Windus, 1968), p. 14. For more details see Daniel Waley, 'Combined operations in Sicily, AD 1060–78', *Papers of the British School at Rome* xxii (1954).
6. Amatus of Montecassino, *The History of the Normans*, ed. Graham A. Loud, trans. Prescott N. Dunbar (Woodbridge: Boydell Press, 2004), p. 138 [book v.15].
7. Malaterra, *The Deeds of Count Roger*, p. 95 [book ii.19].
8. Hubert Houben, *Roger II of Sicily: A Ruler between East and West*, trans. Graham A. Loud and Diane Milburn (Cambridge: Cambridge University Press, 2002), table 2.

Chapter 4: Roger II, King of Sicily and Southern Italy

1. Romuald, archbishop of Salerno, *Chronicon sive Annales, 1153–69*, in Hugo Falcandus, *The History of the Tyrants of Sicily*, trans. Graham A. Loud and Thomas Wiedemann (Manchester and New York, NY: Manchester University Press, 1998), p. 221. Romuald II, archbishop of Salerno 1153–81, was an important figure of Lombard descent who had medical training and acted as a diplomat.
2. Alexander of Telese, *De' fatti di Ruggiero re di Sicilia*, trans. into Italian by M. Naldi, in Giuseppe Del Re, ed., *Cronisti e scrittori sincroni della dominazione normanna nel regno di Puglia e Sicilia* (Naples: Stamperia dell'Iride, 1845), vol. 1, p. 91 [chapter iv] [author's English translation].
3. Ibid., vol. 1, p. 103 [chapters iv, v, vi] [author's English translation].
4. Romuald, *Chronicon sive Annales*, p. 221.
5. al-Edrisi, *L'Italia descritta nel 'Libro del Re Ruggero'*, trans. into Italian by M. Amari and C. Schiaparelli (Rome: Coi tipi del Salviucci, 1883), p. 21 [author's English translation].
6. Romuald, *Chronicon sive Annales*, p. 220.
7. Michele Amari, *Storia dei musulmani di Sicilia* (1854; Catania: Romeo Prampolini, 1933), vol. 3, p. 367 [author's English translation].
8. al-Maqrisi, fifteenth-century Egyptian biographer, quoted in Jeremy Johns, *Arabic Administration in Norman Sicily* (Cambridge: Cambridge University Press, 2002), p. 82.
9. al-Edrisi, *The Book of Roger*, quoted in Frances Carney Gies, 'Al-Idrisi and Roger's book', *Saudi Aramco World* (July/August 1977), pp. 14–19. Available at https://www.saudiaramcoworld.com/issue/197704/al-idrisi.and.roger.s.book.htm (accessed 17 September 2014).

10. al-Edrisi, *L'Italia descritta*, pp. 25, 26 [author's English translation and paraphrase].

11. Romuald of Salerno, *Cronica*, trans. into Italian by Giuseppe Del Re, in Giuseppe Del Re, ed., *Cronisti e scrittori sincroni della dominazione normanna nel regno di Puglia e Sicilia* (Naples: Stamperia dell'Iride, 1845), p. 17 [author's English translation].

12. Ibid., pp. 17, 18 [author's English translation and paraphrase].

13. Two Arab chroniclers refer to Philip: Ibn al-Athir and Ibn Khaldun, as quoted in Johns, *Arabic Administration*, pp. 216–17.

14. On Philip of Mahdia see: Amari, *Storia dei musulmani*, vol. 3, p. 443; John Julius Norwich, *The Kingdom in the Sun, 1130–1194* (London: Faber, 1970), pp. 157–60; and Johns, *Arabic Administration*, pp. 215–18. It is tempting to see Philip's execution as a Greek tragedy in which an atrocious crime leads to the downfall of the Norman kingdom. In reality, while this incident played its part in the downfall, so did many other factors, both internal and external.

15. Erich Caspar, *Ruggero II e la fondazione della monarchia normanna di Sicilia*, trans. into Italian by Laura Mattera Iacono and Monica Musetti (Bari: Laterza, 1999), p. 399 [author's English translation].

16. Hugo Falcandus, *The History of the Tyrants of Sicily*, trans. Graham A. Loud and Thomas Wiedemann (Manchester and New York, NY: Manchester University Press, 1998), p. 59.

Chapter 5: The Last Norman Kings

1. Hugo Falcandus, *The History of the Tyrants of Sicily*, trans. Graham A. Loud and Thomas Wiedemann (Manchester and New York, NY: Manchester University Press, 1998), p. 59. Falcandus' work was probably written in the 1170s and covers the period from February 1154 to the spring of 1169.

2. Ibid., p. 60.

3. Romuald, archbishop of Salerno, *Chronicon sive Annales, 1153–69*, in Hugo Falcandus, *The History of the Tyrants of Sicily*, trans. Graham A. Loud and Thomas Wiedemann (Manchester and New York, NY: Manchester University Press, 1998), p. 225.

4. Falcandus, *History of the Tyrants of Sicily*, p. 97. Maio left a memorial to himself in the church of San Cataldo, built in the Islamic style with red domes, which stands next to the Martorana in Piazza Bellini.

5. Ibid., p. 97.

6. Ibid., p. 136.

7. Ibid., p. 138.

8. Ibn Jubayr, *The Travels of Ibn Jubayr*, trans. R. J. C. Broadhurst (London: Jonathan Cape, 1952), p. 341.

9. Hugo Falcandus, 'A letter concerning the Sicilian tragedy to Peter, Treasurer of the Church of Palermo', in Falcandus, *History of the Tyrants of Sicily*, pp. 258–61.

10. Ibn Jubayr, *Travels*, pp. 339–40, 348–9.

11. Falcandus, *History of the Tyrants of Sicily*, p. 55.

12. For the family tree of the Hauteville dynasty, and the Norman Kings of Sicily, see appendix.

Chapter 6: Frederick II, Wonder of the World

1. Matthew Paris, *Chronica majora*, in Matthew Paris, *The Illustrated Chronicles of Matthew Paris*, trans. and ed. Richard Vaughan (Stroud: Alan Sutton and Corpus Christi College, Cambridge, 1993), p. 198. Matthew Paris was a monk at the Benedictine monastery of St Albans, who completed his chronicle in 1251.

2. Jacob Burckhardt, *The Civilization of the Renaissance in Italy* (London: Phaidon, 1945), p. 2.

3. Salimbene de Adam, *The Chronicle of Salimbene de Adam*, ed. and trans. Joseph L. Baird, Giuseppe Baglivi and John Robert Kane, Medieval and Renaissance Texts and Studies 40 (Binghamton, NY:

Medieval and Renaissance Texts and Studies, 1986), p. 350. Salimbene de Adam was an Italian monk from Parma.

4. Quoted in Georgina Masson, *Frederick II of Hohenstaufen: A Life* (London: Secker & Warburg, 1957), p. 206.

5. Salimbene de Adam, *Chronicle*, pp. 352–3.

6. Paris, *Chronica majora*, p. 202.

7. Geoffrey Barraclough, *The Origins of Modern Germany* (Oxford: Blackwell, 1947), p. 220.

8. Paris, *Chronica majora*, p. 102.

9. Dante Alighieri, *Dante's Inferno: With Translations Broadcast in the BBC Third Programme*, ed. Terence Tiller, trans. Ronald Bottrall et al. (London: BBC, 1966), p. 115 [translation of Canto XIII by Vernon Watkins]. According to David Abulafia, *Frederick I: A Medieval Emperor* (London: Allen Lane, 1988), pp. 401–4, Frederick may not have considered Piero guilty of betrayal but found this a convenient moment to get rid of him, perhaps for financial reasons.

10. Paris, *Chronica majora*, p. 198.

11. Barraclough, *Origins of Modern Germany*, p. 240.

12. H. A. L. Fisher, *A History of Europe* (London: Edward Arnold, 1936), p. 273.

Chapter 7: The Sicilian Vespers

1. For the incident in front of the church see Steven Runciman, *The Sicilian Vespers* (New York, NY: Cambridge University Press, 1958), p. 214, and Michele Amari, *History of the War of the Sicilian Vespers*, trans. Earl of Ellesmere (London: Richard Bentley, 1850), vol. 1, pp. 179–83. The date of 30 March was given by the contemporary chronicler Bartholomew of Neocastro. See Bartholomew of Neocastro, *Historia Sicula*, ed. Giuseppe Paladino (Bologna: Nicola Zanichelli, 1922), pp. 11–12, 185. Bartholomew, a lawyer from Messina who subsequently worked for the Aragonese administration, wrote his chronicle around 1292. The fact that Easter Monday remains a traditional day of celebration lends additional credibility to this date. Runciman followed this version. Not everyone is in agreement. Amari concluded that the incident at the Church of the Holy Spirit took place on 31 March, the Tuesday after Easter. See Amari, *History of the War*, vol. 1, p. 179. 31 March also appears on a commemorative plaque displayed in Palermo in front of Palazzo delle Aquile (the old Senate House) in Piazza Pretoria.

2. Bartholomew of Neocastro, *Historia Sicula*, p. 184 [author's English translation].

3. Amari, *History of the War*, vol. 1, p. 117.

4. Runciman, *The Sicilian Vespers*, p. 212.

5. Brunetto Latini, 'Capitoli del "Tesoro" di Brunetto Latini sul fatti del "Vespro"', in Enrico Sicardi, ed., *Due cronache del Vespro in volgare siciliano del secolo XIII*, Rerum Italicarum scriptores 34/1 (Bologna: Nicola Zanichelli, 1917), pp. 115–16 [author's English translation].

6. John of Saint-Rémy is remembered in Piazza Croce dei Vespri by a plaque on the wall of his palace. He managed to escape to the Palazzo dei Normanni before fleeing the city but his soldiers were attacked and many of them died in the vicinity. A memorial to the French, *La colonna del Vespro* (The Column of the Vesper) was placed in the piazza in 1737. The column that stands there today dates from the late nineteenth century.

7. Bernat Desclot, *Chronicle of the Reign of King Pedro III of Aragon, AD 1276–1285*, trans. F. L. Critchlow (Princeton, NJ: Princeton University Press, 1928), pp. 62–3.

8. Amari, *History of the War*, vol. 2, p. 104.

9. Desclot, *Chronicle of the Reign of King Pedro III*, p. 144.

10. Benedetto Croce, *History of the Kingdom of Naples*, trans. Frances Frenaye (Chicago, IL, and London: University of Chicago Press, 1970), pp. 15–16.

11. At the end of the thirteenth century the population of Sicily was around 850,000. There were

some 50,000 residents in Palermo and 30,000 in Messina, while the other Sicilian cities were considerably smaller. Stephan Epstein, *An Island for Itself: Economic Development and Social Change in Late Medieval Sicily* (Cambridge: Cambridge University Press, 1992), p. 55.

12. Amari, *History of the War*, vol. 1, p. 145.
13. Runciman, *The Sicilian Vespers*, p. 293.

Chapter 8: The Spanish Domination

1. This chapter features aspects of the long Spanish rule from the Sicilian Vespers until the arrival of the British in Sicily in 1798. While the Spanish dominated, other countries briefly ruled Sicily in this period. The sequence of rulers of Sicily in the period is as follows: Aragon (1282–1516); Spain (1516–1713); Piedmont (1713–20); Austria (1720–34); the Spanish Bourbons (1734–98). During the Napoleonic Wars there followed the British protectorate (see Chapter 9). The Spanish Bourbons returned to rule Sicily from 1816 until the arrival of Garibaldi in 1860.
2. Denis Mack Smith, *A History of Sicily: Medieval Sicily 800–1713* (London: Chatto & Windus, 1968), p. 93.
3. Scipione di Castro, *Avvertimenti a Marc'Antonio Colonna quando andò viceré di Sicilia*, quoted in Amelia Crisantino, *Breve storia della Sicilia* (Trapani: Di Girolamo, 2012), p. 126 [author's English translation].
4. The chronicler Senarega, quoted by Francesco Renda, *La fine del giudaismo siciliano* (Palermo: Sellerio, 1993), p. 109 [author's English translation].
5. In the garden of the cloisters of the Magione church in Palermo stands a well, the top of which consists of a marble slab with an inscription in Hebrew. It came from the tomb of a rabbi's son. In Syracuse, there are tombstones with Hebrew inscriptions in the courtyard of the Bellomo Regional Gallery. The Jewish baths lie deep below ground and are to be found in the old Jewish quarter of Ortygia, the historic centre of Syracuse.
6. Renda, *La fine del giudaismo siciliano*, pp. 11, 120, 167. For the statistics on the Jewish community in Sicily, see ibid., pp. 20–6. For the Jewish quarter in Palermo and the synagogue, see Aldo Saccaro, *Gli ebrei di Palermo* (Florence: Editrice La Giuntina, 2008), pp. 69–71 [author's English translation]. Francesco Renda, who died in 2013, was Professor of Modern History at Palermo University and one of Sicily's foremost historians.
7. Mack Smith, *A History of Sicily: Medieval Sicily*, p. 165.
8. Leonardo Sciascia, *Death of an Inquisitor*, trans. Ian Thompson (Manchester: Carcanet, 1990), pp. 13–16. Sciascia tells the story of the monk Diego La Matina and his battle with the Inquisition.
9. Pietro Ransano, *Delle origini e vicende di Palermo*, ed. Gioacchino Di Marzo (Palermo: Stamperia di Giovanni Lorsnaider, 1864), p. 57 [author's English translation and paraphrase].
10. Vincenzo Di Giovanni, *Le fortificazioni di Palermo nel secolo XVI giusta l'ordini dell'ing. Antonio Ferramolino* (Palermo: Tipografia Lo Statuo, 1896), appendix, p. 7 [author's English translation].
11. Xavier F. Salomon, *Van Dyck in Sicily* [exh. cat.] (Milan: Silvana Editoriale; London: Dulwich Picture Gallery, 2012), pp. 24–6. This book was published to accompany an exhibition of Van Dyck's Sicilian paintings at the Dulwich Picture Gallery, 15 February to 27 May 2012.
12. Eliana Calandra, *Il seicento e il primo festino di Santa Rosalia* (Palermo: Città di Palermo Assessorato alla Cultura, 1996), p. 126. This publication, produced for an exhibition in Palermo and backed by the city's historic archive, contains reproductions of original documents relating to the *festino*. The publication states that Geronima La Cattuta lay gravely ill in hospital when she had a vision of Santa Rosalia, who promised she would be healed if she went on a pilgrimage to Monte Pellegrino. After recovering from her illness, she went there and in another vision Rosalia told her exactly where to find her body in the cave. This is based upon a document, dated 20 September 1625, that confirmed an award for Geronima for identifying the location of the bones.

13. For 1170, the date of her death, see the 'Breve storia' section of *Santuario di Santa Rosalia* [website]. Available at http://www.santuariosantarosalia.it/santa-rosalia/in-breve/ (accessed 24 September 2014). Other sources quote the date of Rosalia's death as 1166.

14. Vincenzo Auria, *Diario delle cose occorse nella città di Palermo*, in Gioacchino Di Marzo, *Diari della città di Palermo dal secolo XVI al XIX* (Palermo: Luigi Pedone Lauriel, 1869), pp. 110–11 [author's English translation].

15. Calandra, *Il seicento*, p. 106. For a summary of Rosalia's story see pp. 21–33.

16. La Barbera's painting of Santa Rosalia can be seen in the Museo Diocesano, in the Palazzo Arcivescovile (see Chapter 17).

17. Salomon, *Van Dyck in Sicily*, p. 58.

18. Ibid., pp. 92–106. Van Dyck's painting of the *Madonna of the Rosary* can be seen in Palermo in the oratory of San Domenico (see Chapter 15).

19. See Calandra, *Il seicento*, p. 84 [author's English translation], for the archbishop's statement, and p. 32 for the senate's declaration of the festivals.

20. Patrick Brydone, *A Tour through Sicily and Malta* (1773; London: H. D. Symonds, 1807), p. 237 [letter xxii].

21. Ibid., p. 308 [letter xxx].

22. Johann Wolfgang von Goethe, *Italian Journey*, trans. W. H. Auden and Elizabeth Mayer (London: Collins, 1962), p. 240. This oft-quoted line has been taken to demonstrate Goethe's intuitive understanding of the importance of Sicily in relation to mainland Italy. Sciascia took the concept a stage further. For him Sicily was a metaphor for Italy, representing the best and the worst of its values, culture and society. See Leonardo Sciascia, *Sicily as Metaphor: Conversations Presented by Marcelle Padovani*, trans. James Marcus (Marlboro, VT: Marlboro Press, 1994).

23. Goethe, *Italian Journey*, p. 224. A plaque in Via Butera commemorates where Goethe stayed.

24. Ibid., p. 219.

25. Anthony Blunt, *Sicilian Baroque* (London: Weidenfeld & Nicolson, 1968), p. 30.

26. Denis Mack Smith, *A History of Sicily: Modern Sicily after 1713* (London: Chatto & Windus, 1968), p. 307.

27. Francesco Renda, *La grande impresa, Domenico Caracciolo viceré e primo ministro tra Palermo e Napoli* (Palermo: Sellerio, 2010), p. 49 [author's English translation].

28. Mack Smith, *A History of Sicily: Modern Sicily*, p. 324.

29. Renda, *La grande impresa*, p. 12 [author's English translation].

Chapter 9: Nelson and the British Protectorate

1. Desmond Gregory, *Sicily: The Insecure Base: A History of the British Occupation of Sicily, 1806–1815* (London and Toronto: Associated University Presses, 1988), p. 41. A summary of the British protectorate based on contemporary documents.

2. Letter from Nelson to Henry Addington, First Lord of the Treasury, 28 June 1803, in Horatio Nelson, *Letters and Despatches*, ed. John Knox Laughton (London: Longmans, 1886), p. 309.

3. Gregory, *Sicily: The Insecure Base*, p. 37.

4. Ibid., p. 39.

5. Francesco Renda, *La Sicilia nel 1812* (Caltanissetta: Salvatore Sciascia, 1963), p. 41. This study, which contains an assessment of Sicily under the British in 1812, stresses the backwardness of the island and its extreme social imbalances.

6. James Ridgway, *Sicily and England: A Sketch of Events in Sicily in 1812 and 1848 from State Papers* (London: Davy & Sons, 1849), p. ix.

7. John Wade, *British History, 1812*, quoted in Ridgway, *Sicily and England*, p. viii.

8. John Rosselli, *Lord William Bentinck: The Making of a Liberal Imperialist, 1774–1839* (London: Chatto & Windus, 1974), p. 164.

9. The constitution of 1812 was celebrated in Palermo on its 200th anniversary with a programme of cultural events at the Palazzo dei Normanni. While recognised as ahead of its time, the constitution was seen as a major contributor to the development of government in Sicily and a preparation for the events of 1848 and 1860. See *Cronache parlamentari siciliane* ix/10 (15–30 May 2012). Available at http://www.federicosecondo.org//images/stories/pdf/Cronache_9-10speciale. pdf (accessed 25 September 2014). *Cronache parlamentari siciliane* is the official magazine of the Sicilian parliament.

10. M. I. Finley, Denis Mack Smith and Christopher Duggan, *A History of Sicily* (London: Chatto & Windus, 1986), p. 162.

11. Alexandre Dumas, *I Borboni di Napoli* (Naples: Indipendente, 1862), vol. 2, p. 227.

12. Ridgway, *Sicily and England*, p. xxix.

13. Ruggero Settimo went into exile in Malta and stayed there until his death in 1863. He is honoured in Palermo by a statue in front of the Politeama, in the piazza that bears his name. The adjacent street leading to Via Maqueda is also named after him. Memorabilia from the 1848 revolt can be found at the Museo Risorgimento near the church of San Domenico (see Chapter 16). Francesco Crispi later became the first prime minister from the south, serving two terms during the period 1887 to 1896.

Chapter 10: From Garibaldi to Mussolini

1. Giuseppe Cesare Abba, *Da Quarto al Volturno, noterelle d'uno dei Mille* (Milan: Mondadori, 1980), p. 52 [author's English translation]. Abba joined the Mille and fought at Calatafimi, Palermo and Volturno in the Sixth Company. His memoir of the campaign appeared in 1880.

2. Ibid., p. 81 [author's English translation].

3. Lajos Tüköry died from his wounds, having had his leg amputated, in Palermo on 10 June. He is commemorated with a bust in Piazza Marina and in Corso Tukory, which runs down the south side of Palermo to the railway station. See ibid., pp. 94, 95.

4. Rodney Mundy, *HMS Hannibal at Palermo and Naples during the Italian Revolution, 1859–1861* (London: John Murray, 1863), p. 128. Mundy provides an account of the battle for Palermo and its aftermath.

5. Charles Stuart Forbes, *The Campaign of Garibaldi in the Two Sicilies* (Edinburgh and London: William Blackwood & Sons, 1861), p. 39. Forbes, a commander in the Royal Navy, followed Garibaldi's campaign as an independent witness to events.

6. Mundy, *HMS Hannibal*, p. 174.

7. Abba, *Da Quarto al Volturno*, p. 92 [author's English translation].

8. Mundy, *HMS Hannibal*, p. 194. Garibaldi made a big impact in Sicily. Statues and memorials to him are to be found all over the island. Along the route he followed there are plaques with messages such as 'Garibaldi rested here'. In the Risorgimento Museum near the church of San Domenico (see Chapter 16) there are memorabilia from the campaign, including a statue and portraits of the general. He is remembered by the Garibaldi Garden in the centre of Piazza Marina and by an equestrian statue opposite the Giardino Inglese. His route into Palermo is named the Corso dei Mille, followed by Via Garibaldi. Garibaldi was fortunate in his relations with the British, who significantly aided his campaigns. On his visit to England in 1864 Garibaldi received a hero's welcome, with the excitement lasting for days and crowds cheering him as he passed.

9. Denis Mack Smith, *A History of Sicily: Modern Sicily after 1713* (London: Chatto & Windus, 1968), p. 441.

10. Giuseppe Tomasi di Lampedusa, *The Leopard*, trans. Archibald Colquhoun (London: Collins and Harvill, 1961), p. 146.

11. Mack Smith, *A History of Sicily: Modern Sicily*, p. 397.

12. The origins of the Sicilian mafia have been described by many writers on Sicily, in particular: John Dickie, *Cosa Nostra: A History of the Sicilian Mafia* (2004; rev. edn, London: Hodder & Stoughton, 2007), pp. 24–5, 55; Salvatore Lupo, *History of the Mafia*, trans. Antony Shugaar (New York, NY: Columbia University Press, 2009), pp. 3–5; Norman Lewis, *The Honoured Society* (London: Collins, 1964), pp. 23–6; and Mack Smith, *A History of Sicily: Modern Sicily*, p. 448. For Leonardo Sciascia's claim that the term 'mafia' was imported to Sicily by the Piedmontese (possibly from a Tuscan word, *maffia*, meaning 'distress' or 'poverty') see Leonardo Sciascia, *La palma va a nord* (Milan: Edizioni Quaderni Radicali, 1982), p. 50.

13. Dickie, *Cosa Nostra*, p. 27. © 2004 John Dickie. Reproduced by permission of Hodder & Stoughton Ltd. John Dickie, Professor of Italian Studies at University College London, has made organised crime in Italy the subject of academic study, greatly increasing our knowledge of the subject. Pizzo literally means 'beak'. The mafioso claimed the right 'to wet his beak' in the income of businesses for which he was providing protection.

14. Leopoldo Franchetti and Sidney Sonnino, *La Sicilia nel 1876* (1877; Florence: Vallecchi, 1925), p. 1 [author's English translation]. Attacked at the time for being unpatriotic, the report has since been considered to contain some of the best analysis of the Sicilian condition.

15. Ibid., p. 65 [author's English translation].

16. Ibid., p. 44 [author's English translation]. Anti-government feeling remains strong to this day, as graffiti seen by the author on a wall in central Palermo in June 2013 demonstrates: '*Odio eterno per stato e governo*' (eternal hatred for state and government).

17. Ibid., p. 13 [author's English translation].

18. Sidney Sonnino, whose Christian name came from his English mother, was prime minister twice, in 1906 and in 1909–10. Franchetti, who served as a deputy and a senator in Rome, continued to advise the Italian government on social and economic matters.

19. For the story of Notarbartolo, see Dickie, *Cosa Nostra*, pp. 128–52.

20. On the Sicilian population, see Mack Smith, *A History of Sicily: Modern Sicily*, p. 397, and on emigration, Dickie, *Cosa Nostra*, p. 195.

21. A memorial plaque to Petrosino can be found in Piazza Marina on the side facing the Chiaramonte Palace. His story is told by Dickie, *Cosa Nostra*, pp. 195–212.

22. David Gilmour, *The Last Leopard: A Life of Giuseppe Tomasi di Lampedusa* (London: Harvill, 2003), p. 20.

23. Guy de Maupassant, *Sicily*, trans. Denis Gailor (Palermo: Sellerio, 1990), pp. 25–41, on Palermo, and pp. 63–145, for a summary of Houël's work.

24. Douglas Sladen, *In Sicily* (London: Sands, 1901), vol. 2, p. 65.

25. Ibid., vol. 1, p. xi.

26. Giuseppe Pitrè, *La vita in Palermo, cento e più anni fa* (Palermo: Alberto Reber, 1904), vol. 2, p. 470 [author's English translation].

27. Christopher Seton-Watson, *Italy from Liberalism to Fascism, 1870–1925* (London: Methuen, 1967), p. 503.

28. Mack Smith, *A History of Sicily: Modern Sicily*, p. 514.

29. For Mussolini's campaign against the mafia see Norman Lewis, *The Honoured Society* (London: Collins, 1964), pp. 61–2.

30. Orazio Cancila, *Palermo* (Rome and Bari: Laterza, 2009), p. 250.

Chapter 11: Modern Palermo

1. Carlo D'Este, *Bitter Victory* (London: Collins, 1988), p. 19.

2. Ibid., pp. 579, 606, 609.

3. The deception plan involved placing the dead body of a British officer carrying false documents off the Spanish coast. The documents, purporting to be top-secret Allied invasion plans, convinced the Germans that Sicily was not the intended location for the landings. See Ben Macintyre, *Operation Mincemeat* (London: Bloomsbury, 2010).

4. For the Americans' use of the mafia in Sicily see Rodney Campbell, *The Luciano Project* (New York, NY: McGraw-Hill, 1977), p. 175. The mafia was originally employed by the US Navy to guard the port of New York from German saboteurs landing from U-boats. These contacts were reopened to provide intelligence for the invasion of Sicily. On Luciano's involvement see Tim Newark, *Lucky Luciano* (Edinburgh: Mainstream Publishing, 2011), pp. 169–80.

5. Salvatore Lupo, *History of the Mafia*, trans. Antony Shugaar (New York, NY: Columbia University Press, 2009), pp. 188–9, and John Dickie, *Cosa Nostra: A History of the Sicilian Mafia* (2004; rev. edn, London: Hodder & Stoughton, 2007), pp. 240–4.

6. Gavin Maxwell, *God Protect Me from My Friends* (London: Pan, 1958), pp. 134–9.

7. Aldous Huxley, 'Introduction', in Danilo Dolci, *To Feed the Hungry*, trans. P. D. Cummins (London: Ace Books, 1961), p. 8.

8. Gavin Maxwell, *The Ten Pains of Death* (London: Longman, 1959), p. 8.

9. For the mafia's ability to influence votes, see Jane Schneider and Peter Schneider, *Reversible Destiny: Mafia, Antimafia and the Struggle for Palermo* (Berkeley and Los Angeles, CA: University of California Press, 2003), pp. 51–3.

10. Ibid., p. 246.

11. Saverio Lodato and Roberto Scarpinato, *Il ritorno del principe* (Milan: Chiarelettere, 2008), p. 260 and Dickie, *Cosa Nostra*, p. 358.

12. Corleone has a museum dedicated to the politicians, policemen and magistrates killed by the mafia, which was opened by the president of the Italian Republic, Carlo Azeglio Ciampi, in 2000. In 2013 the mayor of Corleone, Leoluchina Savona, celebrated the 20th anniversary of the capture of Totò Riina, apologising for the blood that was spilled, and asking the mafia to 'leave this land'. See 'Corleone apologises for decades of Mafia murders', *Daily Telegraph*, 15 January 2013.

13. For the story of Dalla Chiesa, see: Dickie, *Cosa Nostra*, pp. 384–6; Alexander Stille, *Excellent Cadavers* (London: Jonathan Cape, 1995), pp. 64–71; and Luciano Mirone, *A Palermo per morire* (Rome: Lit Edizioni, 2012). The sequence of events surrounding the general's death has been repeated many times. A dedicated officer of the law, ignoring all the obstacles put in his way, penetrates the danger zone of the state's secret dealings with terrorists and the mafia. He persists and uncovers new evidence. Slowly but surely he loses the support of the authorities and becomes isolated. Aware of the danger he is in, he confides in people close to him. At this point he is assassinated. The government officials, who have been ignoring him, rush to be seen at his funeral. His family, sickened by the lack of support he received, has nothing to do with the officials. The dead man's personal papers and computers are never seen again. A memorial to the officer is put up at the scene of his death.

14. John Dickie summarises the law's definition of an association of the mafia type as follows: 'a criminal organisation that relied on systematic intimidation, *omertà*, and the infiltration of the economy through extortion rackets carried out on a territorial basis' (Dickie, *Cosa Nostra*, p. 386). According to the mafia collaborator Gaspare Mutolo, the charge of *associazione di tipo mafioso* hit the mafia hard, amounting to a revolution that undermined their impunity. See Gaspare Mutolo, *La mafia non lascia tempo* (Milan: Rizzoli, 2013), p. 88.

15. Dickie, *Cosa Nostra*, pp. 392, 393, 397. Under the Italian judicial system criminal cases are investigated and prosecuted by magistrates supported by the police. Falcone and Borsellino both qualified as judges earlier in their careers before working as prosecuting magistrates, specialising in mafia cases. For an explanation of the system see Schneider and Schneider, *Reversible Destiny*, pp. 128–32.

16. Stille, *Excellent Cadavers*, p. 356. An outstanding account of the judges' battle with the mafia.

17. Giuseppe (Pino) Arlacchi in *La Repubblica*, 25 May 1992 [author's English translation]. Arlacchi, who was a friend of Falcone's, is an MEP and sociologist who has published interviews with mafia collaborators. The suspicion that people other than the mafia were involved in Falcone's assassination was repeated by Maria Falcone, Giovanni's sister, in an interview with Giorgio Bongiovanni. See 'Arlacchi e De Gennaro: una ragione di Stato dietro i loro silenzi?' (22 May 2014). Available at http://www.antimafiaduemila.com/2014052249618/giorgio-bongiovanni/arlacchi-e-de-gennaro-una-ragione-di-stato-dietro-i-loro-silenzi.html (accessed 25 September 2014).

18. Borsellino quoted at a convention of 18 July 2013 in Palermo. See 'Paolo Borsellino: "La mafia mi ucciderà ma saranno altri a volerlo"' (18 July 2013). Available at www.antimafiaduemila.com (accessed 25 September 2014) [author's English translation].

19. John Dickie, *Mafia Republic* (London: Hodder & Stoughton, 2013), p. 406. An expert overview of the major mafia groups (Cosa Nostra in Sicily, the Camorra in Campania and 'Ndrangheta in Calabria) and their impact upon the Italian state.

20. Giovanni Falcone with Marcelle Padovani, *Men of Honour*, trans. Edward Farrelly (London: Warner, 1993), p. 170.

21. Gian Carlo Caselli, *Le due guerre* (Milan: Melampo, 2009), p. 53. This book is a revealing account of Italy's battles with its internal enemies. Its subtitle translates as 'Why Italy beat terrorism but not the mafia'.

22. Mutolo, *La mafia non lascia tempo*, p. 164 [author's English translation].

23. 'Giulio Andreotti: Ex-Italian prime minister dies', *BBC News* [website] (6 May 2013). Available at http://www.bbc.co.uk/news/world-europe-22426199 (accessed 25 September 2014). See also Gian Carlo Caselli and Antonio Ingroia, *Vent'anni contro* (Bari: Laterza, 2013), p. 1.

24. Caselli and Ingroia, *Vent'anni contro*, pp. 1–16.

25. Leoluca Orlando, *Fighting the Mafia and Renewing Sicilian Culture* (San Francisco, CA: Encounter Books, 2001), pp. 190–7. An insider's story of antimafia work in the toughest times.

26. See Addiopizzo's website. Available at http://www.addiopizzo.org/english.asp (accessed 25 September 2014).

27. Export of the various Italian mafia groups' capital is the subject of research at Milan's Università Cattolica. According to their study, in 2013 the Bank of Italy received notification of 60,000 suspect transactions, worth 85 billion euros (*Corriere della Sera*, 2 March 2014). For the comment on Rome, see the interview with the Palermo magistrates Antonino Di Matteo and Leonardo Guarnotta in the *Corriere della Sera*, 23 May 2012.

28. Author's estimates based on data from the *Regione Siciliana* [website]. Their latest report is available at http://pti.regione.sicilia.it/ (accessed 10 October 2014). Visitors on cruise ships, who are on the increase, are not included in these figures. According to Antonio Tajani, from the European Commission in Brussels, in an interview in the *Giornale di Sicilia*, 13 June 2013, the Balearic Islands in Spain, with a comparable length of coastline to Sicily's but without its advantages in terms of history, monuments and food, attract more than ten times the number of international visitors.

29. Article by Sonia Alfano, president of the European Parliament's Antimafia Commission, in *La Sicilia*, 28 January 2014.

30. Interview with Rosario Crocetta, *La Repubblica*, 30 October 2012.

Chapter 12: The Historic Centre

1. Corso Vittorio Emanuele is sometimes known as 'Via' Vittorio Emanuele. The official position is difficult to establish. At the corner of Via Roma and Vittorio Emanuele there are two road signs, one with 'Via' and a more modern one with 'Corso'. The traditional and popular version, Corso, has been used in this book.

2. Rosario La Duca, *Da Panormus a Palermo* (Palermo: Pietro Vittorietti Edizioni, 2006), p. 198 [author's English translation].

Chapter 13: Antiquity

1. See map section.
2. Thucydides, *History of the PeloponnesianWar*, trans. RexWarner (1954; rev. edn, London: Penguin, 1972), p. 410 [book vi]. This text is quoted in Chapter 1. See also Maria Eugenia Aubet, *The Phoenicians and the West* (Cambridge: Cambridge University Press, 1993), p. 200.
3. At the time of writing the Museo Archeologico has been closed for restoration work for five years. Part of the ground floor has recently been reopened. Judging by the quality of the work done to the exterior, visible from Via Roma, this will prove to be another excellent job. However, there is no way of telling what changes are being made to the interior layout.
4. Douglas Sladen, *In Sicily* (London: Sands, 1901), vol. 2, p. 290.
5. R. J. A. Wilson, *Sicily under the Roman Empire* (Oxford: Aris & Phillips, 1990), pp. 156, 157.
6. For the archaeological sites see: Margaret Guido, *Sicily: An Archaeological Guide* (London: Faber, 1967); Gaia Servadio, *Motya: Unearthing a Lost Civilisation* (London: Phoenix, 2000); and Joseph Farrell, *Sicily: A Cultural History* (Oxford: Signal Books, 2012).

Chapter 14: The Norman Era

1. John Julius Norwich, *The Kingdom in the Sun, 1130–1194* (London: Faber, 1970), pp. 401–3 [appendix: 'The Norman monuments of Sicily']. This work contains descriptions of the Norman monuments as part of the main text. A list of all the Norman monuments in Sicily, rated by quality, is contained in an appendix.
2. Otto Demus, *The Mosaics of Norman Sicily* (London: Routledge & Kegan Paul, 1949), pp. 371–2. Demus, the author of *Byzantine Mosaic Decoration*, began studying the mosaics at Monreale in the 1930s. His research, which broadened to include all the Norman mosaics in Sicily, started with the chroniclers and other original sources. He went on to discover documents referring to the foundation and creation of these monuments. An Austrian, Demus moved to England during World War II, where he wrote his study. It was published in 1950 and contains 120 black-and-white photos of the mosaics.
3. David Talbot Rice, *Byzantine Art* (Harmondsworth: Penguin, 1954), p. 126.
4. James Dickie, 'Allah and eternity: Mosques, madrasas and tombs', in George Michell, ed., *Architecture of the IslamicWorld* (London: Thames & Hudson, 1978), p. 34.
5. Guy de Maupassant, *Sicily*, trans. Denis Gailor (Palermo: Sellerio, 1990), p. 28.
6. Romuald, archbishop of Salerno, *Chronicon sive Annales, 1153–69*, in Hugo Falcandus, *The History of the Tyrants of Sicily*, trans. Graham A. Loud and Thomas Wiedemann (Manchester and New York, NY: Manchester University Press, 1998), p. 238. On King William I (1154–66): 'He had the chapel of St Peter in his palace painted with marvellous pictures, covered its walls with different sorts of valuable marble and greatly enriched and ornamented it with gold and silver vessels and precious vestments. He instituted many clerics and prebends there and arranged for the divine office to be properly and carefully celebrated in reverence and fear of God.'
7. Demus, *Mosaics of Norman Sicily*, p. 27.
8. Douglas Sladen, *In Sicily* (London: Sands, 1901), vol. 2, p. 76.
9. Demus, who based his judgement on an analysis of graphic styles, came to the conclusion that the same workshop was employed at all three locations. This is contested in Ernst Kitzinger, *The Mosaics of St Mary's of the Admiral in Palermo*, Dumbarton Oaks Studies 27 (Washington DC: Dumbarton Oaks Research Library and Collection, 1990). Kitzinger acknowledges similarities

in style but doubts that they were done by one workshop. There is agreement, however, that the original work at all three sites was done by craftsmen from Constantinople.

10. Demus, *Mosaics of Norman Sicily*, p. 183.
11. Norwich, *Kingdom in the Sun*, pp. 88–90.
12. Demus, *Mosaics of Norman Sicily*, p. 73.
13. Ibn Jubayr, *The Travels of Ibn Jubayr*, trans. R. J. C. Broadhurst (London: Jonathan Cape, 1952), p. 349.
14. Romuald, *Chronicon sive Annales*, p. 219.
15. Michele Amari, *Le epigrafi arabiche di Sicilia* (Palermo: Luigi Pedone Lauriel, 1875), p. 61 [author's English translation].
16. Demus, *Mosaics of Norman Sicily*, pp. 178–80.
17. John Julius Norwich, *The Normans in the South, 1016–1130* (London: Faber, 1967), p. 178.

Chapter 15: Baroque Palermo

1. Anthony Blunt, *Sicilian Baroque* (London: Weidenfeld & Nicolson, 1968), p. 9.
2. Ibid., p. 10.
3. The figures are based on the monuments listed in the index to Adriana Chirco, *Palermo: la città ritrovata* (Palermo: Dario Flaccovio, 2005).
4. Patrick Brydone, *A Tour through Sicily and Malta* (1773; London: H. D. Symonds, 1807), p. 287 [letter xxvii].
5. The Solomonic column is a twisted column used in architecture, examples of which were brought to Rome by Constantine the Great in the fourth century. According to the legend, these columns came from the Temple of Solomon in Jerusalem. Bernini famously used the design in the *Baldacchino*, a sculpted canopy over the high altar in St Peter's Basilica in Rome. The Solomonic column became a feature of baroque architecture, of which there are many examples in Palermo.
6. Blunt, *Sicilian Baroque*, p. 35.
7. Sacheverell Sitwell, *Southern Baroque Revisited* (London: Weidenfeld & Nicolson, 1967), p. 28.
8. Blunt, *Sicilian Baroque*, p. 35.
9. Ibid., p. 42.
10. Johann Wolfgang von Goethe, *Italian Journey*, trans. W. H. Auden and Elizabeth Mayer (London: Collins, 1962), p. 226.

Chapter 16: The Nineteenth Century

1. Orazio Cancila, *Palermo* (Rome and Bari: Laterza, 2009), p. 167.
2. For the history of the Massimo up until the closure in 1974, see Luigi Maniscalco Basile, *Storia del Teatro Massimo di Palermo* (Florence: Leo Olschki, 1984).
3. Leoluca Orlando, *Fighting the Mafia and Renewing Sicilian Culture* (San Francisco, CA: Encounter Books, 2001), p. 194.
4. For the story of Motya and the Whitakers' involvement, see Gaia Servadio, *Motya: Unearthing a Lost Civilisation* (London: Phoenix, 2000).

Chapter 17: Other Important Monuments

1. Xavier F. Salomon, *Van Dyck in Sicily* [exh. cat.] (Milan: Silvana Editoriale; London: Dulwich Picture Gallery, 2012), p. 90.
2. Maria Grazia Paolini, 'Il *Trionfo* oggi', in *Il 'Trionfo della Morte' di Palermo* [exh. cat.] (Palermo: Sellerio, 1969), p. 21. The powerful impact of the fresco is said to have influenced many painters, possibly including Picasso for his *Guernica*.

3. For background on Antonello and the date of the Palermo *Annunziata*, see Marco Bussagli, *Antonello da Messina* (Florence: Giunti, 2006), pp. 1–33. For Vasari's comments, see Giorgio Vasari, *Lives of the Artists* (New York, NY: Noonday Press, 1957), p. 88, and for Berenson see Bernard Berenson, *Italian Painters of the Renaissance* (London: Phaidon, 1952), p. 143.

4. Andrea Camilleri, *La Vucciria: Renato Guttuso* (Milan: Skira, 2008), p. 54 [author's English translation].

5. Tommaso Fazello, *Della storia di Sicilia*, trans. into Italian by P. M. Remigio (Palermo: Tipografia Giuseppe Assenzio, 1817), vol. 1, p. 500 [author's English translation]. A bronze coin of this description was produced in Palermo under the Romans which featured Zeus and a thunderbolt but there is no evidence of a serpent. Coins from the ancient Greek period in Sicily show a bearded god seated on a rock (Zeus or Poseidon) while from Selinus (modern Selinunte) there are coins showing a nymph with a serpent. The image of the Genius presumably drew upon these ancient designs.

6. Antonella Chiazza, *Il genio di Palermo* (Palermo: Pitti Edizioni, 2010), p. 119.

7. Ibid., p. 55.

8. Further representations of the Genius around the city include two marble panels by the port in Via Emerico Amari, probably the oldest of them all; an eighteenth-century fresco in the ballroom of the Palazzo Isnello and a nineteenth-century mosaic in the Palazzo dei Normanni, located above the entrance to the Palatine Chapel.

9. Opposite the church is one of the gastronomic landmarks of Palermo, L'Antica Focacceria San Francesco, where traditional street food is served. Founded in 1832, it counts among its famous customers Garibaldi and his redshirts.

10. Vasari, *Lives of the Artists*, p. 183.

Further Reading

Sicily

Norman Lewis, *In Sicily* (London: Jonathan Cape, 2000).
Peter Robb, *Midnight in Sicily* (London: Harvill, 1999).

Palermo

Leoluca Orlando, *Fighting the Mafia and Renewing Sicilian Culture* (San Francisco, CA: Encounter Books, 2001). [The mayor's story.]
Roberto Alajmo, *Palermo*, trans. Guido Waldman (London: Haus, 2010). [Reflections on the city by a lifelong resident.]

Travellers' accounts

Patrick Brydone, *A Tour through Sicily and Malta* (1773; London: H. D. Symonds, 1807). [Brydone was in Sicily, including Palermo, in 1770 and left this lively account of his visit.]
Carlo Levi, *Words Are Stones: Impressions of Sicily*, trans. Antony Shugaar (London: Hesperus Press, 2005). [Original: Carlo Levi, *Le parole sono pietre* (Turin: Einaudi, 1955). Sicily, including Palermo, described by one of Italy's foremost writers from the post-World War II period.]

Food and wine

Mary Simeti, *Sicilian Food* (Butler & Tanner Ltd, Frome and London, 1989).
Robert Camuto, *Palmento: A Sicilian Wine Odyssey* (Lincoln, NE, and London: University of Nebraska Press, 2010).
Andrew Graham-Dixon and Giorgio Locatelli, *Sicily Unpacked* (BBC2, January 2012). [This television series, which combines art history with Sicilian food, covers Palermo in episode one.]

Guidebooks

Joseph Farrell, *Sicily: A Cultural History* (Oxford: Signal Books, 2012).
Andrew and Suzanne Edwards, *Sicily: A Literary Guide for Travellers* (London: I.B. Tauris, 2014).

Fiction

Giuseppe Tomasi di Lampedusa, *The Leopard*, trans. Archibald Colquhoun (London: Collins and Harvill, 1961). [Original: Giuseppe Tomasi di Lampedusa, *Il gattopardo* (Milan: Feltrinelli, 1958). Sicily's greatest historical novel, set in the period after Garibaldi's campaign.]

David Gilmour, *The Last Leopard: A Life of Giuseppe Tomasi di Lampedusa* (London: Harvill, 2003). [The story of Lampedusa and his times.]

Leonardo Sciascia, *The Day of the Owl*, trans. Archibald Colquhoun and Arthur Oliver (London: Granta, 2001). [Original: Leonardo Sciascia, *Il giorno della civetta* (Milan: Einaudi, 1961)], and *Equal Danger*, trans. Adrienne Foulke (London: Granta, 2001) [Original: *Il Contesto* (Torino: Einaudi, 1971). Both books are political thrillers.]

Tariq Ali, *A Sultan in Palermo* (London: Verso, 2005). [The story of al-Edrisi, the Arab geographer, during the dying years of the Norman kingdom.]

Bibliography

History

Abba, Giuseppe Cesare, *Da Quarto al Volturno, noterelle d'uno dei Mille* (Milan: Mondadori, 1980).

Abulafia, David, *Frederick I: A Medieval Emperor* (London: Allen Lane, 1988).

Acton, Harold, *The Bourbons of Naples* (London: Prion Books, 1957).

Alighieri, Dante, *Dante's Inferno: With Translations Broadcast in the BBC Third Programme*, ed. Terence Tiller, trans. Ronald Bottrall et al. (London: BBC, 1966). [Italian original written *c*.1314–21. Translation of Canto XIII by Vernon Watkins.]

Amari, Michele, *La guerra del vespro siciliano* (Mazara: Società Editrice Siciliana, 1842).

——— *History of the War of the Sicilian Vespers*, 3 vols, trans. Earl of Ellesmere (London: Richard Bentley, 1850).

——— *Storia dei musulmani di Sicilia*, 3 vols (1854; Catania: Romeo Prampolini, 1933).

——— *Altre narrazioni del vespro siciliano* (Milan: Ulrico Hoepli, Editore-Libraio della Real Casa, 1867).

——— *Le epigrafi arabiche di Sicilia* (Palermo: Luigi Pedone Lauriel, 1875).

——— *Biblioteca arabo-sicula* (Turin and Rome: Ermanno Loescher, 1880).

Amatus of Montecassino, *The History of the Normans*, ed. Graham A. Loud, trans. Prescott N. Dunbar (Woodbridge: Boydell Press, 2004).

Aubet, Maria Eugenia, *The Phoenicians and the West* (Cambridge: Cambridge University Press, 1993).

Barbera, Giuseppe, *Conca d'oro* (Palermo: Sellerio, 2012).

Barraclough, Geoffrey, *The Origins of Modern Germany* (Oxford: Blackwell, 1947).

Bartholomew of Neocastro, *Historia Sicula*, ed. Giuseppe Paladino (Bologna: Nicola Zanichelli, 1922).

Basile, Gaetano, *Palermo è…* (Palermo: Dario Flaccovio, 1998).

Beladiez, Emilio, *Don Pedro Il Grande duca d'Osuna* (Bologna: Edizioni Nobiltà, 1997).

Bianco, Giuseppe, *La Sicilia durante l'occupazione inglese, 1806–1815* (Palermo: Alberto Reber, 1902).

Bosworth, R. J. B., *Mussolini's Italy* (London: Allen Lane, 2005).

Brown, Gordon S., *The Norman Conquest of Southern Italy and Sicily* (Jefferson, NC, and London: McFarland, 2003).

Brown, R. Allen, *The Normans* (Woodbridge: Boydell Press, 1984).

Buttitta, Antonino, *Libro di Palermo* (Palermo: Flaccovio, 1977).

Calandra, Eliana, *Il seicento e il primo festino di Santa Rosalia* (Palermo: Città di Palermo Assessorato alla Cultura, 1996).

Campbell, Rodney, *The Luciano Project* (New York, NY: McGraw-Hill, 1977).

Cancila, Orazio, *Palermo* (Rome and Bari: Laterza, 2009).

Caspar, Erich, *Ruggero II e la fondazione della monarchia normanna di Sicilia*, trans. into Italian by Laura Mattera Iacono and Monica Musetti (Bari: Laterza, 1999). [Originally published in German in 1904.]

Chalandon, Ferdinand, *Histoire de la domination normande en Italie et en Sicile* (Paris: Librairie Alphonse Picard et Fils, 1907, repr. New York, NY: Burt Franklin, 1960).

Comnena, Anna, *Alexiad* [*c*.1148], trans. Elizabeth A. Dawes (London: Routledge & Kegan Paul, 1928). Available at www.fordham.edu/halsall/basis/AnnaComnena-Alexiad.html (accessed 16 September 2014).

Crisantino, Amelia, *Breve storia della Sicilia* (Trapani: Di Girolamo, 2012).

Croce, Benedetto, *History of the Kingdom of Naples*, trans. Frances Frenaye (Chicago, IL, and London: University of Chicago Press, 1970). [Originally published in Italian in 1925 by Laterza.]

Da Lentini, Giacomo, *Poesie*, ed. Roberto Antonelli (Rome: Bulzoni, 1979).

Davis, R. H. C., *The Normans and their Myth* (London: Thames & Hudson, 1976).

Del Re, Giuseppe, ed., *Cronisti e scrittori sincroni della dominazione normanna nel regno di Puglia e Sicilia* (Naples: Stamperia dell'Iride, 1845). [Italian translations of the chroniclers, including Alexander of Telese, Romuald of Salerno, Hugo Falcandus and Falco of Benevento.]

Desclot, Bernat, *Chronicle of the Reign of King Pedro III of Aragon, A D 1276–1285*, trans. F. L. Critchlow (Princeton, NJ: Princeton University Press, 1928).

Di Marzo, Gioacchino, *Diari della città di Palermo dal secolo XVI al XIX* (Palermo: Luigi Pedone Lauriel, 1869).

Diodorus Siculus, *Library of History*, ed. Jeffrey Henderson, trans. Francis R. Walton, Loeb Classical Library 409 (Cambridge, MA: Harvard University Press, © 1957).

Duggan, Christopher, *Francesco Crispi, 1818–1901: From Nation to Nationalism* (Oxford: Oxford University Press, 2002).

Dummett, Jeremy, *Syracuse, City of Legends: A Glory of Sicily* (London: I.B. Tauris, 2010).

Epstein, Stephan, *An Island for Itself: Economic Development and Social Change in Late Medieval Sicily* (Cambridge: Cambridge University Press, 1992).

Falcandus, Hugo, *The History of the Tyrants of Sicily*, trans. Graham A. Loud and Thomas Wiedemann (Manchester and New York, NY: Manchester University Press, 1998).

Fazello, Tommaso, *Della storia di Sicilia*, trans. into Italian by P. M. Remigio (Palermo: Tipografia Giuseppe Assenzio, 1817). [Original written in Latin, 1558.]

Finley, M. I., *Ancient Sicily* (London: Chatto & Windus, 1979).

Finley, M. I., Denis Mack Smith and Christopher Duggan, *A History of Sicily* (London: Chatto & Windus, 1986).

Fisher, H. A. L., *A History of Europe* (London: Edward Arnold, 1936).

Fletcher, Richard, *The Cross and the Crescent* (London: Penguin, 2003).

Forbes, Charles Stuart, *The Campaign of Garibaldi in the Two Sicilies* (Edinburgh and London: William Blackwood & Sons, 1861).

Franchetti, Leopoldo, and Sidney Sonnino, *La Sicilia nel 1876* (1877; Florence: Vallecchi, 1925).

Gilmour, David, *In Pursuit of Italy* (London: Allen Lane, 2011).

Gravett, Christopher, *Norman Knight* (Oxford: Osprey, 1993).

Hazleton, Lesley, *The First Muslim: The Story of Muhammad* (London: Atlantic Books, 2013).

Hibbert, Christopher, *Garibaldi and His Enemies* (London: Longmans, 1965).

——— *Nelson: A Personal History* (London: Penguin, 1995).

Houben, Hubert, *Roger II of Sicily: A Ruler between East and West*, trans. Graham A. Loud and Diane Milburn (Cambridge: Cambridge University Press, 2002). [Originally published in German, 1997.]

Jamison, Evelyn, *Admiral Eugenius of Sicily: His Life and Work* (London: Oxford University Press, 1957).

Johns, Jeremy, *Arabic Administration in Norman Sicily* (Cambridge: Cambridge University Press, 2002).

Kantorowicz, Ernst, *Frederick the Second, 1194–1250* (London: Constable, 1931).

La Duca, Rosario, *Da Panormus a Palermo* (Palermo: Pietro Vittorietti Edizioni, 2006).

La Lumia, Isidoro, *Storia della Sicilia sotto Guglielmo il Buono* (Florence: Successori Le Monnier, 1867).

Lamb, Richard, *War in Italy, 1943–1945* (London: John Murray, 1993).

Lancia di Brolo, Domenico Gaspare, *Storia della Chiesa in Sicilia* (Palermo: Stabilimento tipografico Lao, 1880).

Latini, Brunetto, 'Capitoli del "Tesoro" di Brunetto Latini sul fatti del "Vespro"', in Enrico Sicardi, ed., *Due cronache del Vespro in volgare siciliano del secolo XIII*, Rerum Italicarum scriptores 34/1 (Bologna: Nicola Zanichelli, 1917).

Lupo, Salvatore, *History of the Mafia*, trans. Antony Shugaar (New York, NY: Columbia University Press, 2009). [First published in Italian, 1993.]

Mack Smith, Denis, *A History of Sicily: Medieval Sicily 800–1713* (London: Chatto & Windus, 1968).

———— *A History of Sicily: Modern Sicily after 1713* (London: Chatto & Windus, 1968).

———— *Mazzini* (New Haven, CT, and London: Yale University Press, 1994).

Malaterra, Geoffrey, *The Deeds of Count Roger of Calabria and Sicily and of His Brother Duke Robert Guiscard*, trans. Kenneth Baxter Wolf (Ann Arbor, MI: University of Michigan Press, 2005).

Mallette, Karla, *The Kingdom of Sicily, 1100–1250: A Literary History* (Philadelphia, PA: University of Pennsylvania Press, 2005).

Masson, Georgina, *Frederick II of Hohenstaufen: A Life* (London: Secker & Warburg, 1957).

Miles, Richard, *Carthage Must Be Destroyed* (London: Allen Lane, 2010).

Mundy, Rodney, *HMS Hannibal at Palermo and Naples during the Italian Revolution, 1859–1861* (London: John Murray, 1863).

Nelson, Horatio, *Letters and Despatches*, ed. John Knox Laughton (London: Longmans, 1886).

Norwich, John Julius, *The Normans in the South, 1016–1130* (London: Faber, 1967).

———— *The Kingdom in the Sun, 1130–1194* (London: Faber, 1970).

Palermo Patera, Giuseppe, *Palermo araba* (Palermo: La Bottega di Hefesto, 1994).

Papa Algozino, Rosaria, *Sicilia araba* (Catania: Edizioni Greco, 1977).

Paris, Matthew, *Chronica majora* [extracts], in Matthew Paris, *The Illustrated Chronicles of Matthew Paris*, trans. and ed. Richard Vaughan (Stroud: Alan Sutton and Corpus Christi College, Cambridge, 1993).

Peter of Eboli, *Liber ad honorem Augusti*, ed. and trans. Francesco De Rosa (Cassino: Francesco Ciolfi, 2001).

Pitrè, Giuseppe, *La vita in Palermo, cento e più anni fa* (Palermo: Alberto Reber, 1904).

Quatriglio, Giuseppe, *Breve storia di Palermo* (Palermo: Flaccovio, 2011).

Ransano, Pietro, *Delle origini e vicende di Palermo*, ed. Gioacchino Di Marzo (Palermo: Stamperia di Giovanni Lorsnaider, 1864). [Original written in Latin, 1471.]

Renda, Francesco, *La Sicilia nel 1812* (Caltanissetta: Salvatore Sciascia, 1963).

———— *La fine del giudaismo siciliano* (Palermo: Sellerio, 1993).

———— *La storia della Sicilia dal 1860 al 1970* (Palermo: Sellerio, 1999).

———— *La grande impresa, Domenico Caracciolo viceré e primo ministro tra Palermo e Napoli* (Palermo: Sellerio, 2010).

Ridgway, James, *Sicily and England: A Sketch of Events in Sicily in 1812 and 1848 from State Papers* (London: Davy & Sons, 1849).

Rosselli, John, *Lord William Bentinck: The Making of a Liberal Imperialist, 1774–1839* (London: Chatto & Windus, 1974).

Runciman, Steven, *The Sicilian Vespers* (New York, NY: Cambridge University Press, 1958).

Saccaro, Aldo, *Gli ebrei di Palermo* (Florence: Editrice La Giuntina, 2008).

Salimbene de Adam, *The Chronicle of Salimbene de Adam*, ed. and trans. Joseph L. Baird, Giuseppe Baglivi and John Robert Kane, Medieval and Renaissance Texts and Studies 40 (Binghamton, NY: Medieval and Renaissance Texts and Studies, 1986).

Sciascia, Leonardo, *Death of an Inquisitor*, trans. Ian Thompson (Manchester: Carcanet, 1990). [Original: Leonardo Sciascia, *Morte dell'inquisitore* (Bari: Laterza, 1964).]

Scinà, Domenico, *La topografia di Palermo* (Palermo: Reale Stamperia, 1818).

Servadio, Gaia, *Motya: Unearthing a Lost Civilisation* (London: Phoenix, 2000).

Seton-Watson, Christopher, *Italy from Liberalism to Fascism, 1870–1925* (London: Methuen, 1967).

Trevelyan, Raleigh, *Princes under the Volcano* (New York, NY: William Morrow, 1973).

Wilson, R. J. A., *Sicily under the Roman Empire* (Oxford: Aris & Phillips, 1990).

Modern Era

Aglianò, Sebastiano, *Questa Sicilia* (Verona: Mondadori, 1950).

Alajmo, Roberto, *Palermo*, trans. Guido Waldman (London: Haus, 2010).

Alfano, Sonia, *La zona d'ombra* (Milan: Rizzoli, 2011).

Arlacchi, Pino, *Gli uomini del disonore* (Milan: Mondadori, 1992).

———— *Addio Cosa Nostra* (Milan: Rizzoli, 1994).

Baranski, Zygmunt, and Rebecca West, eds, *The Cambridge Companion to Modern Italian Culture* (Cambridge: Cambridge University Press, 2001).

Bocca, Giorgio, *Annus horribilis* (Milan: Feltrinelli, 2010).

Camilleri, Andrea, *Come la penso* (Milan: Chiarelettere, 2013).

Camuto, Robert, *Palmento: A Sicilian Wine Odyssey* (Lincoln, NE, and London: University of Nebraska Press, 2010).

Caselli, Gian Carlo, *Un magistrato fuori legge* (Milan: Melampo, 2005).

———— *Le due guerre* (Milan: Melampo, 2009).

Caselli, Gian Carlo and Antonio Ingroia, *Vent'anni contro* (Bari: Laterza, 2013).

Consolo, Vincenzo, *The Smile of the Unknown Mariner*, trans. Joseph Farrell (Manchester: Carcanet, 1994). [Original: Vincenzo Consolo, *Il sorriso dell'ignoto marinaio* (Turin: Einaudi, 1976).]

———— *Lo spasimo di Palermo* (Milan: Mondadori, 1998).

Dickie, John, *Cosa Nostra: A History of the Sicilian Mafia* (2004; rev. edn, London: Hodder & Stoughton, 2007).

———— *Mafia Republic* (London: Hodder & Stoughton, 2013).

Emmott, Bill, *Forza, Italia: come ripartire dopo Berlusconi* (Milan: Rizzoli, 2010).

Falcone, Giovanni, with Marcelle Padovani, *Men of Honour*, trans. Edward Farrelly (London: Warner, 1993).

Follain, John, *Vendetta: The Mafia, Judge Falcone and the Quest for Justice* (London: Hodder & Stoughton, 2012).

Gilmour, David, *The Last Leopard: A Life of Giuseppe Tomasi di Lampedusa* (London: Harvill, 2003).

Ginsborg, Paul, *Italy and Its Discontents, 1980–2001* (London: Allen Lane, 2001).

Giudice, Gaspare, *La Sicilia di Leonardo Sciascia* (Palermo: Ugo La Rosa, 1996).

Ingroia, Antonio, *Palermo, gli splendori e le miserie, l'eroismo e la viltà* (Milan: Melampo, 2012).

Jackson, Giovanna, *Leonardo Sciascia 1956–76: A Thematic and Structural Study* (Ravenna: Longo, 1981).

Jones, Tobias, *The Dark Heart of Italy* (London: Faber, 2003).

Lampedusa, Giuseppe Tomasi di, *The Leopard*, trans. Archibald Colquhoun (London: Collins and Harvill, 1961). [Original: Giuseppe Tomasi di Lampedusa, *Il gattopardo* (Milan: Feltrinelli, 1958).]

Lane, David, *Berlusconi's Shadow* (London: Allen Lane, 2004).

Lewis, Norman, *The Honoured Society* (London: Collins, 1964).

———— *In Sicily* (London: Jonathan Cape, 2000).

Lodato, Saverio, and Roberto Scarpinato, *Il ritorno del principe* (Milan: Chiarelettere, 2008).

Macintyre, Ben, *Operation Mincemeat* (London: Bloomsbury, 2010).

Mafai, Simona, ed., *Riflessioni sulla storia della Sicilia dal dopoguerra ad oggi* (Caltanissetta and Rome: Salvatore Sciascia, 2007).

Maxwell, Gavin, *God Protect Me from My Friends* (London: Pan, 1958).

———— *The Ten Pains of Death* (London: Longman, 1959).

Mirone, Luciano, *A Palermo per morire* (Rome: Lit Edizioni, 2012).

Mutolo, Gaspare, *La mafia non lascia tempo* (Milan: Rizzoli, 2013).

Newark, Tim, *Lucky Luciano* (Edinburgh: Mainstream Publishing, 2011).

Orlando, Leoluca, *Fighting the Mafia and Renewing Sicilian Culture* (San Francisco, CA: Encounter Books, 2001).

Robb, Peter, *Midnight in Sicily* (London: Harvill, 1999).

Schneider, Jane and Peter Schneider, *Reversible Destiny: Mafia, Antimafia and the Struggle for Palermo* (Berkeley and Los Angeles, CA: University of California Press, 2003).

Sciascia, Leonardo, *The Day of the Owl*, trans. Archibald Colquhoun and Arthur Oliver (London: Granta, 2001). [Original: Leonardo Sciascia, *Il giorno della civetta* (Milan: Einaudi, 1961).]

———— *To Each His Own*, trans. Adrienne Foulke (Manchester: Carcanet, 1989). [Original: Leonardo Sciascia, *A ciascuno il suo* (Turin: Einaudi, 1966).]

———— *Equal Danger*, trans. Adrienne Foulke (London: Granta, 2001). [Original: Leonardo Sciascia, *Il contesto* (Turin: Einaudi, 1971).]

———— *La palma va a nord* (Milan: Edizioni Quaderni Radicali, 1982).

———— *Fatti diversi di storia letteraria e civile* (Palermo: Sellerio, 1989).

———— *La corda pazza* (Milan: Adelphi Edizioni, 1991).

———— *Sicily as Metaphor: Conversations Presented by Marcelle Padovani*, trans. James Marcus (Marlboro, VT: Marlboro Press, 1994).

Simeti, Mary Taylor, *Sicilian Food* (Frome and London: Butler & Tanner, 1989).

Stille, Alexander, *Excellent Cadavers* (London: Jonathan Cape, 1995).

Monuments

Abbate, Vincenzo, and Michele Cordaro, *Il 'Trionfo della morte' di Palermo* (Palermo: Sellerio, 1989).

Basile, Luigi Maniscalco, *Storia del Teatro Massimo di Palermo* (Florence: Leo Olschki, 1984).

Bellafiore, Giuseppe, *The Cathedral of Palermo* (Palermo: Flaccovio, 1976).

———— *Palermo: guida della città* (Palermo: Punto Grafico, 2009).

Berenson, Bernard, *Italian Painters of the Renaissance* (London: Phaidon, 1952).

Blunt, Anthony, *Sicilian Baroque* (London: Weidenfeld & Nicolson, 1968).

Bussagli, Marco, *Antonello da Messina* (Florence: Giunti, 2006).

Camilleri, Andrea, *La Vucciria: Renato Guttuso* (Milan: Skira, 2008).

Cammarata, Francesco, *Palermo: una strada, un personaggio siciliano* (Palermo: Comunità Nuova Edizioni, 1984).

Chiazza, Antonella, *Il genio di Palermo* (Palermo: Pitti Edizioni, 2010).

Chirco, Adriana, *Palermo: la città ritrovata* (Palermo: Dario Flaccovio, 2005).

De Seta, Cesare, and Leonardo Di Mauro, *Palermo* (Rome and Bari: Laterza, 1981).

Demus, Otto, *The Mosaics of Norman Sicily* (London: Routledge & Kegan Paul, 1949).

Di Giovanni, Vincenzo, *Sul porto antico e su le mura, le piazze e i bagni di Palermo* (Palermo: Tipografia Virzi, 1881).

———— *La topografia antica di Palermo* (Palermo: Tipografia e legatoria del Boccone del povero, 1889).

———— *Le fortificazioni di Palermo nel secolo XVI giusta l'ordini dell'ing. Antonio Ferramolino* (Palermo: Tipografia Lo Statuo, 1896).

Di Natale, Maria Concetta, *Il Museo Diocesano* (Palermo: Flaccovio, 2010).

Di Stefano, Carmela Angela, *Palermo punica: Museo archeologico regionale Antonino Salinas, 6 dicembre 1995–30 settembre 1996* [exh. cat.] (Palermo: Sellerio, 1996).

Dickie, James, 'Allah and eternity: Mosques, madrasas and tombs', in George Michell, ed., *Architecture of the Islamic World* (London: Thames & Hudson, 1978).

Farrell, Joseph, *Sicily: A Cultural History* (Oxford: Signal Books, 2012).

Fiordaliso, Francesco, *Selinunte città di pace* (Marsala: Casa Editrice La Siciliana, 1994).

Giannino, A., *La Chiesa del Gesù a Casa Professa* (Bagheria: Officine Tipografiche Aiello, 2003).

Guido, Margaret, *Sicily: An Archaeological Guide* (London: Faber, 1967).

Kitzinger, Ernst, *The Mosaics of St Mary's of the Admiral in Palermo*, Dumbarton Oaks Studies 27 (Washington DC: Dumbarton Oaks Research Library and Collection, 1990).

La Duca, Rosario, *Cartografia della città di Palermo* (Palermo: Industrie Riunite Editoriali Siciliane, 1962).

Michell, George, ed., *Architecture of the Islamic World* (London: Thames & Hudson, 1978).
Nobile, Marco Rosario, *Antonello Gagini, architetto* (Palermo: Flaccovio, 2010).
Pecoraro, G., P. Palazzotto and C. Scordato, *Oratorio del Rosario in Santa Cita* (Bagheria: Officine Tipografiche Aiello, 2001).
Salomon, Xavier F., *Van Dyck in Sicily* [exh. cat.] (Milan: Silvana Editoriale; London: Dulwich Picture Gallery, 2012).
Scuderi, Vincenzo, *La chiesa della Immacolata Concezione a Palermo* (Palermo: Tipografia Priulla di Palermo, 2011).
Sitwell, Sacheverell, *Southern Baroque Revisited* (London: Weidenfeld & Nicolson, 1967).
Talbot Rice, David, *Byzantine Art* (Harmondsworth: Penguin, 1954).
Trevelyan, Raleigh, *The Companion Guide to Sicily* (Woodbridge: Boydell & Brewer, 1996).
Tusa, Vincenzo, *La scultura in pietra di Selinunte* (Palermo: Sellerio, 1983).
Vasari, Giorgio, *Lives of the Artists* (New York, NY: Noonday Press, 1957).

Travellers

Bonner, Eugene, *Sicilian Roundabout* (Palermo: Flaccovio, 1962).
Brydone, Patrick, *A Tour through Sicily and Malta* (1773; London: H. D. Symonds, 1807).
Consolo, Vincenzo, *Le pietre di Pantalica* (Milan: Mondadori, 1988).
——— *L'olivo e l'olivastro* (Milan: Mondadori, 1994).
Cronin, Vincent, *The Golden Honeycomb* (London: Rupert Hart-Davis, 1954).
Durrell, Lawrence, *Sicilian Carousel* (London: Faber, 1977).
Edwards, Andrew, and Suzanne Edwards, *Sicily: A Literary Guide for Travellers* (London: I.B.Tauris, 2014).
Fallowell, Duncan, *To Noto, Or London to Sicily in a Ford* (London: Gibson Square, 2001).
Goethe, Johann Wolfgang von, *Italian Journey*, trans. W. H. Auden and Elizabeth Mayer (London: Collins, 1962). [First published in German as *Italienische Reise*, 1816–17.]
Hare, Augustus, *Cities of Southern Italy and Sicily* (London: Smith, Elder, 1883).
Houël, Jean-Pierre-Louis-Laurent, *Voyage pittoresque des isles de Sicile, de Malte et de Lipari* (Paris: Imprimerie de Monsieur, 1787).
Hutton, Edward, *Cities of Sicily* (London: Methuen, 1926).
Ibn Hawqal, Muhammad, *Description de Palerme*, trans. Michele Amari (Paris: Imprimerie Royale, 1865). [From Ibn Hawqal's *Cosmology*, written in 977 in Arabic.]
Ibn Jubayr, *The Travels of Ibn Jubayr*, trans. R. J. C. Broadhurst (London: Jonathan Cape, 1952).
Keahey, John, *Seeking Sicily* (New York, NY: Thomas Dunne Books/St Martin's Press, 2011).
Knight, Cornelia, *Autobiography* (London: W. H. Allen, 1861).
Lawrence, D. H., *Sea and Sardinia* (1921; Harmondsworth: Penguin, 1944).
Levi, Carlo, *Words Are Stones: Impressions of Sicily*, trans. Antony Shugaar (London: Hesperus Press, 2005). [Original: Carlo Levi, *Le parole sono pietre* (Turin: Einaudi, 1955).]
Lowe, Alfonso, *The Barrier and the Bridge* (New York, NY: Norton, 1972).
Maupassant, Guy de, *Sicily*, trans. Denis Gailor (Palermo: Sellerio, 1990). [Originally published in Guy de Maupassant, *La vie errante* (Paris: Paul Ollendorff, 1890).]
Prose, Francine, *Sicilian Odyssey* (Washington DC: National Geographic Society, 2003).
Quennell, Peter, *Spring in Sicily* (London: Weidenfeld & Nicolson, 1952).
Russell, George, *A Tour through Sicily in the Year 1815* (London: Sherwood, Neely & Jones, 1819).
Sladen, Douglas, *In Sicily*, 2 vols (London: Sands, 1901).
——— *Sicily: The New Winter Resort* (New York, NY: E. P. Dutton, 1907).

Chronological Table

BC

PREHISTORIC

Palermo region inhabited from Stone Age

*c.*10,000 Monte Pellegrino cave paintings

PUNIC/GREEK

*c.*814 Carthage founded by Phoenicians in North Africa

*c.*753 Rome founded

*c.*750 Panormus, Motya and Solus founded by Phoenicians in Sicily

734–580 Greek settlements founded in Sicily

480–264 Carthaginian–Greek wars in Sicily

415–413 Athenian siege of Syracuse

278–276 Pyrrhus captures Panormus

ROMAN

264–241 First Punic War between Rome and Carthage

254 Romans capture Panormus

218–201 Second Punic War

212 Romans capture Syracuse

202 Romans defeat Carthaginians at Battle of Zama

AD

440–535 Vandals and Goths in Sicily

BYZANTINE

535 Belisarius captures Palermo and Sicily

ARAB

827 Arabs invade Sicily

831 Arabs capture Palermo

878 Arabs capture Syracuse and control Sicily

Palermo becomes capital of Sicily

NORMAN

1061 Normans invade Sicily

1072 Normans capture Palermo

1091 Normans control Sicily

1072–1101 Roger I, Count of Sicily

KINGS OF SICILY	1130–54 Roger II
	1154–66 William I
	1166–89 William II
	1190–3 Tancred
	1194 William III
HOHENSTAUFEN	1194 Germans capture Palermo and Sicily
	1191–7 Henry VI, Holy Roman Emperor, and 1194–1197, king of Sicily
	1198–1250 Frederick II, king of Sicily, and 1220–1250, Holy Roman Emperor
	1250–4 Conrad, king of Sicily
	1258–66 Manfred, king of Sicily
ANGEVIN	1266 Charles of Anjou captures Sicily
	1282 Sicilian Vespers revolt in Palermo
ARAGONESE	1282 Peter of Aragon captures Sicily and crowned king
	1412 Rule by viceroys established
	1453 Turks capture Constantinople
	1479 Ferdinand and Isabella unite Aragon and Castile
	1487 Inquisition in Sicily
	1492 Jews expelled from Sicily
SPANISH	1516–56 Charles V, Spanish emperor
	1535–1600 Redesign and fortification of Palermo
	1556–98 Philip II, Spanish emperor
	1571 Turks defeated at Battle of Lepanto
	1624–6 Plague in Palermo
	1625 Santa Rosalia becomes patron saint of Palermo
	1647 Revolt in Palermo
PIEDMONTESE	1713–20 Victor Amadeus II
AUSTRIAN	1720–34 Charles VI
SPANISH	1734–59 Charles III
BOURBONS	1759–1825 Ferdinand III
	1781–6 Caracciolo, viceroy in Sicily, abolishes Inquisition in 1782
BRITISH	1798 Nelson brings Bourbon king and queen to Palermo
	1799–1815 Napoleonic Wars
	1806–15 Sicily a British protectorate
	1812 New constitution in Sicily

SPANISH	1816 Ferdinand I, king of the Two Sicilies, governs Sicily from Naples
BOURBONS	1820 Revolt in Palermo
	1825–30 Francis I
	1830–59 Ferdinand II
	1848 Revolt in Palermo sets up provisional government
	1849 Bourbon rule re-established in Palermo
	1859–60 Francis II
GARIBALDI	1860 Garibaldi captures Sicily and hands it over to Cavour in Piedmont
ITALIAN	1860 Sicily ruled from Turin
	1861–71 Italian unification
	1866 Revolt in Palermo
	*c.*1880–1914 Belle époque in Palermo
	1914–18 World War I
	1922 Mussolini takes power in Rome
	1939–45 World War II
	1943 British and Americans capture Sicily (Operation Husky)
	1943 Mussolini falls from power and Italy capitulates to the Allies
	1947 Palermo becomes seat of Sicilian Regional Government
	1950s Postwar reconstruction and discovery of oil in Sicily
	1982 General Dalla Chiesa killed by the mafia
	1986–7 Maxi-trial of the mafia
	1992 Judges Falcone and Borsellino killed by the mafia
	1992–3 Mafia bombing campaign
	1990s–current Antimafia campaign successes
	2008–current Economic recession in Sicily

The Norman Kings of Sicily:
The Hauteville Dynasty

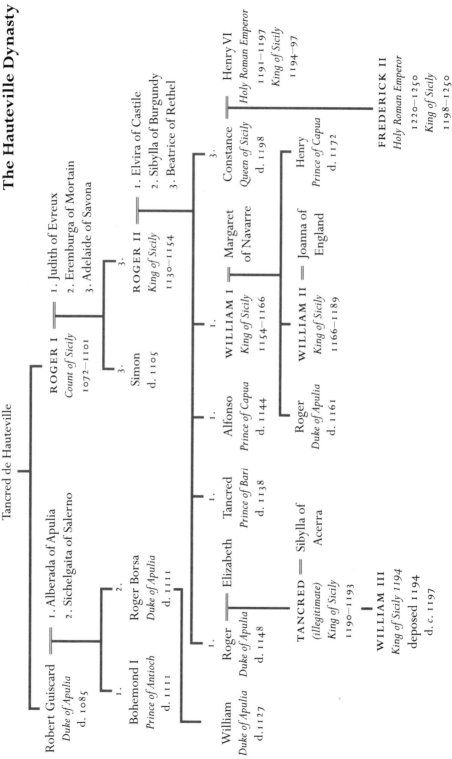

Index

Sicilian cities are listed by their modern names, with their names from antiquity in brackets.

Monuments are listed by their Italian names, with English translations in brackets.